THE ADVE

OF

BIG-FOOT WALLACE

"BIG FOOT WALLACE."—Frontispiece.

THE ADVENTURES

OF

BIG-FOOT WALLACE

THE TEXAS RANGER AND HUNTER

BY

JOHN C. DUVAL

Skyhorse Publishing

First published 1871
First Skyhorse Publishing edition 2015

10 9 8 7 6 5 4 3 2

Library of Congress Cataloging-in-Publication Data is available on file.

Cover design by Rain Saukas

Print ISBN: 978-1-62914-734-5
Ebook ISBN: 978-1-62914-852-6

Printed in the United States of America

PREFACE

THE writer of this little book is well aware that it will not stand the test of criticism as a literary production. A frontiersman himself, his opportunities for acquiring information, and for supplying the deficiencies of a rather limited education, have of course been "few and far between;" and therefore it cannot be reasonably expected that he could make a book under such circumstances which would not be sadly defective as to style and composition. However, it can justly lay claim to at least one *merit*, not often found in similar publications—it is not a compilation of imaginary scenes and incidents, concocted in the brain of one who never was beyond the sound of a dinner-bell in his life, but a plain, unvarnished story of the "'scapes and scrapes" of Big-Foot Wallace, the Texas Ranger and Hunter, written out from notes furnished by himself, and told, as well as my memory serves me, in his own language.

"Big-Foot Wallace" is better known throughout Texas, as an Indian-fighter, hunter, and ranger, than any one, perhaps, now living in the State; which is saying a good deal, when the great number who have acquired more or less notoriety in that way is taken into consideration. Few men now living, I am confident, have witnessed as many stirring incidents, had more "hair-breadth escapes," or gone through more of the hardships and perils of a border life. He has been a participant in almost every fight, foray, and "scrimmage" with the Mexicans and Indians that has taken place in Texas since he first landed on her shores in 1836.

Pioneers, or frontiersmen, are a class of men peculiar to our country, and seem to have been designed especially to meet the exigencies of the occasion. With their "iron nerves," great powers of endurance, and indomitable "go-aheadativeness," they have been essentially useful in clearing the way through the wilderness from such obstacles as would have been perhaps insurmountable to those coming after them. Their mission has been very nearly accomplished. Like the flatboat-men of the Mississippi, who have entirely disappeared as a class since the introduction of steamboats on that river and its tributaries, their numbers are steadily decreasing before the extension of railroads and the area of civilization. Only here and there one is still found in our midst, whom disease, wounds, or old age have rendered incapable of further contests with the Indians and other denizens of the forests and plains, and of enduring the hardships and exposure of a life in the wilderness. As a class, frontiersmen are observant and knowing in all that pertains to their peculiar mode of life, and as deeply versed in all the mysteries of woodcraft as the wily savage himself; but they are guileless and unsuspicious as a child, and whenever they come in conflict with the shrewd, calculating man of business, they are as helpless as a "stranded whale." For this reason, they seldom accumulate property, and those who follow after them generally reap the reward of all their perils, toils, and hardships

Wallace is no exception to this rule. The best days of his life have been freely given to the service of his country; and now that years have "dimmed the fire of his eye," and lessened the vigor of his limbs — now that he is no longer able to follow the buffalo to their distant grazing-grounds, he calls upon a generous public to aid him by patronizing his little book.

THE AUTHOR.

CHAPTER XIX.

CHAPTER XX.

CHAPTER XXI.

CHAPTER XXII.

CHAPTER XXIII.

CHAPTER XXIV.

CHAPTER XXV.

CHAPTER XXVI.

CHAPTER XXVII.

CHAPTER XXVIII.

CHAPTER XXIX.

CHAPTER XXX.

CHAPTER XXXI.

CHAPTER XXXII.

CHAPTER XXXIII.

CHAPTER XXXIV.

CHAPTER XXXV.

CHAPTER XXXVI.

CHAPTER XXXVII.

CHAPTER XXXVIII.

CHAPTER XXXIX.

CHAPTER XL.

CHAPTER XLI.

SKETCH OF WALLACE'S LIFE.

WILLIAM A. WALLACE was born in Lexington, Rockbridge, County, Virginia, in the year 1816. He went to Texas in 1836, a few months after the battle of San Jacinto, for the purpose, he says of taking pay out of the Mexicans for the murder of his brother and his cousin, Major Wallace, who both fell at "Fannin's Massacre." He says he believes accounts with them are now about square.

He landed first at Galveston, which consisted then of six groceries and an old stranded hulk of a steamboat, used as a hotel, and for a berth in which he paid at the rate of three dollars per day. From Galveston, Wallace went on to La Grange, then a frontier village, where he resided until the spring of 1839, when he moved up to Austin, just before the seat of government was established at that place. He remained at Austin until the spring of 1840, when finding that the country was settling up around him too fast to suit his notions, he went over to San Antonio, where he resided until he entered the service.

He was at the battle of the Salado, in the fall of 1842, when General Woll came in and captured San Antonio. The fight began about eleven o'clock in the day, and lasted until night. General Woll had fourteen hundred men, and the Texans one hundred and ninety-seven, under Caldwell, (commonly known as "Old Paint.") Between eighty and one hundred Mexicans were killed, while the Texans lost only one man, (Jett.) Forty men, however, from La Grange, under Captain Dawson, who were endeavoring to form a junction with them, were surrounded and captured by the Mexicans, who massacred them all as soon as they had surrendered their arms.

In the fall of 1842, he volunteered in the "Mier Expedition," an account of which appears in this volume. After his return from Mexico, he joined Colonel Jack Hays's Ranging Company, the first ever regularly enlisted in the service of the "old Republic," and was with it in many of those desperate encounters with the Comanches and other Indians, in which Hays, Walker, McCulloch, and Chevalier gained their reputation as successful Indian-fighters.

When the Mexican war broke out in 1846, Wallace joined Colonel Hays's regiment of mounted volunteers, and was with it at the storming of Monterey, where he says he took "full toll" out of the Mexicans for killing his brother and cousin at Goliad in 1836.

After the Mexican war ended, he had command of a Ranging Company for some time, and did good service in protecting the frontiers of the State from the incursions of the savages. Subsequently he had charge of the mail from San Antonio to El Paso, and, though often waylaid and attacked by the Indians, he always brought it through in safety.

He is now living upon his little ranch, thirty miles west of San Antonio, where, with true frontier hospitality, he is always ready to welcome the wayfarer to the best he has.

WILLIAM WALLACE.

BY DR. F. O. TICKNOR.

HIS life is past the forties—
  His length is six foot two—
And both his feet import he 's
  Not a fly to shoe!
They dubbed him Big-Foot Wallace
  Down in Mexico,
As Liliput would call his
  Brobdignag, you know.

Straight as a rifle-rammer,
  And lightly too he stands,
Though weighted with sledge-hammer
  In each of his great hands!
Grave as his own gun-barrel,
  Yet gracious with the grim,
And when we pick a quarrel
  We must n't pick at him!

A plant of the "red ripper,"
  Whose level eye-light means
A charge of Chili pepper
  Ballasted with "Beans."
A loyal soul! I 'll pound it
  As ever ruled the ranch;
And so the Doodles found it,
  And *also* the Comanche!

And so the little Greasers!
  They say he used to catch
A score of their Mestizoes
  To grease his bullet-patch!
May they be bothered wholly—
  In body and in soul!
For the mills are grinding slowly
  And Wallace takes the toll.

His features so resemble
  His sire's, a cycle back,
That curs and tyrants tremble
  To come upon his track!
Here 's Hope's un-Butlered chalice;
  Here 's loyalty's last wine!
And here 's—To William Wallace
  The Second, by his—"Sign!"

THE ADVENTURES OF

BIG-FOOT WALLACE.

CHAPTER I.

INTRODUCTORY.

IN 1867, while temporarily sojourning in the city of San Antonio, I had a severe attack of fever, from the effects of which I recovered but slowly. Thinking that fresh air and exercise would aid me in regaining my health and strength, I mounted my horse one fine morning in the latter part of October, and set out for the "ranch" of my quondam messmate and *compadre*, "Big-Foot Wallace," who held an uncertain tenure upon a tract of pasture land, situated on the Chacon, one of the head-waters of the Altascoso. I say, uncertain, for his right to and possession of the same is constantly disputed and ignored by predatory bands of savages, and Mexicans, and horse-thieves of all colors, grades, and nations.

Toward sundown, from the top of a considerable hill, I came in sight of Wallace's little ranch, snugly ensconced at the bottom of a valley, near the margin of a small lake, and protected from the northern blasts by a beautiful grove of spreading live-oaks. As I rode up I discovered Wallace under one of these trees, engaged in the characteristic occupation of skinning a deer, which was hanging head downward, suspended from one of its lower branches. Wallace did not recognize me at first, for it was many years since we had last met; but, as soon as I made myself known to him, he gave me a cordial shake of the hand, and invited me into his ranch, where, in a short time, he prepared a supper, to which I sat down, "nothing loath," for my appetite was sharpened by my long day's ride.

I staid with Wallace two weeks, or thereabouts, hunting, fishing, and riding around during the day, and entertained each night with "yarns" of his numerous "'scapes and scrapes, by flood and field." Many years previously, when Wallace and I were messmates together, in the first Ranging Company, enlisted in the service of the "Old Republic," under Colonel Jack Hays, I asked his consent to write out a narrative of his "adventures," to be published for the benefit of the public generally. But he seemed so much opposed to my doing so, that I did not press the matter upon him. His reasons for refusing to accede to my request were characteristic of the man. "He did not think the public would be interested in the history of one so little known;" and, "even if he had vanity enough to believe otherwise, he had not the least desire to see himself figuring in print." I determined once more to approach him on the subject, and this time I had better success than formerly, for finally (though evidently with reluctance) he consented that I should publish the following

WALLACE'S LITTLE RANCH. — Page 14.

narrative of his adventures in Mexico and on the frontiers of Texas.

"There is," I said to Wallace, "one difficulty in the way of writing out your 'adventures,' which I do not exactly know how to get over; and that is, you do not murder the king's English with every other word you speak. Now, in all the books I have ever read, in which backwoodsmen or frontiersmen figure, they are always made to talk without the least regard to the rules of grammar."

"I know," said Wallace, "that my education is a very limited one, but do give me credit for the little I have. People are not such fools as to think that a man cannot be a good hunter or ranger, merely because he speaks his own language passably well."

And so, in compliance with Wallace's request, in the following narrative of his "adventures," I have ignored the time-honored rule of making him speak in slang and misspelt words, and tell the story "just as it was told to me."

CHAPTER II.

Wallace's Initiation into the Mysteries of Woodcraft.

SOON after I came out to Texas, in 1837, said Wallace, being out of employment, and having no inclination to loaf around the "groceries" of a little village, I looked about for something to do; but for several weeks no "opening" presented itself. At length a surveyor, who was preparing for an expedition to locate lands upon the frontier, made me an offer to go with him, which I gladly accepted. At that time, as an Irishman would say, I was "as green as a red blackberry," and I frankly told the surveyor that I knew nothing about the woods, or how to get along in them. But he said that made no difference, as the rest of the party were all old frontiersmen, and it was well enough to have one "green-horn" along to make sport for the balance.

It was a week or ten days before we were ready to start, and in the mean time I prepared myself for the "expedition" as well as I knew how. I had brought with me from Virginia a good rifle, a pair of Derringer pistols, and a bowie-knife, (that you know was before the days of six-shooters,) so that there was no necessity for my hunting up firearms. I bought a good stout Spanish pony, with saddle, bridle, etc., and laid in an ample supply of ammunition and tobacco; and when the surveying party were ready to start, I joined them "armed and equipped as the law directs."

Our party consisted of a guard of two men, well

armed and mounted, together with the surveyor, two chainmen, a marker, a hunter, and a cook, making in all sixteen men — a sufficient force to travel with safety, at that day, in the most dangerous part of the country. At that time, one American, well armed, was considered a match for eight or ten Indians, with their bows and arrows and miserable guns; but now, thanks to the traders, they are well furnished with good rifles and "six-shooters," and can hold their own, man for man.

The first day out, we travelled only a few miles, and encamped on a beautiful little clear stream, where I killed my first deer. I thought I had performed a wonderful feat, for I had never killed anything before larger than a squirrel or a 'possum, and I proudly returned to camp with the deer on my shoulders, trying all the time, though, to look as if the killing of a deer was no unusual thing with me. But the boys suspected me, and when I owned up that it was the first deer I had ever shot, two or three of them seized me, while as many more smeared my face and hands with the blood of the animal — a sort of ceremony, they said, by which I was "initiated" into the brotherhood of "mighty hunters." I suppose I was "initiated," as they called it, for I have killed many a hundred deer since that time, to say nothing of buffalo; bear, elk, wolves, panthers, Mexican lions, catamounts, and other "varmints" too numerous to mention.

CHAPTER III.

ON THE ROUTE — THE OLD LADY AND THE TRUCK-PATCH.

THE next day we started just after sunrise, and travelled twenty-five miles over a beautiful rolling country, watered with clear streams, and encamped at night in a pecan grove near a fine spring. Just at dark, a large drove of turkeys flew up into the trees around, and we killed five or six of them, and spitted them before our fires. These, together with a fat doe killed by our hunter on the way, furnished us with an ample supply of provender, while an abundance of fine mesquit grass in the vicinity enabled our horses to fare as sumptuously as ourselves.

The next morning, after an early breakfast, we saddled up and again took the road, or rather our course, for there was no road, and went about twelve miles to a water-hole, where there was good grass, and where we "nooned" for a couple of hours. The country passed over was all high rolling prairie, interspersed with "mots" of elm and hackberry. While all hands were taking a comfortable snooze here, we came near losing our horses. A wolf or some other wild animal gave them a scare, and they "stampeded," and all broke their halter-ropes, except one, and ran off several miles. One of the men, however, mounted the horse that was left, and, after a chase of several hours, succeeded in bringing them all back. In consequence of the delay caused by this incident, we went only five miles farther this evening, and encamped in the edge of the bottom timber, on a small stream. The country we passed over was of the same character as that we had formerly seen. As soon as we had "staked" out our horses, I rigged up a fishing-line, and in half an hour caught a fine mess of perch, and several "Gaspar Goo," a fish found, I believe, only in the streams of Texas, somewhat similar to the white perch of the "old States." Great numbers of turkeys came at dark to roost in the trees in our vicinity, and they were so tame that we had no trouble in killing as many as we wanted.

[Here we quote from Wallace's journal:]

October 17th.—Made an early start again, and went fifteen miles, when we halted to rest on a little creek, called by the hunters "Burnt Boot." The country passed over high and rolling, and about "half-and-half" prairie and woodland. Here is the last white settlement, I am told, we shall see for many a long day. A man by the name of Benson lives here, and supports himself and family by hunting and trapping, and cultivating a small patch of land. I went up to his house to see if anything in the way of vegetables could be had. Benson was out hunting, but his wife, a tall, raw-boned, hard-favored woman, as soon as she saw me coming, stepped to the door with a gun in her hand, and told me to "stand"—and I stood! A half-dozen little cotton-headed children, who were playing in the yard, discovered me at this moment, and they "squandered," and squatted in the bushes like a gang of partridges!

"Who are you?" asked Mrs. Benson, pointing her gun right at me, "and what do you want here?"

"I am from the settlements below, ma'am," said I, as polite as possible, but keeping a tree between the good lady and myself all the time; for women, you know, are very awkward about handling firearms; "and," I continued, "I want to buy some vegetables, if you have any to sell."

"Well," she answered, "come in. We hain't no vegetables left now," she continued, as I walked into the cabin and took a seat on a bench, "except cowcumbers and mushmillions, and, maybe so, a few 'collards,' the dratted 'varmints' are so uncommon bad on 'em; but if you want any of them, you can go in the 'truck-patch,' and help yourself."

"You seem," I ventured to remark, "from the way you handled your gun, to be a little suspicious of strangers in these parts."

"Yes," she said, "I am, and good reason to be so, too! Only last Saturday was a week ago, some Tonk Ingens, dressed up like white folks, walked into Squire Henry's house, not more than two miles from here, and killed and sculped the whole family; but, as luck would have it, there was nobody at home, except the baby and an old nigger woman that nussed it. And which way are you travelling to?" she asked.

I told her we were going up on the head-waters of the Brazos to survey lands.

"Well," says she, "you 'll be luckier than 'most everybody else that has gone up there, if you 'll need more than six feet apiece before you get back. If I was your mammy, young man, you should n't go one foot on sich a wild-goose chase," — and she looked so determined, I do believe, if she had been my mammy, I should never have got nearer than "Burnt Boot" to the head of the Brazos.

After some further questioning on the part of the old lady, she showed me the way into the "truck-patch," and filled my wallet with "mushmillions" and "cowcumbers," for which I thanked her, as she would take no pay, and started back to camp.

"Good-by, young man!" she called after me; "I feel mighty sorry for your poor mammy, for you'll never see her again."

"Well," I answered, "if I don't, and you do, you must be sure and give her my kindest regards."

"You oudacious young scamp," she replied, "put out from here fast. I'll insure you against everything but hanging, which you are certain to come to."

The "mushmillions and cowcumbers" were a treat to the boys, as well as the account I gave them of the way in which the old lady had made me dodge behind the tree, when she levelled her gun at me.

After dinner, we mounted our horses again, and leaving the last settlement behind us, we rode on ten miles farther into the "wilderness," keeping a bright lookout all the time for "Mr. John;" for we were liable to meet up with him, now, at any moment. The country was more broken and rocky than any we had yet seen. We camped at the foot of a high hill near a little spring of cold water. Our hunter killed an antelope to-day, on which we made a hearty supper. The flesh of the antelope is somewhat coarser than that of the deer, but I think sweeter and more juicy. They are much shyer than deer, and it is consequently more difficult to get in gunshot of them. Some of the boys found a "bee-tree" just before dark, which we cut down, and got four or five gallons of honey out of it, and from this time the boys said we shall have no trouble in supplying ourselves with honey, whenever we have time to look for the "trees." "Bear-meat and honey" is the frontiersman's choicest dish, and I would dislike to say how much of them I have seen an old ranger "worry down," after a hard day's ride, for fear people might think I had no respect for the truth: no one but an old hunter or a starved wolf would credit my story.

There is something singular about the movements of bees. They are never found a great way from the settlements, but usually precede them fifty, sixty, or a hundred miles, so that whenever they make their appearance among the Indians, they know that the white people are coming soon — and yet, they do not remain long in their wild state after the country becomes thickly settled. In many places where "bee-trees" were numerous when I first came to Texas, they are now seldom if ever found.

CHAPTER IV.

A Rattlesnake Bite — Singular Spring — Wild Artichokes — Indian Art Gallery — Wallace's First Bear.

OCTOBER 18*th*. — We were up "by times," and ready to "roll out" at sunrise. Saw some Indian "signs," but they were all old, except one camp, which appeared to have been recently occupied. In going through a thick chaparral to-day, my pony was bitten on the leg by a rattlesnake. An old hunter told me to chew up some tobacco, and tie it on the wound, which I did, and, except a slight swelling, no bad results followed from the bite. (I have seen tobacco used frequently since as a remedy for the bite of a rattlesnake; and there is no doubt it is a good one, but not equal to whisky or brandy taken in large quantities.)

Passed over a great deal of broken, rocky country to-day, watered by little streams that were as clear as crystal, and filled with trout, perch, and other kinds of fish. We "nooned" for a couple of hours on one of these streams, in one of the pools of which we all took a refreshing bath.

In the evening, went on perhaps ten miles farther, and pitched camp on one of the head-waters of Cowhouse Creek. The country passed over is very broken and rocky, with occasional cedar-brakes and "mots" of wild cherry and plum trees.

We passed a very remarkable spring to-day. It breaks out at the extreme point of a high tongue of land that runs down into the bend of a large creek. The water boils up out of a basin the size of a hogshead, which, running over, falls in a beautiful cascade into the creek below. It looked more like an artificial fountain than a natural spring. We saw some fresh Indian signs, but no Indians.

Our camp to-night is under a large, projecting rock, and very fortunate for us it was; for a heavy rainstorm came up about 12 o'clock, which would have "ducked" us thoroughly if it had not been for our stone roof. As it was, we slept dry and comfortably, notwithstanding the heavy rain that fell.

October 19th, Sunday. — Every little creek and gully is swimming this morning, and, as it is Sunday, we have concluded to lay over a day and rest ourselves and animals. After breakfast, one of the boys went out exploring, and in an hour or two came back, bringing with him a large quantity of a vegetable which he called the artichoke. We cooked some for dinner, and found them excellent. It is, I believe, a species of bear-grass; at least, it resembles it very much, except that its leaves or spires are notched like a saw. It grows abundantly everywhere in the hilly and rocky country. The root is the part eaten, and is roasted in the ashes like a potato. Since then I have frequently lived solely on them for days at a time, when out on expeditions, and I can recommend them as a wholesome and nutritious vegetable to all "wayworn wanderers of the Western wilds."

Near our camp there is a perpendicular wall of rock, ten or twelve feet high, with a smooth, even face, on which the Indians have painted, with some sort of red earth, the likenesses of men and animals. Some of the animals are well drawn, particularly a buffalo; others are imaginary beings, unlike anything that was ever seen. One picture represents a fight between the Indians and the whites, and, of course, the Indians are giving the white men a terrible flogging. One white man is represented kneeling down, with his hands lifted up, as if begging for his life, while an Indian warrior stands over him, with tomahawk raised above his head, in the act of dashing out the poor fellow's brains.

Near this place I picked up some small pieces of quartz rock, with shining particles scattered about through them, which I put in my shot-pouch. I afterward had them examined at San Antonio, and the shining particles were said to be gold.

In the evening we all went out "berrying," and gathered quantities of haws, red and black, and a sort of berry that I don't know the name of, which grows upon a little thorny shrub, and is very good to eat, though rather sour.

The weather faired off in the evening, and the night was clear and pleasant. Slept again under our "rock house."

October 20th.—We took our course again, which was about due north, and, crossing a range of mountains at a place called "Walker's Pass," we travelled over a rough, broken country to the South Leon Creek, a distance, I suppose, of fifteen or sixteen miles, where we "nooned." We saw some fresh buffalo signs on the way, and our old hunters began to whet their bills for fat steaks, marrow-bones, and "humps;" but as yet we have seen none of the animals. We found the grass very fine on the bottoms of this creek, and have concluded to lay over until to-morrow, and give our horses a chance to recruit, as they have had but poor grazing for the last forty-eight hours.

We had been in camp but a little while, when one of the boys found a "bee-tree," which we cut down, and took from it at least five gallons of honey.

In the evening I went out hunting, but saw no game to shoot at. On my way back to camp, I stopped to rest for a few minutes in a little cañon that lay between two rocky hills, covered with thick chaparral. After a while, my attention was attracted by a noise in the bushes, and, looking around, I saw a large bear coming directly toward me. I sat perfectly still, and he did not notice me, but came slowly along, now and then stopping to turn over a stick or a rock, in search, I suppose, of insects. When within twenty feet of me, I took sight of his fore-shoulder and fired, and he fell dead in his tracks. This was my first bear. He was very fat, and would have weighed, I suppose, three hundred pounds. I went back to camp, which was not more than half a mile off, and, returning with two of the men to assist me, we butchered him, and, packing the meat on a horse, we soon had some of it roasting before our fires. What a feast we had that night on "bear-meat and honey"! If the mess of pottage that Esau sold his birthright for, was as good as bear-meat and honey, and he had a good appetite, I believe the poor fellow was excusable.

In the night we saw a long line of light to the westward of us, and supposed the Indians had fired the prairie. The night was pleasant and warm.

CHAPTER V.

Buffalo — Fine Grove of Pecan-Trees — The First Buffalo — Bit by a Rattlesnake — The Tarantula — Travelling under Difficulties — A Free Serenade.

OCTOBER *21st.* — We left camp after breakfast, taking what was left of our bear-meat along with us, and steered our usual course, due north, and about twelve o'clock we struck the Leon River, opposite the mouth of Armstrong's Creek. The country passed over to-day was very broken, and but little land on our route is fit for cultivation. We saw a small drove of buffalo, but our hunters did not get a shot at them, and the country where we found them was so broken we could not chase them on horseback. One of our men, who had stopped behind awhile for some purpose, when he came up, reported that he had seen an Indian following on our trail; but he was a "scary" sort of fellow, and we thought his story very doubtful.

We passed a singular chain of high bald hills to-day. Looking at them from a distance, we almost fancied we were approaching a considerable city, so much did they resemble houses, steeples, etc. They were entirely destitute of timber.

The Leon River, where we struck it, is a small, rapid stream, shut in on both sides by high, rocky hills. We crossed over to the northern side, and "nooned" in a grove of pecans. These trees are full of the finest nuts we had ever seen — very large, and their hulls so thin we could easily crack them with our fingers. Before we left, we gathered a wallet-full of them, and strapped it on one of our pack-mules.

In the evening, we continued our route up Armstrong's Creek, and struck camp a little after sundown near one of its head-springs. The valley along the creek is very beautiful, and the soil rich. Our hunter, to-day, killed a fat buffalo-cow on the way, and we butchered her, and packed the meat into camp. That was the first buffalo-meat I ever tasted, and I thought it better even than bear-meat. The flesh of an old bull, however, I have found out since, is coarse, tough, and stringy, but the "hump" is always good, and so are the "marrow-bones" and tongue.

Just after we had encamped, one of our men, named Thompson, while staking out his horse, was bitten on the hand by a rattlesnake. It was a small one, however, and he suffered but little from the effects of the bite. We scarified the wound with a penknife, and applied some soda to it, and the next morning he was well enough to travel. I do not think the bite of the rattlesnake is as often fatal as people generally suppose. I have seen several men and a great many animals bitten by them, and have never known death to ensue, except on one or two occasions. Still, I have no doubt there is great danger, whenever the fangs of the snake strike a large vein or artery. I believe the bite of the tarantula* is much more fatal. I have seen two or three persons bitten by them in Mexico, neither of whom recovered, although many remedies were used. The Mexicans say they will kill a horse in ten minutes.

Night clear and cool — cool enough to make it very pleasant to sleep by our fires. Toward midnight we had an alarm that roused all hands very suddenly. The sentry on post fired his gun off accidentally, and we supposed, of course, that the Indians were upon us. We were all up and ready with our guns by the time the sentinel came in and told us it was a false alarm. I was so completely roused up by the excitement and bustle that I did not get to sleep for more than an hour afterward. The little breeze, that rustled among the leaves and dead grass the early part of the night, had died away, and a dead silence had settled over all. Not a sound could be heard, except the howling of a solitary "cayote" far off among the hills, and the nipping of our animals as they cropped the rank grass that grew around us. The silence was oppressive, and when one of the men muttered in his sleep, or one of our animals coughed or snorted, it was actually a relief. I have frequently observed since, when camping out alone in the wilderness, the dead silence that sometimes prevails on

* A species of spider.

a calm night. It is not so in the "settlements;" for there is almost always some sound to break in upon it — the lowing of cattle, the tinkling of cow-bells, or the barking of a dog.

October 22d. — After an early breakfast, we saddled up, and travelled as fast as the broken and rocky state of the ground would permit. We intended to make a "forced march" to-day, as we expected by night to reach the locality where we were to commence our operations. Our horses had fared sumptuously the last two nights, and were in a condition to do a good day's work, but the farther we went the rougher and more difficult thc way became. Every now and then we would come to a space covered with "honey-comb rock," where we were compelled to travel our horses at the slowest gait. Dense chaparrals, too, frequently obstructed the way, and we either had to turn off and avoid them altogether, or else hunt out a route through them along dim and crooked trails. These causes delayed us so much that by noon we supposed we had only made about fifteen miles. We halted for half an hour at a pool of brackish water, to breathe our horses. We then continued on through the same sort of country, only more rugged still, if possible, and at sundown we found ourselves still half a day's journey from the Palo Pinto, where we expect to begin our work. Luckily, we found a pool of muddy water, on the edge of a small prairie in which there was excellent grass for our animals, where we unpacked and pitched camp for the night. If the night before had been unusually still and quiet, this one was just the opposite. If two or three "menageries" had been turned loose in the vicinity just before we came, monkeys and all, there could not have been a greater variety of sounds. First, a gang of wolves would serenade us for a minute or two, and then a catamount would come in on a high key, and, before he had fairly finished, a panther or a "lobo" would join in the chorus; and so they kept it up until the broad daylight.

CHAPTER VI.

THE PALO PINTO AT LAST — THE CAMP IN THE VALLEY — WALLACE'S LAST LOOK AT THE CAMP — THE INDIANS — A TIGHT RACE — WALLACE KILLS HIS FIRST INDIAN.

OCTOBER *23d.* — We travelled, I suppose, fifteen or sixteen miles to-day, over a better and more open country, and about noon struck a branch of the Palo Pinto Creek, on which we intended to begin our work of locating and surveying land.

We passed, on the way, several large Indian camps, but they were all old. In crossing a little sluggish stream of water to-day, one of our pack animals "bogged" down, and it took us a half-hour's hard work to get him out again on firm ground.

Where we struck the south prong of the Palo Pinto, we found a little valley, surrounded on all sides by high, rocky hills, in the southern extremity of which we determined to build a permanent camp, as a sort of base from which to carry on our work. Game was abundant in the vicinity, and the large pools along the creek were literally swarming with fish. We selected a position for our camp in a bend of the creek, the only entrance to which was by a narrow neck that could easily be guarded and defended against the approach of an enemy. Approach at all other points was almost impossible, on account of the high and perpendicular banks of the creek.

In the evening we hobbled our horses, and all hands went to work to build a camp that would afford us some protection in bad weather. By sundown we had it finished and covered in with a double layer of dry grass. We then covered the floor with a quantity of the same, on which we spread our blankets, and slept like "tops" till morning.

October 24th. — It was thought best that all hands should rest to-day, after our fatiguing journey; so we had nothing to do but to amuse ourselves as we chose. Some "lolled" about camp, passing the time in eating and sleeping. Some rigged up their "tackle" and went off fishing; while others gathered pecans, of which there was an abundance in the vicinity. For my part, I soon got tired of all these things, and determined that I would explore a little of the country around our camp. Taking my gun and hunting equipments, I strolled off in the direction of a pass that seemed to penetrate the hills toward the northern extremity of the valley. At the entrance of the pass, there was a solitary hill, in the shape of a sugar-loaf, which I climbed up, and from the top of which I had a full view of the little valley in which our camp lay, and of the camp itself, about a mile and a quarter off. I could see the smoke rising from it, and our animals grazing round. Little did I think this was the last sight I should ever have of it; but so it was, for I never saw it again. I descended the hill, and took my way up the pass, and, after following it perhaps half a mile, it widened out into a small valley, in which there was a grove of pecan-trees, full of the finest nuts I had yet seen.

I gathered two or three handfuls of pecans, and was sitting down at the foot of one of the trees cracking and eating them, when I happened to look down the pass the way I had come, and saw a party of twelve or fifteen Indians riding up it as fast as the broken nature of the ground would permit. I knew, if I remained where I was, that they would certainly discover me, and there was no chance for me to pass them unobserved. My only hope of escaping from them was in going ahead until I came to some cañon or ravine making into the pass, into which I might dodge and "lay low" until they had gone by.

But there was no time to lose, so I seized my gun and put off up the pass at a brisk trot. The pecan grove concealed me for a while from the Indians; but the moment they passed it they caught sight of me, and came yelling and whooping after me as fast as they could urge on their horses, for the pass was broken and seamed with deep gullies, and for half an hour they gained but little, if any, upon me.

All this time I had looked closely on both sides of the pass for some opening into the hills, but could see nothing of the sort: on both sides there appeared to be a solid wall of rock. At length the pass widened out into a small valley that was smooth and unbroken, and here the race between me and the Indians was a tight one, and a very exciting one to me, for, though I did n't take time to look back, I could tell by the sound of their yells that they were gaining on me.

At length, I saw an opening in the pass on the left,

and made for it as fast as I could, hoping it would lead me into some cañon or ravine that would be impassable for horses, and so it proved; for, after going a few hundred yards, I found great difficulty in getting along, even on foot. The Indians were still after me, I knew from their yells, and would probably dismount and continue the chase on foot when they could ride no farther. I had but little fear, however, of their overtaking me, for, as I have said before, in those days I could run like a scared wolf when I let out the kinks.

The cañon I had entered twisted and turned about among the hills in such a way that I could not see the Indians, but I was satisfied that they were still trailing me, even after I could no longer hear their yells. For this reason, I never slackened my speed until I had penetrated several miles among the hills, when I halted for a few moments to catch my breath at a point from which I could see several hundred yards down the cañon, in the direction I had come. I was just on the eve of getting up to make a start again when an Indian came in sight, travelling along the trail in a sort of "dog-trot," and at a rate which I knew would bring him to where I was in a few moments. The perseverance of this rascal in following me up so long, "stirred my gall," and I resolved to make him pay dearly for it, if I could. Near where I was resting myself, there was a large rock, just about high enough to conceal a man effectually when kneeling down, and behind that I took my position, with the muzzle of my gun resting on its top.

The Indian came trotting along, totally unsuspicious that the "chase" had turned to bay, until he was within twenty paces of me, when I gave a low whistle, and he instantly stopped, looking cautiously round at the same time. I had a dead-rest for my rifle, and I drew a bead about the centre of his breast and touched the trigger. At the crack of the gun, he sprang into the air and dropped dead in his tracks. That was the first Indian I ever killed.

I loaded up my rifle as quickly as possible, for fear others were close behind, and continued on up the ravine. I had gone, I suppose, about half a mile farther, when I came to another cañon, coming in at right angles to the one I was in, up which I took my way; for I thought, if the Indians still continued the pursuit to that point, they would naturally suppose I had gone on in the straight direction. I do not know if this "change of base" deceived them, or whether they followed me so far, but I neither saw nor heard anything of them afterward.

I kept on up this cañon for an hour after the sun went down, and until it grew so dark I found there was great danger of breaking my neck by tumbling into some of the numerous gulches that ran across it, when I turned aside into a little nook, where I laid down without making any fire, and where I intended to rest myself until the moon rose, and then proceed on my way. But I was so exhausted by the long race I had had that I went to sleep, and never woke up until the sun had fairly risen, and was shining above the tops of the hills.

WALLACE KILLS HIS FIRST INDIAN. —Page 34.

CHAPTER VII.

Lost among the Ravines — A Lucky Shot — Comfortable Quarters — A Petrified Forest — The Mexican Gourd — Wallace makes a Friend.

OCTOBER 25*th.* — Here I am, miles away from camp, and not the slightest idea of the direction I ought to travel to reach it. Not daring to go back by the way I had come, for fear of being waylaid by the Indians, who, I was satisfied, would make every effort to capture me, after they found out I had killed one of their party, I scarcely knew which way to turn.* I had not a mouthful to eat, nor had I drank a drop of water since the day before, and I was suffering exceedingly from thirst. Upon investigating the extent of my worldly goods and chattels, I found they consisted of the clothes I had on, my rifle, shot-pouch, a steel for striking fire, a butcher-knife, powder-horn, (filled with powder,) and a memorandum-book and pencil.

Before I left my hiding-place, I reconnoitred the pass cautiously, and seeing nothing suspicious, I started off in the direction I supposed our camp to be. I was suffering very much from thirst, and when I had gone a few hundred yards, I thought myself fortunate in finding a little pool of rain-water in the hollow of a rock. It was clear and cool, and I took a hearty drink of it,

* At that time, you must remember, I was as "green as a cut-seed watermelon," and had no knowledge of the woods, and knew not how to steer my course through them. Under the same circumstances now, I should be as much at home as I would be here in my little ranch.

which refreshed me exceedingly, and gave me new life and strength.

The whole of the country I travelled over was a succession of rugged, rocky hills, separated from each other by narrow gulches and cañons,* and almost impassable even for a man on foot.

About twelve o'clock, tired out and very hungry, I stopped in one of these cañons to rest myself by the side of a small creek that ran briskly for a few steps, and then disappeared in the sand. I had been there but a little while when a large buck came down to the creek to drink, within twenty yards of where I was sitting. I raised my rifle cautiously, and fired at him. He ran off a short distance, as if he was n't hurt at all, when he stopped and began to reel from side to side, and in a moment or so dropped down dead. I dragged him to the bank of the creek, where I skinned and cut him up, and in a little while had a side of his ribs roasting before a fire. He was one of the fattest deer I ever saw, and as I thought it very uncertain when I would reach camp, I concluded it would be good policy to remain where I was the balance of the day, and jerk up as much of the flesh as I could conveniently carry. So, after I had made a hearty dinner on my roasted ribs, I went to work and cut up a quantity of the meat into thin slices, which I placed on a low scaffold made of little poles, and then built a fire under them, and before sundown I had enough meat nicely "jerked" to last me for several days. I then looked around for secure quarters for the night, and a few yards below

* *Cañon.* A deep gorge, or ravine, between high and steep banks, worn by a watercourse. — *Gulch.* A dry watercourse or gully. — WEBSTER.

where I had butchered the deer, I found a shallow cave in a cliff, into which I carried my dried venison and some dry grass for a bed. I was very lucky in finding this cave, for that night a torrent of rain fell, which would have made camping out of doors extremely unpleasant, especially as it was accompanied by a strong and chilly wind; but as it was I slept as "snug as a bug in a rug," and did n't mind the howling of the wind any more than that of the wolves, who were holding a "jubilee" over the remains of the deer I had killed.

October 26th.—When I awoke in the morning, it was broad daylight. The rain had ceased, but it was still cloudy and misty, and I could n't see the sun, which was the only guide I had to indicate the direction I ought to go.*

However, when I had made a breakfast off of my venison, and taken a drink of water from the creek, I packed up my jerked meat, tying it firmly together with thongs of bear-grass, and set out again in the direction I supposed the camp to be. The country continued exceedingly rough and broken, and I was frequently headed off by impassable gulches and cañons, that I could only avoid sometimes by going a long distance out of my course.

* With the experience I now have, I could have pursued my course with as perfect a certainty as if the sun had been visible, for I can tell the points of the compass very nearly at all times, by the bark on the trees, which is generally thicker on the north side, and by the moss growing upon them, or by sticking a pin perpendicularly into a piece of white cloth or paper. In the cloudiest day, the pin will cast a dim shadow opposite the sun, and thus point out its position. But, you see, at that time I was ignorant of all these things, and had to steer my course by guess, when the sun could not be seen; and, unfortunately for me, a spell of misty weather had set in, that lasted for more than a week.

Toward noon, I came to a little valley, in which there was a beautiful bold spring bursting out from the foot of the hills, and round it four or five large pecan-trees, filled with fruit. Here I rested for an hour or so, and made a hearty dinner on venison and pecans, the pecans answering pretty well in the place of bread. In the bed of the little creek formed by this spring I picked up some curious-looking pebbles, about the size of buck-shot, and put them in my shot-pouch. They proved to be "garnets," and I have no doubt that a quantity of them might be collected in that locality; but I am told they are not a very valuable stone. I have found them in several other places in Texas; and at one point on the road from San Antonio to El Paso, I found a number of rubies, but I was ignorant of their value at the time, and only picked up two or three as curiosities.

Near the spring where I had stopped, there was a petrified forest. The trees were all lying upon the ground, as if they had been blown down by a heavy wind, but in some instances they were nearly whole, even the small twigs and branches being petrified.

Toward evening I continued my route, and never stopped for a moment until the sun was about setting, when I began to look out for a convenient place for camping. I had already passed several deep gulches or hollows, in which I expected to find water; but they were all dry. I went on until it grew so dark it was with great difficulty I made any headway at all, and at last I was compelled to stop without finding water. Although pretty hungry, I did not venture on my dried venison, for fear of increasing my thirst, and, having started a small fire, I lay down under a spreading live-oak, and soon forgot all my troubles in a sound sleep.

October 27th. — I woke just at daylight. The morning was cloudy and still, and the first thing I noticed was a pattering sound, as if made by a small stream of water falling from a precipice. I got up and went in the direction of the sound, and in forty or fifty yards from where I had slept I came to one of the finest springs I had ever seen. It broke out at the foot of a huge cliff, in a stream as large as my body, and, after running a little way, it fell fifteen or twenty feet into the bottom of the ravine below, forming a beautiful cascade. Where the stream came out at the foot of the cliff, there was a deep pool of clear, cold water, out of which I took a hearty drink; and after I had bathed my face and hands, I built up a small fire, and roasted some of my venison, and though I had neither bread, nor salt, nor coffee, I made a satisfactory breakfast upon it, with a few of my pecans.

There were one or two Indian camps near this spring, but they did not seem to have been occupied for some time. In one of them I picked up a Mexican gourd that would hold about two quarts of water, which the Indians had evidently forgotten when they left. To my great joy, I found, on examining it, that it was not broken or cracked in any way. I had suffered a good deal for the want of something in which to carry a supply of water along with me, and I looked upon this gourd as a valuable addition to my worldly effects. I fastened a band of bear-grass around it, so that I could carry it conveniently when travelling.

And here, most unexpectedly, I met up with a companion that was never separated from me afterward, (except on one occasion for a few days,) during all my wanderings. While I was sitting down eating my breakfast, I saw some animal poke his head out of a hollow in the rock, a few feet distant, and gaze at me, apparently with considerable curiosity. At first I took it to be a wolf, but, upon closer inspection, I saw that it was a dog, and I whistled and snapped my fingers at him to coax him out of his den. For a while he paid no attention to this, but at length he ventured out, attracted more, I think, by the smell of roasted meat than by the signs I made him. He approached me very cautiously, however, frequently stopping and looking back at his den; but he finally came up to me, and I gave him a piece of venison, which he eagerly devoured. He was the most wretched specimen of a dog I had ever seen. Both of his ears were cut off close to his head, and he had been starved to such a degree that he looked for all the world like a pile of bones loosely packed in a sack of hair and hide. He was too weak to hold his tail up, which dragged upon the ground like a wolf's. I suppose he had been left behind by the party of Indians whose camps I had seen near the spring. I gave him as much venison as I thought he ought to eat at one time, which he swallowed so greedily that he choked himself several times. I named him "Comanche" on the spot, and we were soon upon the most friendly terms.

Comanche's company, ugly and wolfish as he looked, was very acceptable to me, and relieved me, to some extent, from that feeling of loneliness usually experienced by one like myself, unaccustomed to the solitude of the wilderness. I believe the company of a dog, next to that of a man, and more than that of any other animal, seems to satisfy that longing for companionship we feel when circumstanced as I was then.

After breakfast, I filled up my gourd with water from the spring, and took my way again across the hills, Comanche following at my heels. By this time, the breakfast of venison I had given him had improved him amazingly, and his tail began to curl in its usual style.

To-day I passed over the roughest and most desolate-looking country I had yet seen — rocky hills, some of which were entirely bare of all vegetation, and others covered with dense chaparral and thorny bushes, through which I sometimes found it almost impossible to force my way. Game of all sorts seemed to be exceedingly scarce here, for except two or three antelopes I saw no animals on my route; but rattlesnakes were more numerous than I ever saw them elsewhere. I stirred them up every few yards as I walked.

My gourd proved very serviceable to-day, for I did not see a drop of water, after leaving the spring, until night, and we would have suffered without it.

Ever since I had left the pass where the Indians gave me the run, I had scarcely had a glimpse of the sun, for it had been misty and cloudy all the time, but to-day it shone out for a little while, and, to my great disappointment, I found I had been travelling nearly due north, instead of south, which was the direction I ought to have taken. This was exceedingly vexatious, and from that time I abandoned all hope of finding the surveyors' camp. However, I did n't despair of making my way back into the settlements in the course of time, provided the Indians, or the snakes, or the "varmints" did n't get me on the route. I immediately changed my course, steering due south instead of north, passing over a desolate and barren tract of country.

Toward sundown, I came to the top of a high ridge, at the foot of which there lay a little grassy valley, surrounded on all sides by steep rocky hills similar to the one on which I stood. I descended into this little valley just as the sun was setting, and, to my great joy, nearly the first thing I saw after entering it was a fine spring of water, breaking out from the foot of the hill I had just scrambled down.

Near this spring, in a ledge of rocks, I found a sort of shallow cave, walled up in front with loose stones, through which there was a narrow entrance. Inside, there was a comfortable little room about twelve feet square, perfectly protected from the weather, and with a smooth, dry rock floor. It had evidently been built and used by the Indians long ago; but there was nothing about it to indicate that they had occupied it for years.

After supper, I cut a few armfuls of dry grass, which I carried into the cave, and with which I made a soft bed on the floor for myself, and another for Comanche near the entrance, and we slept soundly till morning.

CHAPTER VIII.

MY LITTLE VALLEY — A SAD ACCIDENT — WILD TURKEYS — ON CRUTCHES — ON THE TRAMP AGAIN — A LAST LOOK.

OCTOBER *28th.*—I was up by daylight this morning, and ready to start in half an hour, for it took me but a little while to cook and eat my breakfast, and clear away the dishes.

As I passed through the little valley, I could not but admire its seclusion and beauty. It was shut in on all sides by high hills, covered with cedars and other evergreens. I suppose it was about half a mile long by a quarter in breadth, and a clear, rapid little stream ran through the centre of it. Scattered over it were many beautiful clumps of live-oaks, pecans, and other trees. I saw several flocks of deer grazing among the trees, and a great many wild turkeys, but I did not try to shoot any, as I had some of my jerked venison left, and did not want to waste my ammunition. I had passed through the centre of the valley, and was in the act of climbing up the hill on the opposite side, when my foot slipped on a loose stone, and I sprained my ankle badly. I attempted to go on, but the pain was so great, whenever I put my foot to the ground, that I found it impossible to do so.

Here was a pretty fix. As the backwoodsman said, when the Indians attacked his house just as he had filled his gun with water to swab it out, "It was very ridiculous." But I saw there was no alternative but to stop and remain patiently where I was until my ankle got well enough to enable me to travel again; so I hobbled back with great pain and difficulty to the little cave on the side of the valley I had started from.

By the time I reached my cave, I was suffering very much, and my ankle had swollen out of all shape. I pulled off my shoe, and bathed my foot for half an hour in the cold spring-water, and the pain left me in a great measure. However, I knew it would be days, perhaps weeks, before my ankle would be well enough for me to continue my journey, and knew not how to subsist in the mean time, without being able to hunt for game. This thought was anything but agreeable, and I felt rather despondent that night as I lay down upon my bed in the little cave. I thought, though, after all, I had much to be thankful for; for, if this accident had happened to me anywhere in the barren and desolate country I had lately travelled over, where there was neither water to be had nor game to be found, how much more hopeless and miserable my condition would have been. So I made myself as contented as I could, and was soon fast asleep.

October 29th. — I awoke about daylight, and the first thing I heard was a gang of wild turkeys clucking in the pecan-trees that grew a few steps from my cave. I seized my gun and crawled to the door. The trees were crowded with them, and selecting one of the largest gobblers, I fired at him, and he tumbled to the ground. "Comanche" seemed to understand thoroughly what was up, for as soon as the turkey struck the earth, he pounced upon it, and dragged it up to the mouth of my cave, where I picked and cleaned him nicely, and soon had him spitted before my fire, and in a couple of hours he was done to a turn.

After breakfast, being uncertain as to the length of

time I should be compelled to remain here, I took another "account of stock" on hand, and found that I was the fortunate owner of the following property, viz.: one rifle, in good condition; one shot-pouch, and powder-horn filled with powder; one butcher-knife; twenty-six bullets; steel for striking fire; one Mexican gourd; one memorandum-book and pencil; two plugs of tobacco, and a pipe. Pretty "well to do," thinks I to myself, considering the "tightness of the times." I found it impossible to put my lame foot to the ground at all, without suffering great pain, so I concluded I would try and make a sort of crutch, that would enable me to hobble about on my sound foot. So I crawled out to where there was a bunch of young saplings growing, and, with much labor, at length cut down a forked one with my butcher-knife, which I thought would answer my purpose. By night I had it finished, and, on trial, I found that I could get along with it, after a fashion, on level ground. I have not much fear of starving now, for with my crutch I can follow any game that may come into the valley.

After night, a heavy rain came up from the north, accompanied by much thunder and lightning. The rain never ceased falling till near daylight, but my cave did not leak a drop, and the wall in front prevented the wind from driving it in on me.

From this time, as long as I stayed in the valley, which was until the 20th of November, nothing of importance occurred, and as one day was pretty much like another, I made but few notes in my memorandum-book, only enough to keep from losing the day of the month. On the 2d of November, "I killed a deer;" on the 5th, "gathered about a bushel of pecans;" on the

7th, "killed another deer;" on the 10th, "my ankle improved so much I can walk a little without my crutch," etc.

I never suffered a moment for food the whole time I was in the valley, for I could kill a deer or turkey whenever I wanted one, and could gather, with but little trouble, an abundance of pecans, and various kinds of haws and berries. It was truly lucky for me that the accident happened to me at this place. Had it occurred at almost any other on my route, the probability is I should have starved to death, in my helpless condition.

The day before I left the valley, I jerked up as much venison as I could conveniently carry along with me, and, on the morning of the 20th of November, I bade farewell to my little cave. Before leaving, I carved my name on a rock in front of my old quarters with my butcher-knife, together with the day of the month and year. I felt right sorry to leave my little valley, where I had passed so many peaceful, quiet days. My ankle had got entirely well, and, shouldering my rifle and pack of provisions, and, with "Comanche" following at my heels, I started off across the valley in a southern direction. "Comanche" had lived on the "fat of the land" since he had fallen in with me, and was now quite a respectable-looking dog, and his tail had a fierce and defiant curl.

The sun shone brightly, and I had no difficulty in keeping the course I wanted to go. When I had ascended to the top of the opposite ridge of hills, I turned to take a last look at my little valley. I could see the entrance to my cave, the grove of pecans in front of it, and the smoke still curling upward from the fire I had left burning.

The settlements have now extended beyond this point, and probably by this time some advocate of "squatter sovereignty" has taken possession of it; but when I was there, there was not a log cabin, I suppose, within a hundred miles of it.

I travelled about ten miles this morning, over a very rough and rugged country, covered with thick chaparral, when I halted to rest for an hour or so. There was no water near, but I had a supply along with me in my Mexican gourd, which I had filled from the spring before leaving.

After Comanche and I had eaten a bite, and rested ourselves sufficiently, I continued my route over the same sort of country till near night, when I encamped on the banks of a considerable creek — one of the head branches, I have supposed since, of the Palo Pinto. A small gang of buffalo were grazing in the creek valley, but they discovered me and ran off before I could get a shot at them. I, however, killed a fat doe after I had struck camp, which furnished me with an abundance of fresh meat. I also found some of the "wild artichoke" growing near, which afforded an agreeable addition to my usual bill of fare.

I saw fresh Indian "signs" near my camp, which caused me some uneasiness, and I kept a good lookout for them. Comanche woke me several times during the night with his growling, but I supposed there was nothing more dangerous about than a cayote or catamount, attracted to the camp by the smell of fresh meat.

CHAPTER IX.

GOLD — INDIAN SMOKES — COMANCHE UNEASY — CAPTURED BY THE INDIANS — MYSTERIOUS MOVEMENTS — THE OLD SQUAW — WHAT NEXT?

NOVEMBER *21st.* — Clear and cool. After breakfast I crossed the creek and went on five or six miles, through the most singular-looking country I ever saw. At a little distance, a person would have supposed on approaching it that it was a level plain, but on nearer inspection, though there were no hills or elevations of any size in it, he would have found the whole surface broken and ruptured as if by an earthquake, and seamed with deep gulches and cañons that interlaced and crossed each other at all sorts of angles. I had more difficulty in making my way over these five or six miles than I ever had experienced elsewhere in the same distance. I noticed in the bottoms of many of these gulches a great deal of quartz rock and black sand, which I had been told indicated the presence of gold, and I determined, from mere curiosity, that I would "prospect" a little in one of the gulches, and see if I could not find some of the precious metal itself. I followed one of them down several hundred yards, and amongst a pile of broken rocks and gravel, thrown together by the violence of the torrent that rushed along the bed of the gulch in rainy weather, I picked up three pieces of pure gold, the largest of which weighed nearly a quarter of an ounce.

I have often thought since that, some time or other, I would return to that place and "prospect" it thoroughly, but something has always prevented me from doing so. However, I am determined, just as soon as I can, that I will explore that region of country. I can find it again readily, I know, and I feel confident, from the little examination I made when there, that gold exists there in abundance.

After leaving this locality, I struck a fine open prairie country, through which I travelled without difficulty for twelve or fifteen miles, when I came to a heavily timbered bottom on a considerable stream, which I have since supposed was the Leon.

I saw half a dozen "Indian smokes" on the way, and once I crossed a considerable trail, which was quite fresh. I pitched camp on the edge of the bottom, under the shelter of a spreading live-oak. After dark, Comanche appeared to be very uneasy and watchful. He woke me several times during the night, snuffling and growling, but I paid no particular attention to his movements, supposing his watchfulness was owing to the presence of wolves or other animals in the vicinity of the camp.

About daylight, I was suddenly roused by his furious barking, and looking up, I was horrified to see a dozen Indians coming rapidly toward me, and not more than forty or fifty yards distant. I always slept with my gun by my side, and I seized it instantly, and sprang behind the tree under which I had been sleeping. As I did so, I saw that I was completely surrounded by Indians, and that there was no chance of making my escape. I resolved, however, to sell my life as dearly as I could, and as the circle of warriors drew closer and closer in upon me, I kept dodging from one side of the tree to the other, keeping my gun pointed all the time toward those that were nearest to me. Presently one of the Indians, who I supposed was the chief, said something

5

in a loud voice to the balance, and they all halted. He then advanced a few steps toward me, and asked, in the Mexican language, "who I was, and what I was doing there?" I had picked up a smattering of Mexican after I came out of Texas, and by signs and such phrases as I knew, I told him I was an American, that I had got lost from my party, and was on my way back to the "settlements." He then made signs to me to put down my gun, which I did, for I saw plainly that resistance was hopeless against such numbers, and I thought if I surrendered it was possible they might spare my life. As soon as I laid my gun upon the ground, the chief came up and took possession of it, and then calling to the rest, they all advanced, and one of them seized my hands and bound them firmly with deer thongs behind my back.

Bitterly did I regret that I had not fought it out with them to the last, instead of surrendering, but it was then too late to repent, and I made up my mind to meet my fate, whatever it might be, with as much courage as I could "screw up" for the occasion. Comanche, however, with less discretion than valor, "pitched into" the whole crowd while they were tying my hands, and it was only after they had kicked him and beaten him severely with their spear-handles, that he gave up the contest and retired to a safe distance in the rear.

As soon as my hands were tied, the chief ordered one of the Indians to pick up my shot-pouch and other equipments, and we all started off at a brisk walk up the river, keeping a little trail just outside of the timbered bottom.

We had travelled in this way, I suppose, four or five miles, when the Indians gave three or four loud whoops,

CAPTURED BY THE INDIANS. — Page 50.

which were answered by similar whoops apparently about half a mile ahead, and in a little while we came in sight of the lodges of a large encampment. When within a short distance of the encampment, a mixed crowd of old men, women, and boys came out to meet us, who soon surrounded me in a dense mass, screaming, yelling and hooting, and calling me, I suppose, all sorts of hard names, but of course I could n't understand their "lingo." I was glad when my guard took me away from them and carried me into one of the lodges, where they untied my hands and made signs for me to sit down.

I took a seat on one of the skins scattered over the floor, in no very pleasant frame of mind, as you may well imagine, for I was pretty well satisfied, from the manner in which I had been treated by the Indians since they captured me, that they intended to put me to death. In a little while an old squaw came into the lodge, bringing with her some buffalo-meat and a gourd of water, which she put down by me, and made signs to me to eat and drink; but I had no appetite, and merely took a drink of the water.

I could only see imperfectly what was going on outside of the lodge, but I knew from the whooping and yelling, and the running to and fro, that something was up, and I was very much afraid that my arrival had a good deal to do with it. However, everything quieted down in an hour or so.

A strong guard was placed at night around the lodge in which I was confined, and this confirmed me in my suspicions that foul play was intended me, and at the same time precluded all hope of escape. My reflections during that night were anything but agreeable, as may well be supposed, and my sleep was broken and disturbed.

About sunrise the next morning, the old squaw came into the lodge again with some provisions, which she placed near me on the floor, and she then seated herself and looked at me a long time without saying a word. After a while, she took one of my hands in her wrinkled paws, and rubbed and patted it all the time humming, in a sort of "bumble-bee tone," one of the most mournful ditties I ever heard. At length, she got up to leave, but before she did so she tried very hard by signs to make me comprehend something she wished to say, but I couldn't understand what it was. She was as wrinkled and ugly as an old witch, but still there was something benevolent and kind about her features, that made me think she would willingly befriend me if she had it in her power.

Not long after she had left the lodge, I heard a great "pow-wowing" outside, and then the most terrible racket commenced I ever listened to, yelling, whooping, and beating of drums, and rattling of gourds and the large shields made of dry hides, hung around with bears' tusks and pieces of metal, which the Indians make use of to stampede horses when on their stealing expeditions. In a few moments after the row commenced, several warriors came into the lodge, and one of them proceeded to blacken my face and hands with a mixture he had in an earthen vessel. When they had painted me in this way, they made signs to me to follow them, which I did very unwillingly, for I had no doubt they were going to put me to death, with all the tortures to which I had been told the Indians usually subject those who are so unfortunate as to be made prisoners by them.

CHAPTER X.

Led out for Execution — Saved at the Last Moment — A New Mother and a New Home — Comanche in Luck Again — "Lobo-lusti-hadjo."

MY guard led me out into a sort of square between the lodges, in which all the Indians belonging to the encampment — men, women, and children — were assembled, and proceeded to bind me hand and foot to a post firmly fixed in the ground. I was convinced then what my fate was to be, especially when I looked around and saw the terrible preparations that had been made for the ceremony of burning a prisoner at the stake. Near me there was a great heap of dry wood, and a fire burning, and twenty or thirty grim warriors stood around, painted and blacked up in the most fantastic way, with their tomahawks and scalping-knives in their hands, who, I supposed, were to act as my executioners.

When they had fastened me securely to the stake, the chief to whom I had surrendered rose up from a sort of platform, on which he had been sitting, and made a speech to the crowd. He spoke in his own language, and of course I could understand but little of what he said, but it seemed to me he was telling them how the white people had encroached upon them, and stolen from them their hunting-grounds, and driven them farther and farther into the wilderness, and that it was a good deed to burn every one of the hated race that fell into their hands. After he had finished speaking, the painted warriors formed a ring, and while one of them heaped up the dry wood on all sides of me as high as my waist, the balance danced around me, singing the "death-song" and brandishing their tomahawks and knives.

I thought, sure enough, my time had come, and I tried to summon up courage enough to meet my fate like a man. I don't know how far I would have succeeded in this, for just at this moment the old squaw I had seen in the lodge rushed through the crowd of painted warriors, and began to throw the wood from around me, all the time talking and gesticulating in the wildest manner. One of the warriors seized her and put her out of the ring by main force, but she addressed herself to the crowd, and made them a regular set speech, during which she every now and then turned and pointed toward me. I was satisfied that for some cause, I knew not what, the old squaw was doing her best to save me from burning at the stake, and it is hardly necessary to say I wished her success from the bottom of my heart. The crowd listened to her in silence for some time, when some began, as I thought, to applaud her, and others to cry out against her; but it seems that she at last brought over the majority to her side, for after a great deal of jabbering, a number of women rushed in between the warriors and untied me from the stake in a moment, and handed me over to the old squaw for safe-keeping; and somehow, though I had understood but little of all that had been said on either side for or against me, I knew that I was saved, at least for the time. I felt as much relieved in my mind as when I drew the "white bean" at the city of Saltillo.

I learned afterward that the old squaw had lost one of her sons in a fight with some of the neighboring tribes, and that she had set up a claim to me, according to the Indian custom in such cases, as a substitute. But the Indians, I suppose, were bent on having a little fun, in which I was to play the part of frog, and they the pelters, and, as you have seen, it was only by the "skin of her teeth" that she came out winner at the last quarter stretch. But I was very glad, I can tell you, that their frolic was stopped in this way, for I hadn't the least ambition to perform the part they intended for me in the ceremony.

My adopted mother conducted me to her lodge, patted me on the head, and sang another "bumble-bee ditty" over me, to all of which I made no objection, as I was very glad to get off from being roasted alive on any terms. She then, as I supposed, made signs to me to "consider myself at home," and "as one of the family" from that time. In a little while afterward, some squaws brought me my gun and all my equipments, even to my Mexican gourd, and gave them to me. Even Comanche was hunted up and brought to the lodge, and delivered up to me as a part of my property. Poor Comanche had seen a rough time, as well as myself, since we were separated. He was half starved, and looked as if he had been beaten unmercifully by every urchin in the encampment. He was real glad to see me again, and I "made myself at home" at once by giving him all the cold victuals I could find about the premises.

The old squaw, my mother now, had one son still living with her, "Lobo-lusti-hadjo," or the "Black Wolf," and of course, according to the Indian laws, he was now my brother, and, Indian though he was, he proved a brother to me as long as I lived with the tribe, which was about three months; and when I left, it was with his knowledge, and he did all that he could to aid me in effecting my escape. I have met with few men anywhere that I liked better than Black Wolf. He was a man of good natural sense, and as brave as the bravest, and there was nothing cruel or bloodthirsty in his disposition, and, what is very unusual among the Indians, he was much attached to his old mother, and did everything he could to make her comfortable in her old age.

I might lengthen out my story a good deal by telling of all that occurred to me while I was with these Indians — how I went with them upon their buffalo hunts, and once upon a "foray" with them into Mexico, where I acquired a considerable reputation as a promising young warrior in a hard fight we had there with the Mexican rancheros, etc., — but I am afraid I should grow tiresome, and for this reason, I will bring this part of my story to an end as soon as possible.

The old chief to whom I surrendered in the first instance, for some cause had taken a great liking to me, and offered me his sister for a wife, and a home in his own wigwam; but I preferred staying with Black Wolf and his old mother, for, in fact, the chief's sister wasn't as attractive as some women I have seen. She was tall and raw-boned, and her cheeks looked like a couple of small pack-saddles, and her finger nails were as long as a catamount's claws, and not overly clean at that, and I had no doubt she could have used them just as well "on a pinch" — at least that was my private opinion, though I did not tell the chief so.

When I had been about two months with the tribe, I learned to speak their language pretty well, and Black Wolf never tired of asking me questions about the "white people," and their big canoes, steamboats, railroads, etc., for he had heard about all these things at the trading posts he had occasionally visited. I told him that the white people were so numerous that they had many "permanent camps" in which there were forty, fifty, and a hundred thousand inhabitants, and one in which there was more than half a million.

He said he knew they were a powerful people, but he had no idea before that their number was so great. But he said what I had told him about them confirmed him in the opinion he had had for a long time, that the white people would gradually spread over the whole country, from ocean to ocean, and that the day would soon come when there would be nothing left to show that the Indians had once occupied all this vast territory, except here and there a little mound built over their graves, or a stone arrow-head, ploughed up by the white people where they had once hunted the buffalo or the grisly bear. And as his reason for thinking so, he related to me the following legend, which he said had been told him by his father when he was a little boy.

CHAPTER XI.

BLACK WOLF'S INDIAN LEGEND — DETERMINATION TO ESCAPE — BACK IN THE SETTLEMENTS.

A GREAT many years ago," said Black Wolf, "a young chief, belonging to one of the most powerful tribes of Arkansas, concluded that he would visit one of the nearest white settlements, and see some of the people of whom he had heard so much. So he took his gun and dog, crossed the 'father of waters' in his canoe, and travelled for many days toward the rising of the sun, through a dense forest that had never echoed to the sound of the white man's axe. One day, just as the sun was setting, he came to the top of a high hill, and four or five miles away, in the valley below, he saw the smoke curling up from the chimneys of the most western settlement, at that time, east of the Mississippi river.

"As it was too late to reach the settlement before dark, the chief sought out the thickest part of the woods, where he spread his blanket upon the ground, and laid himself down upon it, with the intention of passing the night there. He had scarcely settled himself to rest, when he heard a 'halloo' a long way off among the hills. Supposing that some one had got lost in the woods, he raised himself up and shouted as loud as he could. Again he heard the 'halloo' apparently a little nearer, but it sounded so mournful and wild, and so unlike the voice of any living being, that he became alarmed, and did not shout in return. After awhile, however, the long mournful 'halloo-o-o' was repeated, and this time much nearer than before. The chief's heart beat loudly in his bosom, and a cold sweat broke out upon his forehead; for he knew that the unearthly sounds that met his ears never came from mortal lips. His very dog, too, seemed to understand this, for he whined and cowered down at his feet, seemingly in the greatest dread. Again the prolonged and mournful 'halloo-o-o' was heard, and this time close at hand, and in a few moments an Indian warrior stalked up and took a seat near the chief, and gazed mournfully at him out of his hollow eyes, without uttering a word.

"He was dressed in a different garb from anything the chief had ever seen worn by the Indians, and he held a bow in his withered hand, and a quiver, filled with arrows, was slung across his shoulders. As the chief looked more closely at him, he saw that his unearthly visitor was, in fact, a grinning skeleton; for his white ribs showed plainly through the rents in his robe, and though seemingly he looked at the chief, there were no eyes in the empty sockets he turned toward him. Presently the figure rose up, and, in a hollow voice, spoke to the chief, and told him to return from whence he came, for their race was doomed — that they would disappear before the white people like dew before the morning sun — that he was the spirit of one of his forefathers, and that he came to warn him of the fate that awaited him and his people — that he could remember when the Indians were as numerous as the leaves on the trees, and the white people were few and weak, and shut up in their towns upon the sea-shore — now they are strong, and their number cannot be counted, and before many years they will drive the last remnant of the red race into the waters of the great western ocean. 'Go back,' said the figure, advancing toward the chief, and waving his withered hand, 'and tell your people to prepare themselves for their doom, and to meet me in the "happy hunting grounds," where the white man shall trouble them no more.'

"As he said this he came up close to the chief, and placed his skeleton fingers on his head, and glared at him out of the empty sockets in his fleshless skull! 'Son of a fading race, the last hour of your unfortunate people is fast approaching, and soon not a vestige of them will be left on all this wide continent. They and their forests, their hunting grounds, their villages and wigwams, will disappear forever, and the white man's cities and towns will rise up in the places where once they chased the buffalo, the elk, and the deer.'

"The chief was as fearless a warrior as ever went to battle; but when he felt the cold touch of that skeleton hand, a horrible dread took possession of him, and he remembered nothing of what happened afterward. In the morning, when he woke up, the sun was shining brightly over head, and the birds were whistling and chirping in the trees above him. He looked around for his gun, and was surprised beyond reason when he picked it up and found that the barrel was all eaten up with rust, and the stock so decayed and rotten that it fell to pieces in his hand. His dog was nowhere to be seen, and he whistled and called to him in vain; but at his feet he saw a heap of white bones, among which there was a skeleton of a neck, with the collar his dog had worn still around it! He then noticed that his buckskin hunting-shirt was decayed and mildewed, and hung in tatters upon him, and that his hair had grown so long that it reached down nearly to his waist.

Bewildered by all these sudden and curious changes, he took his way toward the top of the hill, from which, the evening before, he had seen the smoke rising up from the cabins of the frontier settlement, and what was his astonishment when he saw, spread out in the valley below him, a great city, with its spires and steeples rising up as far as his eye could extend; and in place of the dense, unbroken forests that covered the earth when he came, a wide, open country presented itself to his view, fenced up into fields and pastures, and dotted over with the white man's stately houses and buildings.

"As he gazed at all this in surprise and wonder, he could distinctly hear, from where he stood, the distant hum of the vast multitude who were laboring and trafficking and moving about in the great city below him. Sad and dispirited, he turned his course homeward, and after travelling many days through farms and villages and towns, he at length reached once more the banks of the mighty Mississippi. But the white people had got there before him, and in place of a silent and lonely forest, he found a large town built up where it had once stood, and saw a huge steamboat puffing and paddling along right where he had crossed the 'father of waters' in his little canoe. When he had crossed the river, he found that the white settlements had gone on a long ways beyond it, but at length he came to the wilderness again, and after wandering about for many moons, he at last came up with the remnant of his people, but now no longer a powerful tribe, such as he had left them, for they had dwindled down to a mere handful. His father and mother were dead, his brothers and sisters were all dead, and no one knew the poor old warrior that had appeared so suddenly among them. For a while he staid with them, and talked, in the strangest way, about things that had happened long before the oldest people in the tribe were born; but one day, after telling the story I have told you, he took his way toward the setting sun, and was never seen more."

When I had been about three months with the tribe, I began to long exceedingly to be once more with my own people. I lost all relish for "forays" and "hunting expeditions," and thought only of effecting my escape, and making my way back to the "settlements." I became moody and discontented to such a degree that Black Wolf and his mother at length took notice of it. One day, when Black Wolf and myself were alone together in the lodge, he said to me, "My brother, what is it that makes you so unhappy and discontented; for I have seen for some time that you have had something on your mind? Has any one mistreated my brother?"

"No," said I, "every one has treated me well; but I tell you frankly, my brother," (for I knew he would not betray me,) "I am pining to see my own people again, and I am determined to attempt to make my escape into the settlements, if it should cost me my life."

"My brother," said Black Wolf, "I shall be very sorry if you leave us, and so will my old mother; but it is not strange you should wish to see your own people again, and you must go. I will help you all that I can to reach the settlements in safety. But be careful," said he, "not to say a word about this to anybody, for if you should attempt to escape and be recaptured, nothing could save your life, and I should be put to death for having aided you."

As Black Wolf advised me, I said nothing to any one of my intention of leaving, except to his old mother. She tried very hard to dissuade me from going, but finding I was resolute in my purpose, she gave up the point, and sang two or three more of her "bumble-bee" ditties over me at parting, which seemed to lighten her grief considerably. She also made me a present of a dried terrapin's tail, which she said would protect me from all danger from bullets in battle. I have kept the terrapin's tail, out of respect for the old squaw, but I must say, in the many "scrimmages" I have been in since then with the Mexicans and Indians, I have had more faith in the efficacy of a tree or a stump to protect me from bullets, than in the charm she gave me. She also gave me a necklace made of the claws of the grisly bear and porcupine quills, and a large copper ring to wear in my nose.

Black Wolf and I made our preparations quietly for the journey, but without exciting any suspicions on the part of the other Indians that I had any intention of quitting the tribe, as we told them we were going into the "hills" to take a bear hunt, and would be absent possibly several days. Black Wolf led the way, and Comanche and I followed, and the first day we travelled at least thirty miles from the village, and camped together that night for the last time. In the morning, before we separated, Black Wolf traced out upon the ground a map of the route I had to go, marking down upon it accurately all the ranges of hills and watercourses I would pass on the way. He then bade me good-by, and shouldering his gun, sorrowfully took his course back toward the village, and was soon lost to sight among the hills.

During my stay with the Indians I had acquired considerable knowledge of the woods, and how to steer my course through them even when the sun was not visible, and, in eight days after parting from Black Wolf, I arrived safely at the "settlements," and thus ended my first expedition into the "wilderness." Comanche lived with me till he died of old age, and left a progeny behind him, that, for trailing and fighting "varmints" and "sucking eggs," can't be beat by any dogs in the State of Texas.

CHAPTER XII.

BELATED IN THE WOODS — WOLVES ON THE TRACK — ONE FELLOW OUT OF THE WAY — REINFORCEMENTS COMING UP — A HAND-TO-HAND FIGHT.

HAVE I ever told you, asked Big-Foot, about the "tussle" I had with the wolves a short time after I came to Texas? It was a sort of initiation fee paid for my entrance into the mysteries of border life, and I don't think I have ever been as badly frightened before or since. It happened in this way:

One very cold evening, two or three hours, perhaps, before sundown, I concluded to take a little round in the woods, by way of exercise, and bring home some fresh venison for supper; so I picked up "sweet-lips,"* and started for a rough, broken piece of country, where

* His rifle.

previously I had always found deer in abundance. But, somehow, the deer did n't seem to be stirring that evening, and I walked two or three miles without finding a single one. After going so far, I hated to return without meat, and I kept on, still hoping to find the deer before it got too dark to shoot; but at last I had to give it up, and turned my course back toward home again.

By this time the sun was setting, and I hurried up as fast as possible, to get out of the chaparral and into the prairie before night came on. All the evening I had heard the wolves howling around in an unusual way, but I had no fear of them, as I had been told they seldom, if ever, attacked a man in Texas. When I had gone back perhaps a half mile or so, a large gray wolf trotted out into the path before me, and commenced howling in the most mournful manner; and, in an instant, he was answered by a dozen other wolves in the hills around us. Thinks I, old fellow, if you are hatching a plot for my benefit, I'll make sure of you, anyhow; so I brought "sweet-lips" to range on his shoulder-blade, and at the crack of the gun he gave one spring into the air, and dropped as dead as a hammer in his tracks.

But, somehow, although I can't say I felt any fear of them, my suspicions were aroused as to foul play on the part of the gentlemen who were answering him from the hills, and I loosened "old butch" in the sheath, rammed another bullet down "sweet-lips," and as soon as I had done so, I put out for home again in double-quick time. But the faster I went, the faster the wolves followed me, and looking back after a little while, I saw twenty-five or thirty "lobos" (a large, fierce kind of wolf, found only in Mexico and Texas) trotting along after me at a rate I knew would soon bring them into

6*

close quarters; and in the bushes and chaparral, that bordered the trail I was travelling, I could see the gleaming eyes and pointed ears of at least a dozen others coming rapidly toward me.

I saw in a minute that they meant mischief, but I knew it was useless to try to beat a wolf in a foot-race. However, I resolved to keep on as long as they would let me, and when they closed in, that I would give them the best ready-made fight I had "in the shop." So I stepped out as briskly as I could, and the wolves trotted after me, howling in a way that made my hair stand on end and my very blood run cold. A dozen times I wished myself back again safe in "old Virginny," where a man might travel for a hundred miles without meeting up with anything more dangerous than a 'possum; but wishing didn't stop the wolves, so I let out my "best licks," hoping that I could make home before they could muster up courage enough to attack me.

But, I "reckoned without my host," for one big fellow, more daring or hungry than the rest, made a rush at me, and I barely had time to level my gun and fire, for he was touching the muzzle of it when I pulled the trigger. He fell dead at my feet, but, as if this had been the signal for a general attack, in an instant the whole pack were around me, snarling and snapping, and showing their white teeth in a way that was anything but pleasant.

I fought them off with the breech of my gun, for they didn't give me any chance to load it, retreating all the while as rapidly as I could. Once so many of them rushed in upon me at the same time that, in spite of all my efforts, I failed to keep them at bay, and they dragged me to the ground. I thought for an instant that it was all up with me, but despair gave me the strength of half a dozen men, and I used "old butch" to such a good purpose that I killed three outright and wounded several others, which appeared somewhat to daunt the balance, for they drew off a short distance and began to howl for reinforcements.

The reinforcements were on their way, for I could hear them howling in every direction, and I knew that I had no time to lose. So I put off at the top of my speed, and in those days it took a pretty fast Spanish pony to beat me a quarter when I "let out the kinks." I let 'em out this time with a will, I tell you, and fairly beat the wolves for half a mile or so, but my breath then began to fail me, and I could tell by their close angry yelps that the devils were again closing in upon me.

By this time I was so much exhausted that I knew I should make a poor fight of it, more especially as I could perceive, from the number of dark forms behind me, and the gleaming eyes and shining teeth that glistened out of every bush on the wayside, that the wolves had had a considerable addition to their number. It may be thought strange that I did n't "take to a tree," but there were no trees there to take to — nothing but stunted chaparral bushes, not much higher than a man's head.

I thought my time had come at last, and I was almost ready to give up in despair, when all at once I remembered seeing, as I came out, a large lone oak-tree, with a hollow in it about large enough for a man to crawl into, which grew on the banks of a small cañon not more than three or four hundred yards from where I then was. I resolved to make one more effort, and, if possible, to reach this tree before the wolves came up with me again; and if ever there was good, honest running done, without any throw-off about it, I did it then. The fact is, I believe a man can't tell how fast he can run until he gets a pack of wolves after him in this way. A fellow will naturally do his best when he knows that, if he doesn't, in twenty minutes he will be "parcelled out" among as many ravenous wolves, a head to one, a leg to another, an arm to a third, and so on. At least that was the effect it had on me, and I split the air so fast with my nose that it took the skin off of it, and for a week afterward it looked like a peeled onion.

However, I beat the wolves once more fairly and squarely, and not much time to spare either, for just as I crawled into the hollow of the tree, (which was about as high as my head from the ground,) the ravenous creatures were howling all around me. At the bottom of the hollow I found a "skunk" snugly stowed away, but I soon routed him out, and the wolves gobbled him up in an instant. He left a smell behind him, though, that was anything but agreeable in such close quarters. However, I was safe there, at any rate, from the attacks of the wolves, and all the smells in the city of New Orleans couldn't have driven me from my hole just at that time.

The wolves could only get at me one at a time, and with "old butch" in my hand, I knew I could manage a hundred in that way. But such howling and yelling I never heard before or since but once, and that was when I was with the Keechies, and a runner came in and told them their great chief, "Buffalo Hump," had been killed in a fight with the Lipans! They bit, and gnawed, and scratched, but it was n't any use, and every now and then a fellow would jump up and poke his nose into the hollow of the tree; but just as sure as he did it, he caught a wipe across it with "old butch" that generally satisfied his curiosity for a while. All night long they kept up their serenade, and, as you may well suppose, I did n't get much sleep. However, the noise did n't matter, for I had got several severe bites on my arms and legs, and the pain I suffered from them would have kept me awake anyhow.

Just at daylight the next morning the wolves began to sneak off, and when the sun rose not one was to be seen, except three dead ones at the root of the tree, that had come in contact with "old butch." I waited a while longer, to be certain they had all left, when I crawled out of my den, gave myself a shake, and found I was all right, except a pound or so of flesh taken out of one of my legs, and a few scratches on my arms. I hobbled back home; and for a long time afterward, whenever I heard the howling of wolves, I always felt a little uneasy.

I found out, the next day, why the wolves had attacked me in the way they did. I had a bottle of assafœtida in my trunk, which somehow had got broken and run out among my clothes, and when the wolves pitched into me I had on a coat that had been wet with the confounded stuff, and smelt worse than a polecat. I had often heard that assafœtida would attract wolves, but I always thought, before this, that it was a sort of old-woman's yarn; but it's a fact, and if you don't believe it, go some dark night into a thick chaparral, where wolves are numerous, and pour about a gill over your coat, and then wait a little, and see what will turn up; and if you don't hear howling, and snapping, and snarling, I 'll agree to be stung to death by bumble-bees.

CHAPTER XIII.

A STRUGGLE FOR LIFE—FIGHT WITH THE "BIG INDIAN."

WELL, how was it, Big-Foot," I asked, "about that fight you had with the big Indian in the cañon?"

"The fact is, sir," said he, "I caught a tremendous cold last night, and I 'm so hoarse now I can hardly talk at all. I 've got this cabin chinked entirely too tight, (looking around at the cracks, through which the stars could be seen twinkling in every direction,) and I shall have to knock out some more of the 'daubin'. Nothing like a tight room to give a man a cold. When I went on to the 'States,' five or six years ago, I had a cold constantly from sleeping in rooms that were as tight as a bottle. People want a supply of fresh air just as much as they do their regular meals, and occasionally something to clear the cobwebs out of their throats;" and as he said this, Big-Foot looked longingly toward the corner of the cabin in which the jug was deposited.

I took the hint, and handed over the "red-eye," when he glued the mouth of the jug affectionately to his lips, took an observation of the stars through one of the chinks for about half a minute, and then setting it down with a long breath, he wiped his lips on the cuff of his hunting-skirt, deliberately drew his butcher-knife from its sheath, cut a section from a plug of tobacco, crammed it into his mouth, and giving a preliminary squirt, to see if his spitting apparatus was all in good trim, he began his yarn of the "struggle for life."

In the fall of '42, the Indians were worse on the frontiers than they had ever been before, or since. You could n't stake a horse out at night with any expectation of finding him the next morning, and a fellow's scalp was n't safe on his head five minutes, outside of his own shanty. The people on the frontiers at last came to the conclusion that something had to be done, or else they would be compelled to fall back on the "settlements," which you know would have been reversing the natural order of things. So we collected together by agreement at my ranch, organized a company of about forty men, and the next time the Indians came down from the mountains (and we had n't long to wait for them) we took the trail, determined to follow it as long as our horses would hold out.

The trail led us up toward the head-waters of the Llano, and the third day out, I noticed a great many "signal smokes" rising up a long ways off in the direction we were travelling. These "signal smokes" are very curious things anyhow. You will see them rise up in a straight column, (no matter how hard the wind may be blowing,) and after reaching a great height, they will spread out at the top like an umbrella, and then, in a minute or so, puff! they are all gone in the twinkling of an eye. How the Indians make them, I never could learn, and I have often asked old frontiersmen if they could tell me, but none of them could ever give me any information on the subject. Even the white men who have been captured by the Indians, and lived with them for years, never learned how these "signal smokes" were made.

Well, as I was saying, on the third day out, we found Indian "signs" as plentiful as pig-tracks around a corn crib, and I told the captain we would have to move very cautiously, or we would be apt to find ourselves, before long, in a hornet's nest. That night we camped at a "water-hole," and put out a double guard. Just before the sun went down, I had noticed a smoke, apparently about three miles to the northeast of us, and felt satisfied that there was a party of Indians encamped at that place. So I went to the captain and told him, if he would give me leave to do so, I would get up an hour or two before daylight and reconnoitre the position, and find out whether there were any Indians there or not, and if so, to what tribe they belonged, what was their number, etc. He was willing enough to let me go, and told the guards to pass me out whenever I wanted to leave.

I whetted up "Old Butcher" a little, rammed two bullets down the throat of "Sweet Lips," and about two hours before daylight I left camp, and started off in the direction of the smoke I had seen the evening before. The chaparral, in some places, was as thick as the hair on a dog's back, but I "scuffled" through it in the dark, and after travelling perhaps a mile and a half, I came to a deep cañon, that seemed to head up in the direction I had seen the smoke. I scrambled down into it and waited until day began to break, and then slowly and cautiously continued my course along the bottom of the cañon.

The cañon was very crooked, and in some places so narrow that there was hardly room enough in it for two men to travel abreast. At length I came to a place where it made a sudden bend to the left, and just as

I turned the corner I came plump up against a big Indian, who was coming down the cañon, I suppose, with the intention of spying out our camp. We were both stooping down when we met, and our heads came together with considerable force, and the Indian rolled one way and I the other.

Both rose about the same time, and so unexpected was the encounter, that we stood for a moment uncertain what to do, and glaring upon each other like two catamounts, when they are about to dispute the carcass of a dead deer. The Indian had a gun as well as I, but we were too close to each other to shoot, and it seemed we both came to the same conclusion as to what was best to be done at the same instant, for we dropped our rifles, and grappled each other without saying a word.

You see, boys, I am a pretty stout man yet, but in those days, without meaning to brag, I don't believe there was a white man west of the Colorado River that could stand up against me in a regular catamount, bear-hug, hand-to-hand fight. But the minute I "hefted" that Indian I knew I had undertaken a job that would bring the sweat from me (and maybe so, I thought, a little blood too) before it was satisfactorily finished. He was nearly as tall as I am, say six feet one or two inches, and would weigh, I suppose, about one hundred and seventy-five pounds net, for he had no clothes on worth mentioning. I had the advantage of him in weight, but he was as wiry and active as a cat and as slick as an eel, and no wonder either, for he was greased from head to foot with bear's oil.

At it we went, in right down earnest, without a word being spoken by either of us, first up one side of the cañon, then down in the bottom, then up the other side, and the dust and gravel flew in such a way that if any one had been passing along the bank above, they would have supposed that a small whirlwind was raging below. I was a little the strongest of the two, however, and whenever we rose to our feet, I could throw the Indian easily enough, but the moment he touched the ground, the "varmint" would give himself a sort of a squirm, like a snake, and pop right up on top of me, and I could n't hold him still a moment, he was so slick with bear's grease. Each of us was trying to draw his butcher-knife from the sheath all the time, but we kept each other so busy, neither could get a chance to do it.

At last, I found that my breath began to fail me, and came to the conclusion, if something was n't done pretty soon, I should "have my note taken" to a certainty, for the Indian was like a Lobos wolf, and was getting better the longer he fought. So, the next time we rose, I put out all the strength I had left in me, and gave him a "back-handed trip," that brought his head with great force against a sharp-pointed rock upon the ground. He was completely stunned by the shock for an instant, and before he fairly came to, I snatched my knife from the sheath, and drove it with all my strength up to the hilt in his body. The moment he felt the cold steel he threw me off of him as if I had been a ten-year-old boy, sprang upon me before I could rise, drew his own butcher-knife, and raised it above his head with the intention of plunging it into my breast.

I tell you what, boys, I often see that Indian now in my dreams, (particularly after eating a hearty supper of bear's meat and honey,) grappling me by the throat with his left hand, and the glittering butcher-knife lifted up above me in his right, and his two fierce black eyes gleaming like a panther's in the dark! Under such circumstances, it is astonishing how fast a man will think. He thinks faster than the words can fly over those "new-fangled" telegraph lines. I looked up to the blue sky, and bid it a long farewell, and to the green trees, the sparkling waters, and the bright sun. Then I thought of my mother, as I remembered her when I was a little boy, the "old home," the apple orchard, the brook where I used to fish for minnows, and the "commons," where I used to ride every stray donkey and pony I could catch; and then I thought of Alice Ann, a blue-eyed, partridge-built young woman I had a "leaning to," who lived down in the Zumwalt Settlement. All these, and many more thoughts besides, flashed through my mind in the little time that knife was gleaming above my breast.

All at once the Indian gave a keen yell, and down came the knife with such force that it was buried to the hilt in the hard earth close to my side. The last time I had thrown the Indian, a deep gash had been cut in his forehead by the sharp-pointed rock, and the blood running down into his eyes from the wound blinded him, so that he missed his aim. I fully expected him to repeat his blow, but he lay still, and made no attempt to draw the knife from the ground. I looked at his eyes, and they were closed hard and fast, but there was a devilish sort of grin still about his mouth, as if he had died under the belief that he had sent me before him into the "happy hunting grounds."

I threw him off of me, and he rolled to the bottom of the cañon "stone dead." My knife had gone directly to his heart. I looked at him some time, lying there so still, and stiffening fast in the cool morning air, and I said to myself, "Well, old fellow, you made a good fight of it anyhow, and if luck had n't been against you, you would have 'taken my sign in,' too, to a certainty, and Alice Ann would have lost the best string she 's got to her bow."

"And now," said I to myself, "old fellow, I am going to do for you what I never did for an Indian before. I am going to give you a decent Christian burial." So I broke his gun into a dozen pieces and laid them beside him, according to the Indian custom, so it might be handy for him when he got to the "happy hunting grounds," (though if they have n't first-rate smiths there, I don't think it will be fit for use soon,) and then I pulled up some pieces of rock from the sides of the cañon, and piled them around and over him until he was completely covered, and safe from the attacks of cayotes and other animals, and there, I have no doubt, his bones are to this day.

This is a true account of my fight with the big Indian in the cañon.

CHAPTER XIV.

A TIGHT PLACE — INDIAN SIGNS — BEN WADE'S MOTTO — BEN AND THE BUFFALO RIBS — "INGINS ABOUT" — HERE THEY COME.

I HAVE been in many tight places, said "Big-Foot," but when I was in charge of the mail-coach, running from San Antonio to El Paso, I got into one I thought I should never squeeze out of with a whole hide, but I did.

In all the rows and scrapes I 've been in since I came to Texas, I have never been seriously wounded either with an arrow or a ball, which, considering I am a good-sized mark to shoot at, is something strange. I have known a great many men who, as General Scott said of General Johnston, had an "unfortunate knack" of getting wounded in every fight they went into, but I have not been one of that sort. They say those who are born to be hung won't be shot or drowned, and perhaps that may account for it.

But I am flying off from my story before I have fairly commenced it. We had been travelling hard ever since 12 o'clock at night, in order to make the watering-place at Devil's River, where I intended to "noon it" and graze our animals for two or three hours. After daylight I noticed several "Indian smokes" rising up and disappearing; but apparently they were a long ways off, and once we passed a considerable "trail," where at least fifteen or twenty horses had crossed the road. Altogether, I did n't like the sign, and I told the boys to keep a bright look out, as I felt sure the Indians were hatching some devilment for our benefit. However, we reached the "water-hole" in safety about noon, watered all our animals, and hobbled them out to graze. I had eight men with me, most of them old frontiersmen, who had seen much service, and were as good fighters (with one exception) as ever drew a bead upon an Indian, for I had seen them tried on several occasions before.

Near the watering-place there was about a quarter of an acre of very thick chaparral, and after we had taken a bite to eat, I told the boys to drag the coach up to the edge of it, and that they could then spread down their blankets and take a "snooze," for they had been up all night before, and were pretty well "beat out." I was considerably "fagged" myself, but somehow, although I had seen nothing in particular to excite my suspicions since we stopped at the watering-place, I felt uneasy, and determined to keep watch while the balance slept.

If there had been nothing else, the appearance of the country around our encampment was enough to make one uneasy, for it had a real "Inginy look" — broken rocky hills, covered here and there with clumps of thorny shrubs and stunted cedars, and little narrow valleys or cañons between them, in which there was nothing but a few patches of withered grass, from which our poor animals were picking a scanty repast. On all sides these rugged, rocky hills shut in the little cañon where we were encamped; so that we could see but a short distance in any direction. I picked up my rifle and walked off to a little knoll about fifty or sixty yards to the right of our encampment, from which the best view could be had of the approach of an enemy, where I seated myself, resolved that I would watch everything closely that looked at all suspicious.

I don't know how it is with others, but with me there are times when I feel low-spirited and depressed, without being able to account for it, and so it was on this occasion. The breeze rustled with a melancholy sound through the dead grass and stunted bushes around me, and the howling of a solitary cayote among the hills appeared to me unusually mournful. Nothing else could be heard except the snoring of Ben Wade in camp, who was one of the most provident men, where eating and sleeping were concerned, I ever met with. Ben's motto was, "Never refuse to eat or sleep when you are on the 'plains,' if you should have a chance forty times a day, for you can't tell how soon the time may come when you will have to go forty days without any chance at all. In that way," says Ben, "you can keep up and stand the racket a good while." Ben was n't like a good many people I have known, whose preaching and practice did n't agree; he was always on hand when there was anything to eat, and the minute he was off guard, you might hear him snoring like a wild mule.

One night, when Ben and I were on a spying expedition in one of the Waco villages, the dogs discovered us, and soon roused the whole tribe with their barking. In a little while, the warriors began to pour out of their lodges, with their bows and arrows in their hands, and we concluded we could find a healthier locality a few miles off, and made tracks for the bottom timber, about two miles from the village. But just as we were passing the last lodge, Ben discovered a side of buffalo ribs roasting before a fire in front of it.

"Cap," says he, "let's stop and take a bite; there's no telling when we may get another chance," and at that very minute we could hear the red devils yelling behind us like a pack of hungry wolves.

"Well," said I, "Ben, if you are willing to sell your scalp for a 'mess of pottage,' you can stop, but I set a higher price on mine, and can't tarry just now."

"But," says he, "Cap, it's a rule I've always stuck to, never to let slip a chance of taking a bite when I'm 'on the war-path,' and I don't like to break through it this late in the day."

Seeing I made no signs of stopping, for some of the Indians where then within a hundred yards of us, screeching like so many catamounts, he said:

"If you won't wait, I must take the ribs along with me," and I wish I may be cut up into bait for mud cats if he did n't grab them up and sling them over his shoulder, though half a dozen of the foremost Indians were in sight of us.

Ben and I were both pretty hard to beat in a foot-race at that time, but for about a mile and a half, the Indians compelled us to put in our best licks to keep ahead of them: still the darkness of the night was in our favor, and we got safely into the bottom. As soon as I thought we were out of immediate danger, I stopped to catch my breath a little, and said to Ben:

"Ben, as you would bring those ribs along, I believe I'll take one of them now. My run has given me an appetite."

"I'm sorry," says he, "Cap, but you spoke too late; I've polished them all."

And, if you'll believe me, it was a fact! While we were running for dear life, with a dozen red devils screeching after us, Ben had picked the ribs as clean of meat as the ivory-handle of my six-shooter.

Notwithstanding all this, Ben was as true blue as ever fluttered, and would do to "tie to" when danger was about. Feeling pretty sure that it was about now, though I did not know exactly why, I determined to go and wake Ben up, and get him to help me bring in the horses and mules. Just as I came to this conclusion, I saw one of the horses raise up his head and look for a long time in a certain direction, and a few minutes afterward a deer came running by as if it had been frightened by something behind it. I waited long enough to see that no wolves were after it, and then hurried to camp and gave Ben a shake by the shoulders.

"Get up, Ben," said I, in a low voice, for I did n't want to wake up the other boys.

"Hello!" said he, raising himself up with one hand and rubbing his eyes with the other—"Hello, Cap, what's the matter? Dinner ready?"

"No," I replied, "you cormorant, it has n't been half an hour since you ate dinner enough for six men. Get up, and help me bring in the horses."

"Injins about?" says Ben.

"I have n't seen any yet," I said, "but they are about here, certain."

"Why, Cap," said he, "if I did not know you so well, I should think you were a little too cautious; but if you say fetch in the horses, here goes."

And between us we brought them all in, and tied them securely in the chaparral, without waking up any of the other boys.

After we had got them all well fastened, Ben laid down again to finish his nap, but had scarcely coiled himself in his blanket when he sprang up as suddenly as if a stinging lizard had popped him.

"Crackey!" says he, "Cap, they are coming! I hear their horses' feet!"

I listened attentively, and sure enough, I could hear the sound of horses' feet clattering on the rocky ground, and the next minute we saw twenty-three Comanche warriors coming as fast as their horses could bring them right for our camp.

CHAPTER XV.

A WARM RECEPTION—"FIRE AND FALL BACK"—HOT WORK—A NATURAL COWARD—FOUR AT A SHOT—LASSOING DEAD INDIANS.

IN an instant we had roused up the boys, and were ready for them. They evidently expected to take us by surprise, for they never checked their horses until they had charged up within a few feet of the chaparral in which we were posted, and began to pour in their "dogwood switches" as thick as hail. But we returned the compliment so effectually with our rifles and six-shooters, that they soon fell back, taking off with them four of their warriors that had been "emptied" from their saddles. They wounded one of our men, named Fry, but not badly, and killed a pack-mule.

The Indians went off out of sight behind a hill, and most of the boys supposed they had left for good, but I told them they were mistaken, and that we should have a lively time of it yet; that the Indians had only gone off to dismount, and would come back again soon and give us another "turn." And so it turned out, for we had scarcely got our guns and pistols loaded again when they rose up all around the little thicket in which we were, yelling and screeching as if they thought we were a set of "green-horns" that could be frightened by a noise.

But I saw plainly they were in earnest this time, and told Ben Wade to take three of the boys and keep them off from the far side of the thicket, while I kept them at bay with the rest from the side next the coach. We both had our hands full, I can tell you. I rather think we must have killed some noted warrior in the first charge they made upon us, and that they were bent on having revenge, for I never saw the red rascals come up to the "scratch" so boldly before. Three or four times they charged us with great spirit, and once they got right among us, so that it was a hand-to-hand fight; but the boys never flinched, and poured the six-shooter bullets into them so fast that they could n't stand it long, and retreated once more out of sight behind the hills.

During the time the Indians were charging on us so fiercely, I saw one of my men skulking behind a bunch of prickly-pear. I won't mention his name, for the poor fellow could n't help being afraid any more than he could help feeling cold when a hard "norther" was blowing.

"Come out of that," said I, "and stand up and fight like a man."

"Cap," said he, "I would if I could, but I can't stand it."

I saw by the way his lips quivered and his hands shook that he told the truth, so I said, for I really felt sorry for him:

"Well, stay there, then, if you must, and I'll say nothing about it."

But some of the other boys noticed him too, and I actually believe, if I had not interfered, they would have shot him after the fight was over, and I might just as well have let them, for the poor fellow had no peace of his life after that.

I have seen two or three men in the course of my life who were naturally "scary-like," and they could n't help it, any more than they could help having bandy legs or a snub nose. They were made that way from the jump, and they are more to be pitied than blamed. You might just as well blame a man because he is n't as smart as Henry Clay, as because he is n't as brave as Julius Cæsar. However, it is mighty aggravating to have them act in that way when the service of every one is needed, as it was on this occasion. And, after all, they are generally more unlucky than those who are braver and expose themselves. With the exception of Fry, this man was the only one in the crowd that was wounded. An arrow went through his arm and pinned him hard and fast to the prickly-pear behind which he was skulking.

After the Indians had retreated the second time, the boys concluded, of course, that they had given up all idea of attacking us again, but I told them I did n't think so; that I thought they would wait for us to make a start, when they intended pouncing upon us at some place where we could get no shelter.

"But," said I, "boys, we can soon satisfy ourselves about this," and I ordered every man to take his gun and lie flat down under the coach, and keep perfectly quiet. The boys had begun to get a little tired of this position, (except Ben, who was fast asleep,) when suddenly we saw an Indian cautiously poke his head out of the chaparral, about seventy yards from where we were lying. He looked for a long time toward us, and seeing no one moving he ventured out, and stood straight up, to have a better view.

"Don't fire at him, boys," I said; "there will be some more of them directly, and we may get two or three."

In a little while, another Indian stepped out by the side of the first, and then another and another, until five of them were standing side by side, all looking intently toward the coach, and wondering, I suppose, what had become of us.

"Now score 'em, boys," says I, and we let them have it.

Four fell dead at the crack of our guns, and the fifth scrambled back into the chaparral as fast as if he had had a heavy bet on doing it inside of a second.

I told the boys to load up again as quick as possible, for that more of them would be sure to come out to take off the dead ones; but I made a miscalculation this time to a certainty. Not a thing could be seen or heard for fifteen or twenty minutes, when all at once we saw an arm rise up out of the bushes on the edge of the chaparral, and make a sort of motion, and the next instant one of the dead Indians was "snaked" into the thicket; and I wish I may be kicked to death by grasshoppers, if they did n't rope every one of them and drag 'em off in that way, and we could never see a thing except that Indian's arm, motioning backward and forward as he threw the lasso.

"Boys," says I, "that gets me! I have been in a good many 'scrimmages' with the Indians, but I never saw them 'snake off' their dead in that way before. However," I continued, "it shows they 've had enough of the fight, and I think now we may venture to make a start, without any fear of being attacked by them again." But there was new danger ahead, as you will soon see.

CHAPTER XVI.

MORE COMANCHES ON THE WAR-TRACK — KEEPING A STIFF UPPER LIP — ON A FALSE TRAIL — BEN WADE WANTS HIS DINNER — "MR. JOHN" OUTWITTED.

WHILE the boys were harnessing up, I took my rifle and stepped out a short distance to reconnoitre, and well for us it was that I did, for on reaching the top of the little "rise" where I had first taken my stand, I saw and counted forty warriors coming down a cañon not more than four hundred yards off. I was satisfied it was not the same party we had been fighting, but a reinforcement coming to their assistance. They rode slowly along directly toward me, and when within about one hundred yards of me, I rose up from where I was sitting and showed myself to them. They halted instantly, and one of them, who I supposed was the chief, rode forward thirty or forty yards in advance of the rest, and in a loud voice asked me in Mexican (which most of the Comanches speak) what we were doing there?

There is nothing like keeping a "stiff upper lip" and showing a bold front, when you have to do with Indians; so I told him we had been fighting Comanches, and that we had flogged them genteelly, too!

"Yes," said he, "you are a set of sneaking cayotes, and are afraid to come out of the brush. You are afraid to travel the road. You are all squaws, and you don't dare to poke your noses out of the chaparral."

"If you will wait till we eat our dinner," I answered, "I 'll show you whether we are afraid to travel the road. We shall camp at the California Springs to-night, in spite of the whole Comanche nation!"

And with this I turned round and walked slowly back to the coach, as if I did n't think they were worth bothering about any further.

I was satisfied if I could only make them believe we had no fear of them, and that we would take the road again that evening for the California Springs, they would hurry on there for the purpose of waylaying us at that place; and so it turned out, for they immediately put off for the Springs, (eight miles distant,) leaving only three warriors behind to watch our motions.

When I got back to the coach I told the boys what I had said to the Indians, and that I had no doubt they would hurry off to the California Springs, with the intention of waylaying us there, and that when I thought they had had time enough to make the distance, we would put out and take the back track to Fort Clarke:

"They are too strong for us now, boys," said I, "for they have had a reinforcement of forty warriors, and they will fight like mad, to revenge the death of those we have killed."

"Cap," said Ben Wade, "I heard you make one sensible remark to that Indian you were talking with."

"What was that?" I asked.

"Why," says Ben, "you told him as soon as we got

some dinner we would go to the California Springs, in spite of the whole Comanche nation."

"Yes," I said, "I told him that because I wanted him to think we were delaying here of our own accord, and not because we were afraid of him and his warriors, and I believe they have gone off under that impression."

"It was a pretty smart dodge in you, Cap, to put 'em on the wrong scent in that way, I 'll admit, but you see, as we may not be able to get to the California Springs after all, and *we can get dinner*, we had better make sure of doing what is in our power; besides, Cap," he continued, hauling out a chunk of venison and some hard-tack from his wallet, "they have probably left a spy to watch us, and I 'll 'make pretend' to eat a bite, so he won't have any reason to think we are 'throwing off' on them."

"There 'll be no danger of that, Ben," said I, "if he 's where he can get a good look at you. There 's no 'throw off' in you when eating and sleeping is to be done."

"Nor fighting either," he said. "If I had n't shot that Indian on the last charge they made on us, just as he was drawing his bow on you, not six feet off, you would have had a quill sticking out of your back now as long as a porcupine's."

"That 's a fact, Ben," I replied, "and it is n't the first time you have done me a good turn in that way, and I ain't the man to forget it; and when we get back to Fort Clarke, I will stop over a day, just to give you a fair chance to lay in a good supply of provender."

Ben was "mollified," and as soon as he had finished the venison and hard-tack he tumbled over on his blanket, and was fast asleep in two minutes.

After waiting about half an hour longer, we took the road back to Fort Clarke, instead of going on to the Springs, and travelled as rapidly as we could urge on the animals. Just as we started, we saw two of the warriors that had been left behind to watch our movements put off at full speed toward the Springs, no doubt with the intention of letting the Indians know we were taking the back track. The other — for they had left three behind — followed on after us at a safe distance from our rifles, for seven or eight miles, when we lost sight of him.

We had so much the start of the Indians, and the road was so firm and good, and we rattled along at such a rate, they had no chance to overtake, even if they pursued us, which I suppose they did. At any rate, we saw nothing more of them, and the next morning reached Fort Clarke safely, where our wounded men were taken care of. We had outwitted "Mr. John" completely.

The commandant at Fort Clarke furnished us with an escort of twelve men and a sergeant, and we made the trip back to San Antonio without any further trouble from the Indians at that time.

CHAPTER XVII.

A Night Visit from the Indians — Afoot, and Ten Miles to Travel — On the Trail — A Curious Specimen.

DID I ever tell you (asked Big-Foot) about a curious sort of character I fell in with at the "Zumwalt Settlement," on the La Vaca, a year or so after I came out to Texas? I have met with many a good honest hater in my time, but this fellow hated Indians with such a "vim" that he had n't room left even for an appetite for his food. But he had a good reason for it and if they had served me as they did him, I am afraid I should have taken to scalping Indians myself for a livelihood, instead of being satisfied with "upping" one now and then in a fair fight.

A party of eight of us had been out on an exploring expedition to the Nueces River, (which was then almost unknown to the Americans,) and the night we got back to the La Vaca we encamped on its western bank, and all went to sleep without the usual precaution of putting out a guard, thinking we were near enough the settlements to be safe from the attacks of Indians. I told the boys I thought we were running a great risk in not having any guard out, as I had already found that when you least expected to meet up with Indians, there they were sure to be; but the boys were all tired with their long day's ride, and said they did n't think there was any danger, and if there was they were willing to take the chances. So, after we had got some supper and staked our horses, we wrapped our blankets around us, and, as I have said before, were all soon fast asleep.

I was the first one to rouse up, about daylight the next morning, and, looking in the direction we had staked our horses, I discovered that they were all gone. I got up quietly, without waking any of the boys, and went out to reconnoitre the "sign." I had gone but a little ways on the prairie when I picked up an arrow, and a few yards farther on I came across one of our horses lying dead on the grass, with a dozen "dogwood switches" sticking in various parts of his body. This satisfied me at once that "Mr. John" had paid us a sociable visit during the night, and, with the exception of the one they had killed, (he was an unruly beast,) had carried off all our stock when they left.

I went back to camp and stirred up the boys, and gave them the pleasing information that we were ten miles from "wood and water" and "flat afoot." But there was no use in crying over the matter, so we held a "council of war" as to what was best to be done under the circumstances; that is, flat afoot, with all our guns, saddles, bridles, and other equipments on hand, and ten miles to the nearest settlement. At length, it was decided that each man should shoulder his own "plunder," or leave it behind, as he preferred, and that we should take a "bee-line" to the "Zumwalt Settlement" above us on the river, borrow horses if we could, follow the Indians, and endeavor to get back from them those they had stolen from us. So we took a hasty snack, and, each man shouldering his pack, we put out on a "dog-trot" for the settlement.

It was a pretty fatiguing tramp, hampered as we were with our guns and rigging, but we made it in good time. Fortunately for us, a man had just come into the settlement, from the Rio Grande, with a large "caballada,"*

* Drove of horses.

and when we made known our situation to him, he told us to go into the corral * and select any of the horses we wanted. They were only about half broke, and it took us fully an hour to catch, bridle, and saddle them, and fifteen minutes more to get on their backs. I was more lucky than most of the boys, for I only got two kicks and a bite before I mounted mine.

When all was ready, we put spurs to our steeds and galloped back to our encampment of the night previous, where our horses had been stolen, and took the Indian trail, which was plainly visible in the rank grass that grew at that day along the bottoms of the river. Several men belonging to the settlement had volunteered to accompany us, so that our number (rank, but not file, for we were all colonels, majors or captains, except one chap, who was a judge,) amounted to thirteen men, well armed and mounted.

As long as the Indians kept to the valley we had no trouble in following the trail, and pushed on as rapidly as we could. When we had travelled perhaps eight or ten miles, I had to halt and dismount for the purpose of fixing my girth, which by some means had become unfastened. While I was engaged at this, I heard the tramp of a horse's hoofs behind me, and looking back the way we had come, I saw a man riding up rapidly on our trail. When he got up to where I was he reined in his horse, evidently intending to wait for me, and I had a chance of observing as curious a looking "specimen" as I ever saw before in any country. He was a tall, spare-built chap, dressed in buckskin hunting-shirt and leggings, with a coonskin cap on; a long, old-fashioned flint-and-steel Kentucky rifle on his shoulder, and a

* Enclosure, or fence.

THE INDIAN HATER.—Page 92.

tomahawk and scalping-knife stuck in his belt. His hair was matted together, and hung around his neck in great uncombed "swabs," and his eyes peered out from among it as bright as a couple of mesquite coals. I have seen all sorts of eyes, of panthers, wolves, catamounts, leopards, and Mexican lions, but I never saw eyes that glittered, and flashed, and danced about like those in that man's head. He was mounted on an ugly, raw-boned, vicious-looking horse, with an exceedingly heavy mane and tail; but, notwithstanding his looks, any one could see, with half an eye, that he had a great deal of "let out" in him on a pinch.

As soon as I had patched up my girth, I mounted my horse again, and rode along sociably with this curious specimen for a mile or so, without a word passing between us; but I got tired of this, and, although I felt a little "skittish" of this strange-looking animal, I at length made a "pass at him," and inquired if he was a stranger in these parts.

"Not exactly," said he. "I have been about here 'off and on' for the last three years, and I know every trail and 'water-hole' from this to the Rio Grande, especially those that are used much by the Indians going and coming."

"And ain't you afraid," I asked, "to travel about so much in this country alone?"

He grinned a sort of sickly smile, and his fingers clutched the handle of his tomahawk, and his eyes danced a perfect jig in his head.

"No," he answered; "the Indians are more afraid of me than I am of them. If they knew I was waylaying a particular trail, they would go forty miles out of their way to give me a wide berth; but the trouble is, they never know where to find me. And, besides," he continued, "the best horse this side of the Brazos can't come alongside of 'Pepper-Pod' when I want him to work in the lead."

As he said this, he touched up Pepper-Pod smartly with his spurs, who gave a vicious plunge, and started off like a "shot out of a shovel." But he soon reined him up, and we rode on together again in silence for some time. Finally, I said to him:

"Man of family, I suppose?"

Gracious! if a ten-pound howitzer had been fired off just then at my ear, I could n't have been more astonished than I was at that chap's actions. He turned pale, and his lips quivered, and he fumbled with the handle of his butcher-knife, and his eyes looked like two lightning-bugs in a dark night. He did n't answer me for a while, but at length he said:

"No, I have no family now. Ten years ago, I had a wife and three little boys, but the Indians murdered them all in cold blood. I have got a few of them for it, though," he went on, "and if I am spared, I 'll get a few more before I die;" and as he said this he clicked the triggers of his rifle, and pushed the butcher-knife up and down in its scabbard, his eyes danced in his head worse than ever, and he gave Pepper-Pod another dig in the ribs, who reared and plunged in a way that would have emptied any one out of the saddle, except a number-one rider.

After a while, he and Pepper-Pod both quieted down a little, and he said to me:

"You must n't think strange of me. I always get in these 'flurries' when I think of the way the Indians murdered my poor wife and my little boys. But I will tell you my story."

CHAPTER XVIII.

Story of the Indian-hater — The Move from Kentucky — New Home in Texas — Wife and Children Murdered by the Indians — Terrible Revenge — A Dangerous Companion — The Indian Camp.

"TEN years ago," said the strange-looking man, "I was as happy a man as any in the world; but now I am miserable except when I am waylaying or shooting or scalping an Indian. It 's the only comfort I have now.

"I had a small farm in Kentucky, not far from the mouth of the Beech Fork, and though we had no money, we lived happily and comfortably, and had nothing to fear when we laid down at night. But, in an unlucky hour for us, a stranger stopped at my house one day on his way to Texas, and told me about the rich lands, the abundance of game, and the many fortunes that had been made in this new country. From that time I grew restless and discontented, and I determined, as soon as possible, that I would seek my fortune in that 'promised land.'

"The next fall I had a chance to sell my little farm for a good price, and we moved off to Texas, and, after wandering around for some time, finally settled on the banks of a beautiful little stream that runs into the Guadalupe River. My wife had left Kentucky very unwillingly, but the lovely spot we had chosen for our home, the rich lands and beautiful country around, and the mildness of the climate, at length reconciled her to the move we had made.

"One lovely morning in May, when the sun was shining brightly, and the birds were singing in every tree, I took my rifle and went out for a stroll in the woods. When I left the house, my wife was at work in our little garden, singing as gayly as one of the birds, and my three little boys were laughing, and shouting, and trundling their hoops around the yard. That was the last time I ever saw any of them alive. I had gone perhaps a mile, entirely unsuspicious of all danger, when I heard a dozen guns go off in the direction of my house. The idea flashed across my mind in a moment that the Indians were murdering my family, and I flew toward the house with the speed of a frightened deer. From the direction in which I approached it, it was hid from view by a thick grove of elm-trees that grew in front of the house. I hurried through this, and rushed into the open door of the house, and the first thing I saw was the dead body of my poor wife, lying pale and bloody upon the floor, and the lifeless form of my youngest boy clasped tightly in her arms. She had evidently tried to defend him to the last. The two older boys lay dead near by, scalped, and covered with blood from their wounds.

"The Indians, who had left the house for some purpose, at that instant returned, and, before they knew I was there, I shot one through the heart with my rifle, and, drawing my butcher-knife, rushed upon the balance like a tiger. There were at least a dozen of the savages, but if there had been a thousand of them it would have made no difference to me, for I was desperate and reckless of my life, and thought only of avenging the cruel and cowardly murder of my poor wife and children.

"I have but a faint recollection of what happened after this. I remember hearing the yells of fright and astonishment the Indians gave as I rushed upon them, and that I cut to pieces several of them with my butcher-knife before they could escape through the door—and then all was a blank, and I knew nothing more. I suppose some of those outside fired upon me, and gave me the wounds that rendered me senseless, but I gave them such a scare it was evident they never entered the house again, as otherwise, you know, they would have taken my scalp, and carried off the dead Indians.

"Some time during thc day, one of my neighbors happened to pass by the house, and noticing the unusual silence that prevailed, and seeing no one moving about, he suspected something was wrong, and came in, and the dreadful sight I have described to you met his eyes.

"He told me afterward he found me lying on the floor, across the body of an Indian, still grasping his throat with one hand, and with the other the handle of my knife, which was buried to the hilt in his breast. Near by lay the bodies of three other Indians, gashed and hacked with the terrible wounds I had given them with my butcher-knife. My kind neighbor, observing some signs of life left in me, took me to his house, dressed my wounds, and did all that he could for me.

"For many days I lay at the point of death, and they thought I would never get well; but gradually my wounds healed up and my strength returned; although for a long time afterward I was n't exactly right here, (tapping his forehead,) and even now I am more like a crazy man than anything else, when I have to go a long time without 'lifting' the scalp from the head of an Indian; for then I always see (especially when I lay down at night) the bloody corpses of my wife and poor little boys."

"I hope, my friend," I replied, for I did n't like the way his eyes danced in his head, and the careless manner he had of cocking his gun and slinging it around—"I hope you have had your regular rations lately, and that you don't feel disposed to take a white man's scalp when an Indian's can't be had handily."

The fellow actually chuckled when I said this, the first time I had heard anything like a laugh from him.

"Oh, no," he said; "I have been tolerably well supplied of late, and could get along pretty comfortably without a scalp for a week or so yet. I have forty-six of them hanging up now in my camp on the Chicolite, but I shan't be satisfied unless I can get a cool hundred of them before I die; and I 'll have 'em, too, just as sure 's my name is Jeff Turner."

Again his eyes glared out of his bushy locks, and his fingers again began to fumble about his knife-handle, in a way that, if I had had a drop of Indian blood in my veins, would have made me feel exceedingly uneasy. At last, to change the subject, I asked him which way he was travelling, though, of course, I knew very well he was going along with us.

"Any way," he replied, "that these Indians go. I 'd just as soon go in one direction as another. I always travel on the freshest Indian trail I come across. You and your company may get tired and quit this trail without overtaking the Indians, but I shall stick to it until I get a scalp or two to take back with me to my camp on the Chicolite."

By this time we had come up with our companions, and all rode on in silence. At length we came to a hard, rocky piece of ground, where the Indians had scattered, and we lost the trail altogether, for not the least sign was visible to our eyes. At that time, you see, none of us had had much experience in the way of trailing and fighting Indians, except Jeff Turner, the "Indian-hater."

We soon discovered that he knew more about following a trail than all of us put together, and from this time on, we let him take the lead, and followed him wherever he went. Sometimes, where the ground was very hard and rocky, and the Indians had scattered, he would hesitate for a little while as to the course to pursue, but in a moment or so he was all right again, and off at such a rate that we were compelled to travel at a full trot to keep up with him.

About half an hour before sundown, he came to a halt, and when we had all gathered around him, he told us to keep a sharp lookout, and make no noise, as the Indians were close by; and, in fact, we had scarcely travelled three hundred yards farther when we saw their blanket tents in the edge of some post-oak timber, about a quarter of a mile to our right. We put spurs to our horses, and in a few moments we were among them.

CHAPTER XIX.

Attacking the Indians — Narrow Escape — The Indian-hater at Work — Forgot to Untie his Horse — A Dying Struggle — Worse Scared than Hurt — Dinner Ready Cooked — Return to the Settlements and Disappearance of the Indian-hater.

THE Indians did n't see us until we were within fifty yards of their encampment, but still they had time to seize their guns, and bows and arrows, and give us a volley as we charged up; but luckily no damage was done except slightly wounding one of our horses. We dismounted at once and commenced pouring a deadly fire into them from our rifles.

Just as I sprang from the saddle to the ground, a big Indian stepped from behind a post-oak tree and drew an arrow upon me that looked to me as long as a barber's pole. I jumped behind another tree as spry as a city clerk in a dry-goods store when a parcel of women come around shopping, and not much time had I to spare at that, for the arrow grazed my head so closely that it took off a strip of bark from it about the width of one of my fingers. I levelled my rifle and drew a bead upon him as he started to run, but his arrow had rather unsettled my nerves, and I missed him fairly.

The fight was kept up pretty hotly on both sides for fifteen or twenty minutes, when the Indians "soured on it," and retreated into a thick chaparral, leaving seven of their warriors dead upon the ground.

I noticed my friend Jeff several times during the fight, and each time he was engaged in "lifting the hair" from the head of an Indian that either he or some one else had shot down. They say that "practice makes perfect," and it was astonishing to see how quickly Jeff would take off an Indian scalp and load his rifle in readiness for another. One slash with his butcher-knife and a sudden jerk, and the bloody scalp was soon dangling from his belt. At the same time, he never seemed to be in a hurry, but was as cool and deliberate about everything he did as a carpenter when he is working by the day and not by the job.

When the Indians began to retreat, one of them jumped on one of our horses, (which they had tied hard and fast to post-oaks near their camp,) forgetting, in his hurry, to unfasten the rope, and round and round the tree he went, until he wound himself up to the body, when, just at that instant, Jeff plugged him with a half-ounce bullet, and had his scalp off before he had done kicking.

After the Indians had retreated to the chaparral, a little incident occurred that shows the pluck of these red rascals when they have been "brought to bay." We were standing all huddled up together, loading our rifles, for we did not know but that the Indians had retreated on purpose to throw us off our guard, when all at once we were startled by a keen yell and the firing of a gun, and at the same instant a tall chap by the name of B——, who had come with us from the "settlement," dropped his rifle, and, clapping his hands to his face, cried out:

"Boys, I am a dead man!"

I looked around to see from whence the shot had come, and discovered an Indian lying on the grass, about thirty yards off, with his gun in his hand, slowly

9*

sinking back upon the earth again, from which he had partially raised himself by a dying effort, to take a last pop at the enemies of his race. I had seen this Indian fall during the fight, and supposed, of course, that he was dead — as he was, in fact, an instant after he gave the yell and fired his gun; for I went up immediately to where he lay, and found that he was dead as a door nail, with his gun still tightly clasped in his hands; and yet at the time he fired at B—— he had no less than seven rifle-balls through various parts of his body, for the wounds were plainly to be seen, as he had nothing on to speak of, except his powder-horn and shot-pouch.

Our "Indian-hater," Jeff, came up to him about the same time I did, and lifted the hair from his head before you could say "Jack Robinson," and strung it on his belt to keep company with three other scalps that were already dangling from it. The scalps seemed to ease the mind of Jeff considerably, as he told me they would, and he got quite sociable with the boys after the fight, and once actually laughed outright, when one of them told a funny story about shooting at a stump three times for an Indian before he discovered his mistake; but either the unusual sound of his own laugh frightened him, or else he had used up all his stock on hand, for I never saw him crack a smile afterward.

As it turned out, B—— was worse scared than hurt, for the Indian's bullet had only grazed his head, but, striking the black-jack tree near which he was standing, it had thrown the rough bark violently into his eyes, the pain from which led him to suppose "he was a dead man."

The Indians had killed a fat buck, and when we pounced upon them they had the choice pieces spitted before the fire, and after the fight we found them "done to a turn." We hadn't eaten a bite all day, and seized upon the venison as the lawful spoils of war, and made a hearty supper upon it, together with some hard-tack which we had brought along with us in our haversacks. While I was eating supper, I couldn't help feeling a little sorry for the poor creatures who had cooked it only half an hour before, and who were now lying around us cold and stiff on the damp grass of the prairie, so soon to be devoured by vultures and cayotes. However, this thought didn't take away my appetite, or, if it did, a side of roasted ribs and about five pounds of solid meat disappeared along with it.

As soon as we had finished supper, we changed our saddles from the horses we had ridden to those the Indians had stolen from us, (which had been resting for some time,) and mounting, we took the trail back towards the settlement, where we arrived about sun-up the next morning, making seventy-five miles we had travelled in part of a day and night, without ever getting off our horses except for a few moments, when we fought the Indians.

Jeff, the Indian-hater, left us here for his camp on the Chicolite, and I never saw him again. I was told when I was at the settlement, several years after this, that he staid around there for a good while, occasionally coming into the settlement for his supplies of ammunition, etc., and always bringing with him four or five scalps. At length, he went off and never returned, and it is supposed that the Indians finally caught him napping. At any rate, that was the last that was ever seen or heard of Jeff Turner, the "Indian-hater."

CHAPTER XX.

WALLACE MAKES A TREATY WITH THE LIPAN INDIANS — THE INDIANS BREAK IT — PREPARATION TO PUNISH THEM — FIRST APPEARANCE OF A LIVE AUTHOR.

A FEW months after I had settled on the Medina River, I concluded that it would be good policy to enter into a regular treaty with the Lipans, who, at that time, occupied all the adjacent country. So I made my preparations for a grand dinner, to which, upon a certain day, I invited all the chiefs, and after I had feasted them to their hearts' content, on "bear-meat and honey" and "sweetened coffee," of which they are exceedingly fond, I broached the subject to them, stating briefly that I was a lone man, and they were a powerful tribe, and that I wanted to make a treaty with them, by which they should guarantee never to interfere with me or my stock so long as I conducted myself peaceably toward them!

Whereupon, the head chief, Coyo-lopto-hajo, or literally, "Smells-bad-when-he-walks," (I suppose he had some Congo blood in him,) rose up from the buffalo robe on which he was sitting, and made a speech in reply, in which he praised me in the highest terms, saying I was a great warrior and hunter, and a good friend to the Lipans; that I did not have two faces, like a great many of the white people, and that, therefore, they had confidence in what I told them; that they knew no Lipan had ever come to my ranch and gone away hungry, but that I had always filled their stomachs (patting his own) with fat bear-meat and honey, as I had done that day.

He then turned to the other chiefs, and asked them if they were willing to enter into the treaty I proposed, and they all grunted out their readiness to do so. So the treaty was formally made and ratified, and though the expenses attending it were much less than the cost of a majority of the "treaties" made by "Uncle Sam," it was probably as faithfully kept — at least for a long time.

When the chiefs got up to leave, they all shook me by the hand, and told me that henceforth I was just the same as a Lipan in their estimation, and that I must *steal* plenty of horses and cattle, (the only mode, as they supposed, of getting them,) and that they would never steal them from *me;* and that no other Indians would dare to do so on their "hunting grounds." But before the chiefs left, I produced a jug of whisky, (in order to "clinch" the treaty effectually,) and told them they had to take a parting drink with me. From the length of time that "Smells-bad-as-he-walks" held the jug to his lips, I think he must have swallowed at least a pint — indeed, I am certain of it, for before they were out of sight, I saw him charge his mustang over the other chiefs, and go off whooping and yelling like a maniac.

Well, for several years, the "treaty" was faithfully kept on both sides, and I never lost a horse or a hoof of any sort, although my neighbors (for after a while several families settled within six or eight miles of me) could not keep an animal on their ranches. But, in the course of time, the Lipans concluded to emigrate from that part of the country to the head-waters of the Guadalupe River, and as I had then collected quite a stock of horses and mules around me, the temptation to steal from me was too great to be resisted; and a night or so after the tribe had left they sent back a party of warriors, who made a clean sweep of every thing I had in the shape of a horse on my ranch. At first I did not suspect the Lipans, supposing that the stealing had been done by other Indians; but on following their trail a short distance the next morning, I picked up an arrow which I knew, from its peculiar make, had belonged to a Lipan; and also the tail of a fox fastened to a carved wooden handle, such as the chiefs of that tribe generally carry with them on all occasions of public ceremony. I was indignant, of course, at being served such a scurvy trick by my old friends and allies, particularly as I had always kept the "treaty" made with them in good faith myself, and I determined to make them pay dearly for it if I could. So the next morning I went into San Antonio, where there was a ranging company stationed, in which I had many old acquaintances, and I told them how the Lipans had served me, and proposed that we should make up a party and follow the Indians, and give them a lesson that would teach them that they could not break their "solemn treaties" with impunity.

The captain of the company (who was an old friend of mine) readily consented that any of his men should go with me who desired to do so, and about thirty of the "right sort" volunteered at once, by whom I was unanimously elected "commander in-chief" for the expedition. The captain also furnished us with four fine pack-mules, and rations enough to last us a month.

Just as we were leaving San Antonio for my "ranch," a queer-looking customer rode up to me, and introduced himself by saying:

"Captain Wallace, I believe."

AUTHOR RIDING UP TO WALLACE'S RANCH. —Page 107.

"At your service, sir," I replied.

"Well," said he, "captain, I have understood you were about starting on a trip into the 'wilderness,' and if you have no objection, I should like to go along with you. I am an author, sir, and am now engaged in writing a novel entitled the 'Wayworn Wanderer of the Western Wilds,' and never having, as yet, been outside of the 'settlements,' I am anxious to accompany you on your trip, in order to acquire some practical information of the subjects to be treated of in it."

"Well," I replied, "Mr. Author, I have not the least objection to your going with us, if you wish it; but I will tell you beforehand, that you will have a very rough road to travel, and no taverns on the way to put up in at night."

"Oh!" said he, "I understand all about that, and if it is agreeable to you I shall certainly go along."

Seeing that it was evidently his intention to go along with us at once, I said to him:

"Of course, Mr. Author, I have not the least objection in the world to your company; but you surely do not think of starting on such a trip in the dress you have on."

(He was dressed in a stove-pipe hat, light cloth coat and pantaloons, and patent-leather gaiter shoes. Just think of a fellow, will you, in that costume, among the chaparrals on the head-waters of the Guadalupe River, one of the roughest little scopes of country in all the borders of Texas.)

"Why," said he, looking down at himself, in an admiring sort of way, "what is the matter with my dress?"

"Oh, nothing now," I replied, "but by the time you

get through the first chaparral on the way, you will not have a rag on you big enough to patch a bullet with; and besides," I continued, "you ought, by all means, to have your 'implements' with you," (meaning, of course, a rifle and revolver.)

"Oh, I have got them," he said, hauling out of his pocket a portable ink-stand and a memorandum-book. "I always carry them with me."

I could not, to save my life, help laughing right out in the fellow's face. It was too ridiculous to think of a man starting out on the "war-path" without a gun or a pistol, or even a butcher-knife — with nothing, in fact, except an "ink-bottle" and a memorandum-book.

"My friend," I said, "if you are determined to go on this trip, take my advice, and go back to San Antonio, and get you a gun and pistol, and a buckskin suit of clothes, and then join us at my ranch on the Medina, where we shall remain until to-morrow evening."

"Captain," he replied, "I reckon you are right, and I will go back into town and 'fix up' as you advise, and then meet you at your 'ranch' at the time appointed, provided I can find my way out there."

"Oh, there will be no trouble about that," I said, and then gave him the necessary directions to enable him to find the road.

"Well, good-by, captain," he said; "you may look for me to a certainty, for I am resolved to go along with you, and pick up all the information I can on the subjects I shall treat of in my great novel of the 'Wayworn Wanderer of the Western Wilds.'"

"All right, Mr. Author," I replied; "and I have no doubt you will be able to pick up a good deal before you get back;" and with that, he turned his pony and cantered off toward town. I was rather anxious that the fellow should go with us, for it struck me there was considerable fun to be had out of him, if he was rightly "handled," and I hoped what I had told him of the dangers and hardships of the trip would not prevent him from meeting us as he had promised.

CHAPTER XXI.

The Author Again — The Boys Make Fun of his Umbrella — His Pistol "Goes off" and Creates an Excitement — Mr. Cooper's Indian Characters — Some Sage Reflections on Character — The Author wants a Bed, and gets Tige's Buffalo Robe — "Something like a Pillow" — Troublesome Bedfellows — The Start after the Indians.

SURE enough, late in the evening our author rode up to my ranch dressed in a suit of buckskin, with a little double-barrel gun on his shoulder, and an umbrella strapped behind his saddle! He came up to me smiling, and shook me by the hand.

"Well, captain," said he, "you see I am 'up to time,' and 'armed and equipped as the law directs.'"

The men gathered around him as he dismounted from his pony, to see, as I overheard one of them remark, if they could make out what sort of a "varmint" he was.

"I am glad to see you, Mr. Author," I said, "and in a few days I think I can promise you a little insight into the ways of the wilderness."

"Hello, stranger," said one of the men, pointing to

the umbrella, "what's that you have got strapped to your saddle there?"

"That," said our author, "is what is commonly termed an 'umbrella,' and is used as a protection against the sun and rain."

"Run here, everybody!" cried the fellow. "Here's a man going on a scout with an umbrella."

"Yes," says another, "and when he gits it 'histed,' he won't care a snap if it rains Injins."

"Hurray, boys!" said another, "if we can only come up with them thieving Lipans, they might as well 'knock under' at once, for we have got a man and his 'umbrell' along with us. It's worth a dozen of Uncle Sam's mountain howitzers."

"I'd rather have it," said another, "than that bird-gun he's got on his shoulder, for if he was to open it suddenly on an Injin, he would run certain, thinking it was some new-fangled 'weepin' of the white people; at least, I know his horse would."

"My friend," said I, seeing nothing like a revolver buckled around him, "why didn't you bring a pistol with you?"

"Pistol," he answered, rummaging about in his pockets; "I have got one somewhere, I know."

I wish I may be kicked to death by grasshoppers if he didn't fish up out of his breeches pocket a little pepper-box of a thing about the size and length of my big toe.

"Here it is," said he, fingering at the trigger as he pulled it out, when "pop" it went, right in the midst of the crowd. This frightened or excited our author so much that he kept on pulling the trigger, and bang! bang! it went, until all six of the barrels were emptied, when he dropped it like a hot potato, and made tracks for the house. While it was firing off the men dodged behind everything that was handy, some of them hallooing, "Hobble the thing," "Rope it," "Pitch it into the creek," etc.

Fortunately, there was no one hit, which was a wonder, for things of this sort, I have noticed, are very apt to hurt somebody when they go off accidentally, but you cannot strike the side of a house with them at ten paces when you shoot at it on purpose.

The men were tickled to death with our author, and some of them proposed having him out of the house again for their further amusement; but I objected to this, and told them that he belonged to me, for I had "found him first," and that it would not do to use him too extravagantly, for fear he wouldn't last us the trip through. They thought this was reasonable enough, and let him alone the balance of the night.

After supper, as the weather was pleasant and dry, the men spread their blankets under the trees around, and soon a general snoring gave evidence that they had all emigrated to the "land of Nod."

"Captain," said our author to me, when we were left alone in the ranch, "you have read Mr. Cooper's novels, of course: what do you think of his delineation of the Indian character?"

"Yes," I replied, "Mr. Author, I have read some of his novels, and from my recollection of them, I rather think his Indian characters are a little too highly colored. His Indians stalk about in a lofty sort of way, wrapped up in their robes, with an eagle's feather on their heads, and talk in a manner that the Indians of this country couldn't comprehend at all. Besides, his Indians, if I remember well, never laugh, nor steal horses, while I have always found Indians to be uncommonly fond of a joke, (especially of a certain kind,) and the most arrant and expert thieves that ever went unhung. I believe they could almost steal a horse out of a 'corral' if there had not been one in there for a week."

"You astonish me greatly," said the author; "and if what you tell me about the Indians be true, I have been cruelly deceived by Mr. Cooper, and shall have an immense deal of work to do in writing over the characters of those that figure in my novel of the 'Way-worn Wanderer of the Western Wilds,' for they are drawn after his models. I shall hate to 'rub out' my principal hero, particularly 'Hopa-Tuki-lika-hajo,' or the 'Rushing River,' for he is my beau ideal of an aborigine — haughty and reserved, and always dressed in fringed hunting-shirt, beaded moccasins and wampum-belts, and never says two words without beginning, 'Brother, listen.' Oh, it will be too bad," he continued, "if I shall have to blot out my 'sheff-duvver,"* (whatever he meant by that,) Hopa-Tuki-lika-hajo, after all the trouble I have had to fix him up to my notion; but I'll do it if I find his character overdrawn, for the 'Way-worn Wanderer' is not intended for a sensation novel, and its scenes and characters must be true to nature."

Our author and I sat up, I suppose, till ten o'clock, talking on various matters, and though he was as green as a "cut-seed watermelon" on everything pertaining to a frontier life, I found him to be well informed upon

* "Chef-d'œuvre," French for "masterpiece."

many subjects of which I was totally ignorant. I am not in the habit of "putting a man up" as an ignoramus, merely because he is verdant in some things which my profession or peculiar mode of life has given me thorough knowledge of, and yet I know there are many men who judge of one entirely by this standard. If a man is ignorant of woodcraft, a poor shot with a rifle, and cannot manage a wild mustang, backwoodsmen are very apt to think he is "no great shakes" any way.

After a while, our author said to me: "Captain, I'm not much used to riding on horseback, especially on such horses as you have here in Texas, that 'pitch,' as you call it, half the time, like a boat beating against a head sea, and I feel a good deal worried in consequence; so if you will show me my bed, I believe I'll retire for the night."

"A bed," I replied, "Mr. Author, is a piece of furniture that has never darkened the doors of this ranch yet; but there is a buffalo robe in the corner yonder, where you can lie down, if you can get 'Tige' off of it; but I see he has 'nine points of the law' in his favor."

"Captain," said our author, after he had with some difficulty ousted Tige, "I hate to trouble you, but if there is anything in the shape of a pillow about the ranch, I should like to get it, as I cannot sleep well without something of the sort under my head."

I stepped out into the yard, and picked up a wooden maul, which I brought in and stuffed under his buffalo robe, telling him there was something in the *shape of* a pillow, though not quite so soft as it might be, and that I hoped he would rest well, as he had a long ride before him the next day.

10*

In a little while he was sound asleep, and dreaming, I suppose, of his novel, for I heard him muttering something about the "Wayworn Wanderer of the Western Wilds."

In the morning, as soon as he awoke, he said:

"Captain, this is a substantial pillow of yours here; they must last a long time."

"Yes," said I, "they do, when you are careful to keep them out of the weather, and don't split more than two hundred rails a day with them. And how did you rest last night?" I asked.

"Well, only tolerable," says he; "I 've got a 'crick' in my neck this morning," (and no wonder, for the maul was made of ebony wood, and was as hard as a flint rock,) "and besides, there was some sort of an insect here that bit me cruelly during the night."

"Did they seem to hop, or did they appear to crawl?" I asked.

"I think," he replied, "that they did more crawling than hopping, and more biting than either."

"Where did you get that buckskin suit you had on?" I inquired.

"From a Mexican," said he, "who sold it to me as a great favor."

"Then," said I, "Tige is n't to blame! you are lousy, sure!"

"What!" he cried, jumping up as if a stinging lizard had popped him in the back. "You don't say so! What am I to do, for I 've nothing else here to wear but that miserable buckskin suit?"

"Oh," I said, "they are all off of the clothes by this time, and on you, and if you will step down to the lake and take a good wash, you will be all right again."

Away he went, as if he had been on fire, or had swallowed a dose of No. 6, and pitched headforemost into the water, where he washed, combed, and scrubbed faithfully for half an hour. All the while I knew very well that Tige was at the bottom of his troubles, but of course I didn't tell him so.

After we had got some breakfast, we saddled up our horses and mounted, and took the trail of the Indians. Our author rode alongside of me, on a white-eyed "paint pony," with his bird-gun slung across his shoulders, and his "umbrell" tied behind him.

He didn't present a very formidable appearance, as you may well suppose, and the men were highly amused at the figure he cut; but they held in as much as possible on my account.

Notwithstanding all this, as we found out afterward, the little author was as "true blue" as ever fluttered, though of course he couldn't do much damage with his bird-gun and pepper-box.

CHAPTER XXII.

The Sudden Storm — Sad Fate of the "Author's" Umbrella — What he Thought of Mr. Cooper — The Author Goes a-Hunting, and what he Found — He Pronounces Mr. Cooper a Humbug.

I WAS satisfied, the Indians having had so much the start of us, that it was useless to "hurry up" with the expectation of overhauling them before they reached the country they intended to occupy permanently, and I determined to travel along leisurely, and keep our horses in as good plight as possible for the long "scout" that I knew was ahead of us; so we travelled only about twenty-five miles that day, and encamped just before sundown in a little valley where there was a bold running creek and plenty of good grass for our horses. When we had got some supper, we staked out our animals, placed the usual guard over them, and laid down under the trees upon our blankets, the author and I occupying one bunk together.

In a little while after we had "gone to roost," the author said to me:

"Captain, what is that roaring I hear like a charge of cavalry?"

I rose up and saw a dense black cloud coming rapidly toward us from the north, and I knew we were about to have one of those sudden squalls common at that season of the year in the hilly country, and invariably accompanied by a heavy fall of rain.

"We are in for a ducking, my friend," I said, "unless you can manage to protect us with your umbrella."

"Oh, I can do that," said he, jumping up; "and you will find that an umbrella is not such a bad article to have on a scout, after all."

So he unstrapped it from his saddle and hoisted it over us; but scarcely had he done so when the squall struck us with the force of a tornado, and the first gust of wind turned the umbrella wrong side out, wrenched it from his hand, and carried it out of sight in a moment.

"Captain," said he, "what's to be done now? The umbrella has been whisked off like an old witch upon a broomstick, and we shall be drenched to the skin."

"I know it," I replied, "but there's no help for it, and all we can do is to 'lay low' and take it quietly."

"Why, captain," he answered, "it will be the death of us! I never caught a wetting but once in my life, and then as soon as I got home, I did n't feel safe until I was tucked into bed with the 'sheets aired,' and had swallowed a couple of hot toddies. Oh, dear! the water is running down my back in a stream now, and I shall certainly perish from such horrible exposure."

"Not a bit of it, Mr. Author," I replied; "you 'll wake up as fresh as a lark in the morning. There 's a stream running down my back, too, but it is n't quite as big as the Colorado, and I'm not the least afraid of its drowning me. All you 've got to do is to keep quiet, and you will very soon be comfortable enough."

"Well," said he, after a while, "if this is what you call 'comfortable,' your ideas and mine differ very widely on the subject. The water is half-way up my sides. I begin to think," he continued, shivering and scrouging closer up to me, to borrow a little of my warmth, of which in fact I had n't much to spare—"I begin to think there was a good deal of humbug about Cooper, after all, for in all his descriptions of the woods and frontier life, he never says a word about a fellow's having to sleep in a puddle on the ground, with a damp blanket smelling of horses over his shoulders, and a stream of cold water trickling down his back. When people 'bivouac' in his novels, the nights are always serene and clear, the stars twinkle overhead, the turf is green and soft, (there 's a bowlder as big as my fist exactly under my hip,) and everything is pleasant and agreeable. I 'm losing my confidence in Mr. Cooper rapidly."

In about an hour the rain ceased, the puddle disappeared from around us, and notwithstanding his "uncomfortable" situation, our author slept like a top the balance of the night.

The first thing we saw in the morning, when we woke up, was the "umbrell" on the top of a mesquite bush, where the wind had lodged it, about fifty paces from where we had slept. The men discovered it about the same time, and as they wanted to fire off their guns and pistols, which had got damp in the rain, they pretended to think it was a turkey on its roost, and every one took a crack at it. As soon as the firing ceased, our author went out and lifted it from its roost with a long pole, and though sadly damaged by the bullets and wind, he carefully strapped it on his saddle again.

That day we travelled only about twenty miles on the trail, to a small creek where I thought it advisable to camp, as I knew it was doubtful about finding any water for a long distance beyond it. The sun was two or three hours high when we got to the creek, and several of the men went out hunting, and so did our author, though what he expected to kill with his little bird-gun is more than I can say. He had been gone but a short while when we heard both barrels of his gun go off quickly one after another, and soon afterward we heard him halloo a dozen times in rapid succession.

Supposing something extraordinary had happened to him, I seized my rifle and hurried off in the direction of the sound. When I had gone about half a mile, I came to the top of a ridge, and looking over in the valley beyond, I saw our author dodging from one side to the other of a small mesquite-tree, while a big buck trotted around it, every now and then making furious lunges at him with his horns. Our author, however, displayed more activity and skill in dodging than I had given him credit for, and thinking he was in no immediate danger, I walked along very leisurely toward him.

When I had got within about fifty yards of him, he sang out to me, in the most pleading tones, "to make haste and shoot the buck."

"Hurry, captain," said he, "and shoot the outrageous thing, for I can't keep up this dodging much longer."

But the fact is, I was in no hurry to shoot, for it was rather a funny sight to see how spry the little author would "squirrel" round the tree whenever the buck made a pass at him. At last he lost all patience, and sang out:

"Captain, why in the world don't you shoot? Shoot, and that pretty quick too, if you don't want to see me murdered in 'cold blood' by this horrid beast."

"That's hardly possible, Mr. Author," I said, "as you certainly have taken exercise enough to warm it up a little."

But the buck kept him so busy he paid no attention to anything I said, but continued to sing out:

"Shoot, captain! shoot the horrid beast."

The little author was amazingly expert and nimble at dodging, but, fearing he might accidentally get hurt if the game was kept up too long, I raised my gun, deliberately took sight at the buck, and fired. At the crack of the rifle, he made one last and desperate plunge at the author, grazing him so closely that he carried away a piece of the tail of his hunting-shirt on his horns, and then fell as "dead as a door nail" a few feet from the root of the tree.

Our author threw himself on the ground, completely "beat out," and panting and blowing like a stag-hound after a long chase. I walked up to where he lay, and as soon as he could catch his breath a little, he said:

"Captain, will you please tell me exactly how long it took you to walk from the top of that hill to this place, and how long you took sight at that buck after you got here? I am anxious to know, for I wish to make a note in my book of the 'slowest time on record.'"

I saw in a minute that our author was as mad as a hornet, (and no wonder, either,) so I said:

"Until I got up close to you, I actually thought you were after the buck, and not the buck after you; that it was the buck dodging round the tree, and you were trying to get hold of him to cut his throat." *

"Well," he replied, "it may have looked so to 'a man on a hill,' but it was just the contrary, I can tell you. If you had put off shooting one moment later, the world would never have seen the conclusion of the 'Wayworn Wanderer,' and you would have been responsible to posterity for the loss they would have suffered in consequence. But it's all owing to Mr. Cooper," he continued, "for I never would have ventured to attack a beast with

* Big-Foot "stretched his blanket" considerably here.

such a head of horns if it had not been for him. In all his novels he describes the deer as 'a timid, innocent animal, that is startled at its own shadow in the sun.' I only wish he had been here in my place! Why, sir, I never saw so furious a beast in all my born days, and I am pretty well convinced now that Mr. Cooper was a humbug; and as certain as I live I will expose all his fallacies in the 'Wayworn Wanderer.' He has imposed on the world quite long enough."

"That's all right, Mr. Author," said I; "but how do *you* intend to describe the deer?"

"Just as he is," said he, "a peaceable-looking animal enough before you attack him, but, the moment you fire upon him, a great fierce creature, with a head of horns like a brush-heap, eyes as green as grass, and his hair all turned the wrong way, and so active that nothing but a monkey or a squirrel can dodge fast enough round a tree to keep out of his way."

"That's a description, sir, that for truth and correctness would do to go in 'Goldsmith's Animated Nature.'"

While our author was running on in this style, I proceeded to skin the buck, and to cut off some choice pieces to carry back with us to camp. When I got through, I pretended just then to discover the tail of our author's hunting-shirt hanging to the buck's horns.

"Hello!" said I, "what's this?"

"Oh, that," he said, "is nothing but the tail of my hunting-shirt, which that 'timid, innocent animal, that is startled at its own shadow in the sun,' carried away on its horns when he made the last furious lunge at me. I'll thank you to hand it over to me, if you please, and I'll splice it on when we get to camp. Mr. Cooper's a humbug, sir!"

CHAPTER XXIII.

Our Author has an Appetite — Scarcity of Water — The Author takes Notes, and the Men get Riled — The Mud-Puddle.

WHEN we got back to camp with our author's venison, we found that some of the boys had cut down a "bee-tree," from which they had taken five or six gallons of excellent honey, and with some of the steaks from the buck that had exercised our author so much, we made a bountiful supper. I never in my life saw a man eat heartier than the author.

"Captain," said he, as he sat sipping his coffee, after having stowed away about five pounds of venison, not to mention "hard-tack" and other things, "this wandering about in Western wilds seems to give one a wonderful appetite. I feel like a frog that had swallowed shot, and I should make a poor out at dodging a buck now, for I should have him on both sides of me at once, inside and outside."

"Oh, my friend," said I, "you have not come fairly to your appetite yet. When you have been out a couple of weeks or so, and have exercised yourself at dodging bucks a few times more, you will be very nearly able to eat a 'mule and a hamper of greens' at a single meal."

"I shall not take any more exercise in that way," he replied, "particularly if I've got to depend upon you to help me out of the scrape. I shall certainly not interfere again with Mr. Cooper's 'timid, innocent animals, that are frightened at their own shadows in the sun.'"

After a while, our author took out his memorandum-book and pencil, as was his custom every night, and noted down all that had happened during the day, which he said was the "material" for the revised edition of the "Wayworn Wanderer."

The night passed off quietly, and the next morning we were again on our way by the time the sun had fairly risen.

We had entered upon a country that at that time was entirely destitute of water, and we travelled all that day and until an hour after dark without finding any. As the weather was warm, men and animals suffered severely for want of it. The next morning we were up betimes and again on the road, but mile after mile was passed over, and still not one drop of water could we find in the bottoms of the deepest gullies and cañons that lay on our way.

Toward sundown, both men and horses were suffering severely from thirst, and I began to feel some uneasiness at the prospect of having to pass another night without water. Our author stood the "racket" like a man; in fact, he seemed rather to enjoy the situation than otherwise.

"Captain," said he, riding up to me, "I wouldn't have missed this for a great deal. I can work up from the material I have collected in the last twenty-four hours a thrilling chapter on the suffering produced by intense thirst, that will add much to the interest of the 'Wayworn Wanderer.' But, I have one thing to ask of you, which will enable me to complete the information I want, and make this chapter (unlike Mr. Cooper's) true to nature. Will you please order the men to halt for a moment?"

Not having the slightest idea what he wanted, I did

as he requested, and called out "Halt!" The men drew up very unwillingly, for they were parching with thirst, and were anxious to get on as fast as possible, in the hope of finding water before night.

As soon as they had come to a halt, our author rode out in front of them, like an enrolling officer, and deliberately drawing forth his memorandum-book and pencil, he said to them:

"My friends, I hope you will not think I have taken too great a liberty in halting you in this way, and I am sure you will not, when I explain to you my reasons for so doing."

"Well, say it out quick," said some one in the crowd, "for this is no time for long talks, and we are in a hurry to get to water, if there is any left in this miserable country."

"Well, my friends," said our author, "I will not detain you more than ten minutes. All I want of you is to keep still long enough to enable me to get a correct expression of the human countenance when distorted by the pangs of intense thirst, which will aid me materially in working up one of the most thrilling chapters of my forthcoming novel, the 'Wayworn Wanderer.'"

And I wish I may be kicked to death by grasshoppers if he didn't ride along the line, every now and then stopping before a fellow and putting down in his book such notes as these: "Eyes inflamed and bloodshot," "Lips purple and contracted," "Countenance pale and anxious," etc.

The men, for a little while, didn't seem to understand what he was up to, but when they did, I verily believe they would have murdered him on the spot if it had not been for me. As it was, they contented themselves with giving him a hearty cursing, and, wheeling their horses, rode on rapidly, to make up for lost time. Said one of them to another:

"If that fellow had n't been a sort of pet of the captain's, if I would n't have shot him off that wall-eyed 'paint' of his'n! Only think of the fellow's impudence, will you, to stop the whole crowd when we have n't had a drop of water for two days, just to see how a man looked when he was dying from thirst!"

Said another: "If I had only suspicioned what he was up to at the start, he would have heard a gun fire certain; but when he came out in that way, with his book in his hand, I made sure he was going to tell us where there was a gold mine, or at least that he had a 'way-bill" to some water-hole."

Our author seemed a little disconcerted at first by the unceremonious manner in which the men had treated him, but he soon recovered his usual self-complacency, and took it all in good part.

"My friend," said I, as I rode up to him, "the men did n't seem very well pleased at your halting them in the road to make a note of their looks."

"No," he replied, "and I can't blame them much for being a little impatient, under the circumstances; but if I had only taken the precaution to read them a chapter or two from the 'Wayworn Wanderer' before I told them what I wanted, I have no doubt they would willingly have put themselves to some inconvenience to aid me in perfecting such a work."

"Oh, no doubt of that," I answered.

"The fact is," continued the author, "I 'm beginning to lose some of my interest in the book myself, for this wretched thirst torments me so I can think of nothing but water, in some shape or other — river water, lake water, spring water, or even a duck-puddle would have more interest for me now than I ever took in one of Cooper's novels before I found him out. Captain," he went on, " don't you see any signs of water hereabouts at all?"

"No," I answered, "but I hope we won't have to pass another night without it, for if we should, our animals will be seriously injured, to say nothing of what we will have to suffer ourselves."

Luckily, just before night, we struck a sort of lagoon, or the dry bed of a branch, which we followed down for some distance, and at length came to a little pool of muddy water. With great difficulty, we kept our horses from plunging into it until we had filled our canteens, when we turned them loose, and in a few moments they drank it dry. They did not get half as much as they wanted, but still there was enough to partially slake their thirst.

What we had taken up in our canteens was so thick with mud that we could scarcely pour it out, and yet out author declared it was the best water he ever drank, and that the flavor of the mud was rather an addition to it than otherwise; of which fact he said he intended to make a "note," as it controverted the popular idea that the water of "crystal streams" and "purling brooks" was the best.

We encamped near this lagoon for the night, and at daylight the next morning we were on the way again, for we did not wait for breakfast, as there was not water enough left in our canteens to make a cup of coffee.

CHAPTER XXIV.

Plenty of Water — A Halt for Refreshment — Our Author Among the Rocks — He Meets with an Adventure — Treed by Mexican Hogs — He grows Desperate — Is Released at last — Adventure with a Rattlesnake — More Scared than Hurt.

WE had travelled but a few miles, when our trail led us into a narrow pass in the hills, and after going up this two or three miles farther, we came to one of the most beautiful little valleys I had ever seen, through the midst of which there ran a bold stream of water, bordered by fine large cypress and pecan trees. The grass in this valley was luxuriant, and the Indians we were following had stopped in it some time to recruit their horses, after passing over the desert country we had just come through, as was evident from the quantity of bones and other offal around their camps. As our own horses had had but little grass for the last two days, I thought it would be good policy to follow their example, and rest them here until the next day. So we picked out a suitable place for a camp-ground, in a grove of pecans, and staked the animals out to graze.

Our author was a great geologist, I think he called it, as well as a book-maker, and would frequently talk to me about the "stratas" and the "primary" and "tertiary" formations, though I told him I did not know anything of such matters; and whenever we stopped to camp, he would frequently "boge" about for hours among the caverns and gulches, hunting what he called "specimens," and come back with his pockets filled with rocks, which he would sort out and label, and then store them away carefully in his saddle-bags. On one occasion I heard one of my men say to another, "Bill, what in the thunder do you suppose the 'author' has got in his saddle-wallets, that makes them so heavy?"

"Don't know," said Bill, "unless they are nuggets."

"Nuggets?" said the other; "they are rocks just like these you see laying all around here. I know it is so, for I looked into them this morning!"

"Why," answered Bill, "what do you reckon the fool is packing them about for?"

"No idea," said the other, "unless he has no faith in that 'bird-gun' and 'pepper-box' he totes, and intends to fight with them when we catch up with these Ingens. The truth is, Bill," he continued, "the fellow is as crazy as a bed-bug, sure, and if he only had any weepins about him that could hurt a body, I should keep my eye skinned on him, certain"

In fact, by this time the belief was prevalent among the men that our author was really "unsettled" in his mind, which supposition proved, in the end, of service to him, for of course they could not hold a crazy man responsible for anything he did.

As soon after our halt as he had unsaddled and staked his horse, he went out, as usual, hunting "specimens" in the ravines and gullies among the hills. I was just settling myself upon my blanket, to take a comfortable snooze, when we heard him "halloo" repeatedly about half a mile from camp.

"There," said one of the men, "there is that crazy chap got into a scrape with another buck, I suppose, and somebody will have to go and help him out of it."

"Yes," said another, "and the first thing he knows he will have his 'hair lifted,' 'boging' about alone, with nothing but that 'pop-gun' of his to fight with. He had better trust to his 'umbrell.'"

I was satisfied, however, it could not be a buck that was after him this time, for I had noticed, when he left camp, that he did not take his "pop-gun" along with him, and as he continued to "sing out" louder and louder, I at length picked up my rifle, and started off to see what sort of a scrape he had got into. At the bottom of a deep ravine, I found him sitting on the top of a chaparral bush, with his memorandum-book in his hand, and about a dozen Mexican hogs around him. He was barely out of their reach, and every now and then, one of them would make a pass at his legs, whenever he stretched them down to relieve them a little from the constrained position in which he was compelled to keep them.

As soon as I appreciated the situation of affairs, I scrambled up into a mesquite-tree, about thirty paces from where our author was roosting, for I knew very well these "havilinas," when excited and roused, were the most dangerous of all our wild animals. When in considerable numbers, they frequently attack a man with great ferocity, and are almost certain to cut him to pieces with their terrible tusks, unless he can effect a timely retreat, for they are much more active and swift on foot than the common wild hog.

When I found myself safe from their attacks, I called out to our author to know what he was doing on the top of that bush?

"Hallo! Captain!" he called out, "is that you?" (for the hogs had kept him so busy he had not noticed me till then.) "I am as glad to see you as I was when the buck was after me. I hope, though, you will not be quite so deliberate as you were on that occasion."

"Yes," I answered, "but what are you doing on the top of that bush?"

"Doing!" said he. "Can't you see that I am trying to keep my legs out of the reach of these outrageous wild pigs, and it is as much as I can do at that. There! did you see that scoundrel make a pass at me?"

"Why don't you drive them away?" I asked.

"Drive them away!" replied our author. "I have thrown all my specimens at them, and everything else I had about me except my memorandum-book, and it only makes them worse. They are not afraid of anything."

Said I, "Mr. Author," fixing myself comfortably on a limb, "this reminds me of a scrape I once got into with these 'havilinas,' that would do for a chapter in the 'Wayworn Wanderer;' and as we are comfortably fixed out here, all by ourselves, I could not have a better chance of telling it to you."

"Comfortable!" he exclaimed. "You have strange ideas of it, if you think a man can be comfortable, sitting on the top of your abominable Texas chaparral, with his knees drawn up to his chin, a thorn in each leg as long as my finger, and a dozen wild hogs making lunges at them whenever he stretches them down for a moment's ease. For heaven's sake, shoot them," he implored, "and let me out of this nest of thorns."

"I can't," I replied. "I have only the bullet that is in my gun, and if I shoot one of them, it will make the rest ten times worse."

"You don't tell me so, captain," he answered; "then, what in the world shall we do?"

"Why," said I, "the only thing we can do now, is to be patient, and wait until the moon rises to-night, and I think then the 'havilinas' will leave us."

"Oh! do not talk to me about the moon's rising. It will not be up till twelve o'clock, at least, and I cannot stand this fifteen minutes longer, no how. Crackey! that fellow gave me a grazer! He has taken off the heel of my boot on his tusks!"

"You see, Mr. Author," I continued, pretending not to hear what he said, "it was about six years ago, that Bill Hankins and I were out 'bear-hunting' on the head-waters of the Leon, when — "

"Plague take that fellow, he brought blood that time, certain!" said our author. "Their teeth are as sharp as razors."

"As I was saying," I went on, "it was about six years ago that Bill Hankins and I were out bear-hunting on the head-waters of the Leon, when we fell in with a large drove of these 'havilinas.'"

"They are gnawing my bush down," said our author, in a pitiable tone; "they will have it down in less than ten minutes."

"As I was saying," I continued, "it was about six years ago that Bill Hankins and I were out bear-hunting on the head-waters of the Leon, when we fell in with a large drove of havilinas, and before we were aware of our danger — "

"Shuh! you devils," said our author, flinging his last missile, his memorandum-book, at the hogs, as they made a general rush on his bush.

"Mr. Author," I said, in an offended tone, "you are not paying the slightest attention to what I am telling you. You might learn something even from the Indians in this respect, for, according to Mr. Cooper, they never interrupt a man when he is talking.

"As I was saying," I continued, "it was about six years ago that Bill Hankins and I were out bear-hunting on the head-waters of the Leon —"

"Oh! bother Mr. Cooper and Bill Hankins and the head-waters of the Leon," said our author, losing his temper at my persistence in relating the anecdote. "Cooper's a fool. Oh, my! there's a thorn clean through my back, into the hollow!"

"But, my friend," said I, changing my tactics, "you ought to bear your troubles with patience, for you should remember what a thrilling chapter you will be able to make out of this adventure for the 'Wayworn Wanderer.'"

"Oh, yes," said he; "but who will there be to write it, when I am chawed up by these infuriated pigs like a handful of acorns? Oh, dear! they 'll have me directly. I can feel the bush giving way now. Captain," said he, "you will find the manuscript of the 'Wayworn Wanderer' in my saddle-bags. Take it, and publish it for the benefit of the world, and tell them of the melancholy fate of the poor author. But tell them, for mercy's sake, that I was devoured by a lion, or a panther, or a catamount, or some other decent sort of a beast, and not by a gang of squealing pigs. It won't sound romantic, you know."

"I 'll do it, Mr. Author," said I; "but I hope you will live long enough yet to tell them all about it yourself. You have a first-rate chance now to study the habits and appearance of these 'havilinas,' and can write a chapter on them that will be very interesting, and true to nature. How will you describe them?" I asked.

"They look to me," he answered, "like a couple of butcher-knives about as long as my arm, stuck into a handle covered with hair and bristles!"

"And can you tell me," I said, "what particular tribe of animals they belong to?"

"Captain," he answered, "I don't feel inclined to discuss the subject just now, particularly as the subject is so eager to discuss me; and besides, to tell you the truth, I think you have selected a most unsuitable time for propounding your questions in natural history. Oh, my! there goes the leg of my pants, and a strip of the hide with it!"

"Mr. Author," I said, pretending not to hear his remarks, "I recollect once reading a chapter in one of Mr. Cooper's novels, in which he gives a very interesting account of the immense droves of wild pigeons that were migrating from one part of the country to another, and—"

"Oh, bother Cooper, I say!" said our author, becoming perfectly frantic, as a thorn touched him up in the rear, and a pig made a dash at his legs in front. "Cooper is an unmitigated humbug, and I begin to think you are not much better. Oh, I can stand this no longer," said he, "and I'll make a finish of it at once;" and I verily believe he would have jumped down right among the hogs in another moment; but just then I saw several of my men coming toward us from camp, and said to him:

"Hold on a minute, Mr. Author; there come some men to help us, and we'll soon rout the beasts now."

Seeing that we were both treed by some sort of "varmints," the men hurried up, shot several of the hogs, and the balance, finding we mustered too strong for them, quickly retreated into the chaparral.

Our author came down from his roost, and threw himself at full length upon the ground, for the purpose, as he said, of getting the tucks out of his legs After he had rested himself for awhile, and picked out all the thorns that had been left sticking in his flesh, he rose up considerably refreshed in mind and body, and we walked back toward camp.

"I am afraid, Mr. Author," said I, as we sauntered along, "you will begin to think you are paying pretty dearly for the information you are collecting in the wilderness."

"Not at all, captain," he answered, "for I know that no great undertaking was ever accomplished without labor and many difficulties to be overcome. A novel such as I intend the 'Wayworn Wanderer' to be, cannot be written except by one thoroughly posted on the subjects of which it treats. I will confess, however, that once or twice since I came out, (particularly when I was in that disagreeable position on top of the chaparral-bush,) I have wished I had never undertaken the job; but that, you see, was only a momentary weakness, and I shall not give way to it hereafter. 'Richard's himself again,'" he said, flapping his arms across his breast like a play-actor.

Now, there was one thing of which our author was exceedingly afraid, and that was a snake. He was in constant fear of them, day and night, and, like all people who have a great dread of snakes, he could find more of them in the course of the day than any six men in the company. He was forever finding snakes, at all times, and in localities, where nobody else could have found one if he had hunted closely for a week. Now, it so happened that just as he made this last heroic speech, and in the very act of flapping his arms against his breast, he put his foot upon a large rattlesnake that was coiled up in a bunch of grass. The snake rattled, and struck his teeth into his buckskin leggings.

"Oh! oh!" he sang out, dropping his feathers like a strutting gobbler when he hears a gun go off, at the same time making a most extraordinary leap to one side; "I am gone now to a certainty. This reptile has bitten me to the bone."

When the snake struck him, thc fangs penetrated partially into the tough, spongy buckskin of his leggings, and as our author sprang off he dragged the snake along with him. The moment he discovered that the snake was fastened to him, he kicked out frantically with his legs, and exclaimed, in the most piteous accents:

"Take him off, captain, for heaven's sake; take him off before he swallows me alive."

The snake was torn loose after the first vigorous kick: in the excitement of the moment, however, our author never noticed it, but continued his kicking and ground and lofty tumbling, until at last he fell to the ground from pure exhaustion, where he lay rolling and squirming apparently in the greatest agony. I ran up to him, and taking hold of him, said:

"Mr. Author, are you bit?"

"Bit!" said he; "you can't put your finger on a place that is n't bit. I 'm poisoned from head to foot by the reptile! The jig is up with me now, certain. Oh! what a fool I was to venture out into this howling wilderness, where you can't go forty yards from camp without running a great risk of being devoured by some wild beast, nor put your foot down without treading on a snake."

I really feared at first that the snake had bitten him,

and I hastily rolled up his leggings and looked for the wound, but could n't find the slightest sign of one, except some scratches made by the thorns of the chaparral bush.

"Mr. Author," said I, "you are all safe; the snake has n't even grazed the skin."

"Are you sure he has n't bit me?" he asked.

"Yes," I replied, "I 'll warrant your life for a gingercake. Why, Mr. Author," I continued, "you are in luck to-day. You have scarcely finished your adventure with the havilinas when here you are collecting material enough for another thrilling chapter of the 'Wayworn Wanderer.'"

"Yes," said he, "that 's true enough, and I can work up a very interesting chapter on 'snakes' out of this, there is no doubt; but, let me tell you, I don't want to collect 'material' quite so rapidly. I would rather these incidents would occur a little wider apart, and give me time enough to catch my breath. 'Enough is as good as a feast.' I am willing to make a martyr of myself now and then for the sake of immortality, but I can't afford to do it every fifteen minutes in the day."

We got back to camp without any further incident happening on the way, but I caught an idea from the last which I resolved to carry out for the benefit of our author, the first good opportunity that might present itself, and thus furnish him with the "material" for another thrilling chapter of the "Wayworn Wanderer."

CHAPTER XXV.

ANOTHER RATTLESNAKE — HOW TO MANAGE RATTLESNAKES — TERRIFIC ADVENTURE WITH A GRAPE-VINE RATTLESNAKE.

THE next day I rode along with our author, knowing if there was a rattlesnake on the road he would be sure to find it; and in fact he soon stirred up one, and I got down and killed it, and pulled off its rattles, which I slipped into my pocket, unnoticed by our author. "Captain," said he, as I remounted, "how in the world have you managed to live so long and camp out so much at night in this wilderness without ever having been bitten by a rattlesnake?"

"Why, you see," I answered, "if you don't lose your presence of mind, there 's very little danger of a rattlesnake's biting you, even when he crawls to bed with you at night. When you discover one crawling under your blankets, all you 've got to do is to lie still and let him fix himself to his notion, (and they always pick out the warmest places,) and as soon as he is fast asleep, you can jump up without the least danger of being bitten; but if you should move a peg before he has settled himself, he 'll 'nip you' to a certainty."

"Yes," replied our author, "but who could lie still under such circumstances?"

"I have," said I, "a hundred times. One dark night, about a year ago, when I was camping near the edge of a thick chaparral, I felt a fellow crawling under my blanket. I lay perfectly still, and let him select his own locality, and nothing would do him but a place right along side of my face. I tell you it was pretty hard work to keep quiet when I felt his scaly sides rubbing up against my neck and face, as he slowly wound himself in his coil. After he had fixed himself to his notion, I lay perfectly still a few moments longer, to make sure he was asleep, and then sprang up suddenly, and striking a light, soon had the gentleman's head mashed as flat as a pancake. Remember, Mr. Author," I continued, "there 's no danger at all of a rattlesnake's biting you at night, if you only lie still and keep quiet until he settles himself."

"Yes," said our author; "but who could lie still and keep quiet (unless he was made out of cast-iron) while a rattlesnake was slowly coiling itself up in his bosom? Ugh! the bare idea makes me shudder from head to foot."

I saw that my "snake story" had produced the desired effect upon him, and for the time I dropped the subject. The next night we encamped in a very snaky-looking locality, and I cut off a piece of grape-vine about as thick as an ordinary rattlesnake, which I slyly slipped under the edge of our blanket just before we "turned in." About half an hour after we had lain down, I drew out the slip of grape-vine and ran it slowly along the author's back, at the same time gently shaking my rattles, which I held in the other hand. He was just on the eve of dropping off to sleep, but the crawling motion and the "rattling" aroused him in an instant.

"Oh! murder, captain," said he, "there 's a rattlesnake crawling along my back! What in the world am I to do?"

"I know it," I answered, "I hear him rattling now,

(and I gently shook the rattles I held in my hand.) Lie still, and don't move a muscle until he coils up."

"Oh, yes," said the poor fellow, (and his teeth fairly chattered from fright,) "it 's easy enough for you to say lie still when I am between you and the snake, but it is n't so easy for me, for I can feel him squirming along my back now."

"I know that," said I, "but you must lie still, for the first motion you make, he will have his fangs into you, sure."

"Oh!" said the poor fellow, as I gave the vine another serpentine twist along his back, "this is more than human nature can bear — ugh! ugh! Captain, can't you do anything for me?"

"There 's no danger at all," I said, "if you will only keep still; he will soon settle himself, and then you can jump up without the least risk of being bitten. When he quits rattling altogether," said I, shaking the rattles in my hand, "you will know that he 's asleep."

"Captain," he replied, in a faint and husky voice, as I gave the vine another twist and shook the rattles, "this is past endurance. I *must* get out of this at all hazards."

"Unless you want to die," said I, "don't do it, but lie as still as a mouse when puss is about. By the way, Mr. Author," said I, "can you tell me whether the rattlesnake is confined to the American continent, or if he is to be found also in other countries? I have heard a great many opposite opinions on the subject, and some pretend to think," I continued, giving the vine another twist, "that they are a species of the Cobra di Capello, the most poisonous serpent in the world."

"Captain," said our author, getting the better of his

fright for the moment, in his indignation at being asked such an untimely question, "I like an inquiring mind, but I must say that you select the strangest occasions imaginable for obtaining information upon such subjects. Why, man," he continued, in a rage, and totally unsuspicious that I was playing upon him, "do you suppose a man is in a condition to answer any question rationally with a rattlesnake spooning up to his back?"

"There is no doubt," said I, pretending not to notice what he had said, and giving the vine another rake along his back, "that if they are not a species of the Cobra, they are just as poisonous, for I have seen a man die in twenty minutes after he had been bitten by one of them. There was Jake Thompson, who was bit on the foot by one, when we were scouting a year or two ago on the Nueces, and he did n't live long enough to say 'Jack Robinson, Junior;' and yet in that little time he turned as black in the face as a negro, and his body swelled up till he was as big as a 'skinned horse.'"

"Captain," said he, "will you do me the favor to postpone the balance of that interesting story for another occasion? I 'll back you against the world for picking out the most unsuitable times for telling your yarns."

"Oh! I beg your pardon," said I, "I forgot you was n't broke into the ways of the wilderness yet. When you have 'bunked' with a hundred rattlesnakes, as I have done, you won't mind it a bit. I recollect about six years ago, when Bill Hankins and me were out hunting on the head-waters of the Leon, we camped one night —"

"Oh! good gracious," said our author, "Bill Hankins again, and the head-waters of the Leon! Captain, I want you to distinctly understand that I 've heard just as much as I desire of Bill Hankins and the head-waters of Leon, and — "

"Oh! very well," I said, interrupting him in turn, and shaking my rattles, and screwing the vine into the small of his back, "I 've no wish at all to force my stories upon you."

"Ugh!" said the poor fellow, "this is past all endurance. Captain, remember me to all inquiring friends, and don't forget that the manuscript of the 'Wayworn Wanderer' is in my saddle-bags. Give it to the world with all its imperfections!"

"Hold on just one minute longer," I said, giving the rattles a vicious shake, "and you will be all right."

"Not another second," he cried, "it 's no use talking, I may just as well die one way as another," and he made a desperate bound from under the blanket, and pitched head foremost on the ground ten or twelve paces off.

I seized a bottle of "Chili pepper-sauce" and ran to where he was lying. "Here, Mr. Author," I said, "drink this quick!" He took it, and in the hurry and excitement of the moment, hastily swallowed about a pint of the contents.

"Gracious," said I, "you have made another wonderful escape."

"I don't know so well about that," said he, sputtering and gasping for breath. "I 'm afraid I 'm bit."

"Do you feel," I asked, "as if you were up to your waist in a kettle of melted lead?"

"Not exactly," he replied, drawing his breath through his teeth, "but I feel as though I had swallowed a quart or so of it."

"Then," said I, "you are all safe, and you have made the most wonderful escape on record. No one before has ever missed being bit, who sprang off as you did, before the snake had coiled himself up. A most extraordinary escape, truly," I continued.

"What in the world," said he, "was that stuff you gave me just now?"

"That," replied I, "is an antidote I always keep for the bite of snakes. I got it from 'Puppy's Foot,' the Tonkawa chief, and if taken in time it will kill the poison of the most venomous snake."

"I have no doubt of it," said our author; "it would kill old Satan himself. It is hot enough to scald the throat out of a brass monkey. For mercy's sake, give me some water to cool my coppers."

I handed over the gourd to him, and he took a long swig at it, then seating himself on a log by the fire, in spite of my remonstrances, he persisted in sitting up the balance of the night.

CHAPTER XXVI.

Fresh Signs of the Indians — Our Author in Trouble Again — Scatter Guns Compared with Bows and Arrows.

THE next morning, the little author looked so pale and haggard, after his terrible encounter with the snake, I really felt sorry for him, and inwardly resolved that I would play no more such practical jokes upon him. However, he had got such a scare that from that time until his return to the "settlements," he never slept again upon the ground. By means of a blanket and a staking rope, the first thing he did of an evening when we stopped to camp was to rig up an impromptu hammock, which he would stretch between two trees, out of the reach of snakes and other varmints, and in this airy roosting-place he would safely swing till morning.

Day after day, we followed our Indian trail with dogged perseverance, never leaving it for a moment, except when we were in search of a suitable camping-place for the night. On the morning of the fifteenth day after leaving my ranch on the Medina, we struck the range of high hills in which the head-waters of the Guadalupe take their rise. Here, the trail was so fresh, and other indications of the proximity of the Indians were so apparent, that I determined to move forward with the utmost caution, as I could hope to effect nothing of importance with the small force I had with me, except by taking the Indians by surprise. I therefore struck camp in a little valley, shut in on all sides by high hills, and sent forward, on foot, two of my most experienced trailers to reconnoitre.

I had issued strict orders against the firing of guns, for fear some straggling Indians might be in the vicinity and give the alarm, and I was, therefore, much astonished when, a short time after we had halted, I heard the report of a gun in camp; and looking round I discovered our little author running toward me for dear life, and a big fellow by the name of Bill Hawkins in close pursuit of him, with a poking stick in his hand, which he evidently intended to make use of as soon as he could get within striking distance. It was "nip and tuck" between them, but the little author fairly kept the lead until he reached me, when he jumped behind my back as nimbly as he had done behind the tree when the buck was after him upon a former occasion.

"Hello!" said I to Hawkins, as he came up, puffing and blowing, "what's the row now?"

"Look here, captain," said he, pulling at a few crisped remnants of hair that still hung to one side of his head, "look what that dratted author has done to me! He's let off his little 'scatter gun' right into my face, and has n't left hair enough on my head for a nit to hatch in. Phew! I smell worse than a singed 'possum! The little varmint ain't no more fit to handle a gun than a ribbed-nose baboon."

"See here, my friend," said our little author, stepping boldly forward, and beginning to shuck off his coat, "the firing of my gun was entirely accidental, and I am sorry I singed your hair off in that way; but if you are determined to make a fighting matter of it, you can 'pitch in' as soon as you please."

Bill weighed about two hundred pounds, exclusive of accoutrements, and was known all over the country as the toughest hand in a bear-fight west of the Colorado River; but when he saw the little author spunking up to him in that way, and beginning to peel in readiness for a fight, his anger was gone in a moment, and a good-natured smile spread over his weather-beaten features.

"Well," said he, "my little fellow, I 'spose the gun did go off accidentally, but I've noticed they always do so (unless they snap) when they are loaded, and somebody cocks 'em and pulls the trigger. However, we 'll not fight about it this time, for the fact is," Bill continued, winking at me, and looking down upon the "scant pattern" of the little author, "you rather 'oversize my pile;' so you kin just put on your coat agin for the present. I'm snapped, though, if you ever git another showing at my head with that pop-gun of yourn;" and saying this, Bill stalked back to his camp, smoothing down as he went along the singed and crisped remnants of his yellow locks.

"It's too bad," said the little author, in a vexed tone, "but that is certainly the most perverse gun of mine that was ever made. Whenever I want it to shoot, I can't get it to go off unless I stick a chunk of fire to the touch-hole; but when I least expect it, bang! it goes without the least provocation in the world. I wish I could swap it for a good bow and arrows! They never go off till you are ready; and, besides, there is a sort of romance associated with archery that carries one back to the days of chivalry — of cloth-yard shafts, and the good old times of Robin Hood."

"Well," said I, not understanding exactly what our author meant by all this rigmarole, "I have seen a great many men in my time spitted with 'dogwood switches,' but I never heard one of them yet complain of feeling anyways romantic under the circumstances. But the truth is, Mr. Author, if you only understood the use of 'em, you might have a worse weapon than a good bow and arrows; at least, I know they are pretty dangerous in the hands of an Indian. They can shoot their arrows faster than you can fire a revolver, and almost with the accuracy of a rifle at the distance of fifty or sixty yards, and with such force, that I have frequently seen them drive a shaft through and through a full-grown buffalo.

"I remember once, in a little scrimmage we had with the Indians on the head of the Leon, ('Oh, my!' exclaimed the author, 'there's the head of that Leon again!') I saw one of them drive an arrow through a man at the distance of seventy-five or eighty paces, and into another, who was standing just behind him; and there they were, fastened together like a couple of Siamese twins. The man in front was killed instantly, but the one behind at length kicked loose from the traces and eventually got well, though he carries the head of the arrow in his breast to this day.

"The heads of the arrows used in war are barbed, and fastened on very slightly with deer sinews, so that when an attempt is made to extract them from anything into which they may be driven, they are almost always left behind in the wound. The only alternative is to *push them through*, whatever may be in their way—heart, liver, or lungs: but this, as you may well suppose, is a very dangerous operation, and besides, not a very pleasant one, even when not followed by fatal consequences. There is one serious drawback, however, to the bow and arrows in the hands of the Indians, and that is, that they are almost useless in very damp or rainy weather, owing to the fact that the strings they use are made of deer sinews, which stretch so much when wet that it is almost impossible to keep the bow properly strung; and, for this reason, it is always most prudent to attack an Indian force in misty or rainy weather, for they have to rely, then, mainly upon their old flint-and-steel shot-guns, which are poor weapons except at very close quarters. There," said I, "Mr. Author, are some facts in regard to archery which you may note down in the 'Wayworn Wanderer' as beyond dispute."

CHAPTER XXVII.

THE INDIANS OVERTAKEN — DESPERATE FIGHT — THE AUTHOR PROVES HIMSELF A GOOD SOLDIER — THE INDIAN GIRL — THE AUTHOR HAS A RACE FOR HIS LIFE — THE UMBRELLA COMES IN PLAY — GATHERING UP THE SPOILS — THE HORSES RECOVERED — FAREWELL TO THE AUTHOR.

A LITTLE before sundown, the trailers I had sent out reported that they had discovered a large Indian camp about six miles beyond where we were, and that they were confident the Indians had no suspicion of our proximity. I at once determined to make an early start the next morning, so as to reach the Indian camp, about daylight. Everything was got in readiness for the move, and by three o'clock we were all mounted and on the trail again. There was no moon, and the night consequently was very dark, but we found no difficulty in following the trail, as our guides had so recently passed over it.

Just as the first streak of daylight became visible in the east, we came in view of the Indian encampment, situated in a pecan grove in the centre of a beautiful valley, which was hemmed in by high rugged hills on all sides, except in the direction we were approaching it. The smokes from their smouldering fires rose up in slim straight columns above the trees, and not a sound disturbed the deep silence that reigned around, except the occasional yelp of a cur in the encampment, or the distant howling of a wolf among the hills.

The Indians evidently had had no notice of our approach. As I gazed upon the quiet and peaceful scene, I could not help feeling some compunctions of conscience for the "bloody awakening" that was soon to rouse up my old friends and allies from their morning slumbers; but then, when I thought of the "scurvy," rascally trick they had played me, I dismissed all such ideas from my mind, and made my arrangements for an immediate attack upon the encampment.

About one-half of my men, led by Nathans, an old Rocky Mountain hunter, I sent around to the left, under cover of a low range of hills, with instructions to attack the Indians in the rear, whilst I slowly moved forward with the balance to assail them in front. A discharge of guns from the first party was to be a signal for a general assault.

I advanced with my party to within one hundred and fifty yards of the encampment, under cover of a thicket of dogwood, and there halted to wait for the concerted signal. In a few minutes the keen report of a dozen rifles was heard on the opposite side of the encampment, warning us that the time for action had arrived, and putting spurs to our horses, we dashed furiously into the Indian village, and dismounting from our horses, we poured in a deadly fire from our rifles and "repeaters" upon the warriors, as they rushed out, confused and frightened, from the doors of their lodges. But, although taken completely by surprise, they fought with great desperation and obstinacy, and for half an hour the possession of the camp was hotly contested by both parties. At one time I thought I should be compelled to beat a retreat, for the Indians greatly outnumbered us, but just at this juncture the fall of one of their head chiefs threw them into momentary confusion, and taking advantage of it, we charged them so vigorously that they at length slowly and sullenly retreated into a thick chaparral in the vicinity of their camp, leaving twenty-seven of their warriors dead upon the ground. Their wounded they carried off with them.

During the fight, I noticed our author several times busily "pegging away" with his little bird-gun, and every now and then yelling like a "tiger cat," whenever he saw an Indian fall, but I am very sure (although I believe his will was good) that nothing ever fell before his fire, except the top of a mesquite-bush, a few feet from the muzzle of his gun. He was, however, evidently under the impression himself that everything depended upon his personal exertions, and he "blazed away" and hurrahed, and jumped around, ordering this one to do that, and that one to do this, until he was in a lather of sweat, and looked like a stunted coal-heaver, on account of the way in which he had smeared his hands and face with gunpowder. The men, of course, paid no attention to his orders; nevertheless the little author evidently had risen a hundred per cent. in their estimation from the courage he displayed, and the recklessness with which he exposed himself to the fire of the Indians.

In the very height of the engagement, and just at the time I began to think seriously of quitting the field, I heard a shrill voice exclaim, "Oh, que, Wallace!" and a young Indian girl darted out of a lodge near by, and seizing the skirt of my hunting-shirt, she clung to it frantically until the fight was over, and the warriors were in the act of retreating.

I felt sorry for the poor little thing, and tried my best, by keeping her behind me, to shield her from the bullets and arrows that were flying about thick and fast; but unluckily, in the very last volley the Indians gave us, a stray bullet struck her full in the breast, and she sank to the ground. I dropped my rifle, and raised her up in my arms, but I saw in a moment that she had received a fatal wound, for her eyes were already glazing, and she was gasping for breath. I laid her down upon the soft green grass at the foot of a pecan-tree, and for an instant she seemed to revive. Looking sorrowfully at me, she said, in broken English and Spanish:

"Oh, Captain Wallace, I know you. Mi madre — mi pobrecito padre — no kill 'em — adios" — and then a slight shudder passed over her, her head gently fell back upon my arm, and the poor little thing was beyond the trials and troubles of this wicked world.

The sort of life that I had led had not been one particularly to soften a fellow's heart, but I am not ashamed to own, as I gazed upon the stiffening form of this forest child, so cruelly cut down by the hands of her own friends and relatives, that my eyes were dimmed with tears, and I sincerely wished on her account that I had permitted her tribe to go unpunished for breaking the treaty they had made with me.

However, it was too late then to indulge in useless regrets; and in fact I had no time to do so, for the Indians, when they retreated, had quickly made off for some place in the vicinity where their horses were staked out, and mounting them, they returned and renewed the fight with greater obstinacy than ever. We mounted our horses, also, and in this way the contest for the possession of the village was continued for half an hour longer. But, although they outnumbered us still at least two to one, the superiority of our weapons (especially our revolvers, which at that time were almost unknown to the Indians,) more than made up for our deficiency in numbers, and they at length gave way. Breaking up into little squads, they fled in every direction before my men, who followed them in the same disorderly manner.

Just at this stage of the game, having seen nothing of our little author for some time, I looked around to ascertain what had become of him. Casting my eyes up the open valley to our left, I saw him coming "full split" toward me, on "Old Paint," * bare-headed and apparently unarmed, and a half dozen mounted Indians in close pursuit of him. Two or three of us, who happened to be near by, immediately spurred our horses and galloped out to meet him, to help him in any way we could in making good his retreat, although from the rapidity with which the Indians lessened the distance between the little author and themselves, I had but faint hopes that we could reach him

* His horse.

before they came up with him. "Old Paint," however, held his own much better than any one would have supposed possible; but at length the foremost Indian rode up so near that we saw him draw back his lance, for the purpose of driving it through our little friend. At that moment I gave him up for lost, but the little author, it seems, had his wits fully about him, and had been closely watching the motions of the Indians over his shoulder, for just at this crisis he snatched his "umbrell" from behind his saddle, and suddenly wheeling old Paint, he flopped it open right in the eyes of the Indians' horses.

The effect of this masterly movement was instantaneous and magical. The Indians' horses stopped for a second as suddenly as if they had been turned to stone, and gazed with terror and astonishment upon the strange-looking object presented toward them; then wheeling as quick as lightning, in spite of all the efforts of their riders, they dashed off like mad in the direction they had come. In a few minutes the little author trotted up to where we were, looking as pleasing as a basket of chips, and smiling as complacently as if he thought it no ways strange at all that he should have routed a half dozen warriors with no other weapon than his much-abused "umbrell."

The men were so much "tickled" with his recklessness and daring (for by this time a crowd had gathered around us, who had witnessed the whole proceeding,) that they welcomed him as he rode up with a shout that might have been heard for a mile.

"Darn my hind sights," said Bill Sykes, an old frontiersman and Indian-fighter, "ef this ain't the first time I ever knowed or hearn tell of a gang of Ingins bein' whipped with nothing but an 'umbrell.' I never seed horses so badly 'stampeded' before in my life! They'd just as soon run over a bluff forty feet high as — up a tree, any way to git out of reach of that 'umbrell.' Ef the fellow would only put it up at auction, I'd bid high on it myself, I would; I'd rather have it than a pair of Deringers, any day."

"And who'd have thought it?" said another; "the little cuss has got sand in his craw certain, and back-bone enough for a feller three times his length. If Big-Foot gits 'upped' * on this scout, or resigns, I'll vote for him to be captain of this squad, sure — don't care if he does fill his saddle-wallets with rocks, and totes a 'pepper-box' for a repeater. He's true blue and no mistake."

"Well, Mr. Author," said I, as he rode up, "you have had a closer shave for your life this time, than you did when the buck was after you. I began to think sure enough that you would never live to finish your great novel of the 'Wayworn Wanderer.'"

"Yes," he answered, "I was in a pretty tight place for a while, and I began to think myself that the world would never see the revised edition of the 'Wayworn Wanderer.' The fact is though, captain, this 'scrimmaging,' as you call it, with the Indians, is a very exciting business, and forgetting the old saying 'that discretion is the better part of valor,' I followed a party of them too far, and before I was aware of my danger, they turned upon me; and dropping my gun and pistol, which were both empty, I had, as you saw, to depend on the heels of 'Paint' to take me out of the scrape. But, didn't I send 'em to the right-about though, when I

* Killed.

unmasked my 'battery' on them? They went back a good deal faster than they had come!"

"Yes," said I, "Mr. Author, you have saved your scalp pretty cleverly this time; but I would advise you not to be so venturesome in the future, for fear your 'umbrell' might not serve you as well on another occasion."

When we got back to the village, we found the men busily engaged in collecting the "plunder" the Indians had stowed away in their lodges, and piling it up in the centre of the square, previous to distribution, and the amount of it was truly astonishing. Kegs of powder, sacks of lead, bales of blankets, dry goods, brass kettles, beads, skins, and buffalo-robes, cutlery and hardware of various sorts, and a great variety of camping and hunting equipments, mostly of their own manufacture. About this time a party of my men came in from following the retreating Indians, bringing with them one hundred and seventy head of horses and mules, which they had found penned up in a corral near by, and among them were most of those that had been stolen from me.

Whilst the men were engaged in dividing out the "plunder" among themselves, or such of it as they could carry along with them, the little author and I took an old spade we picked up near one of the lodges, and going to where I had left the lifeless form of the Indian maiden, we dug a grave at the foot of a pecan-tree, and wrapping her up in a clean white blanket, we gave her as decent a burial as we could. The little author seemed very sorry when I told him how she had been accidentally killed in the fight by her own people, but said he would make her all the amends in his power for the melancholy fate, by immortalizing her under the name of "Pa-ha-tal-ca" or the "Soft Wind," in his great novel of the "Wayworn Wanderer."

In the second fight with the Indians, they lost twenty-one warriors, making altogether forty-eight of them killed and left upon the ground. I had but two men killed and five wounded. The Lipans never recovered from the fatal blow we gave them on this occasion. From having been, up to this time, a formidable tribe, able to send out six or eight hundred warriors into the field, they rapidly dwindled away until now they scarcely number a hundred souls, men, women, and children, all told.

Nothing worthy of note occurred on our way back home. I parted with our little author at San Antonio, and he promised me faithfully to send me a copy of his book as soon as it was published; but I never got it, nor do I know to this day whether or not he has ever exposed (as he threatened to do) the "humbugeries" of Mr. Cooper, in his great novel of the "Wayworn Wanderer of the Western Wilds."

CHAPTER XXVIII.

WALLACE SURPRISES A PARTY OF INDIANS WHO WERE MAKING THEMSELVES "COMFORTABLE" NEAR HIS RANCH.

INDIANS are sometimes monstrous impudent, and will run the greatest risks without anything to gain by it. Would you believe, that not more than six months ago a party of five Tonkawa warriors came within half a mile of my ranch, and in broad daylight killed one of my fattest "mavericks," pitched their camp, and set in for a general jollification?

It happened that morning that Tom Jones, Bill Decker, Jeff Bonds, and myself were out looking after the stock, when all at once Jeff remarked that he smelt meat roasting on the coals. I then turned up my nose to windward and smelt it too as plainly as I ever whiffed fried middling of a frosty morning with the breeze dead ahead, when I 've been coming into camp after a three-hours' hunt before breakfast. Talk about your "Hostetter's Bitters," and your "patent tonics!" the best tonic I know of is a three-hours' hunt among the hills on a frosty morning. It gives a fellow an appetite that nothing less than a "mule and a hamper of greens" can satisfy.

Well, as I was saying, just as soon as I smelt roasted meat, I knew there were Indians about, although the last place I should have looked, if I had been hunting for them, would have been the vicinity of my ranch. Still, I was certain they were there somewhere, for wolves, and panthers, and catamounts, and other varmints, you see, always take their meat raw; so I told the boys to keep quiet and get down and fasten their horses. We then recapped our guns and revolvers, and cautiously crept along through the bushes until we discovered the Indians, not more than fifty yards from us, where they were making themselves as much at home and as comfortable around their fire as if they were in the mountains about the head of the Guadalupe River, which is undoubtedly the roughest little scope of country to be found in the State of Texas.

I whispered to Jeff, who was nearest to me:

"Well, don't this beat you? Did you ever know such impudence before in your life? To kill one of my fattest 'mavericks' and barbecue it in broad daylight, within half a mile of my ranch! Well, if I don't let 'em know I am the landlord of these 'diggins' yet, and bring in a bill for the entertainment they have had, you may call me 'short stock,' if I am six feet three in my stockings!"

All this time the Indians never suspected we were near them. There was one big fellow among them, who must have been six feet two or three inches high in his stockings, (though of course he never had on a pair in his life,) and he was making himself very prominent around the fire, broiling the fat steaks of my "maverick" upon the coals, and turning and basting the joints of meat on the spits, all the while laughing and talking just as if he did n't know he was within a mile of Big-Foot's ranch.

I don't think I ever felt less like giving quarter in my life but once, and that was when a big buck-nigger, with a nose like a "dormant" window, and a pair of lips that looked like he had been sucking a bee-gum and got badly stung in the operation, objected to my registering as a voter. He was one of the Board of Registrars at

Castroville, but he was n't in a condition to object to any one else registering that day, and probably the next, for I took him a "clue" over the head that would have stunned a beef, but he never winked; and changing my tactics, I gave him twelve inches of solid shoe-leather on the shins that brought him to his milk in short order. The "Buro" fined me fifty dollars and costs, but the amount is n't paid yet, and probably won't be until they can get a crowd that is good at trailing and fighting Indians to pilot the sheriff to my ranch.

But, to come back to the Indians that were barbecuing my maverick; I determined to take the impudent chap that was making himself so "prominent" around the fire into my especial keeping, and I whispered Jeff to draw a bead on the one sitting down, and to tell Bill and Tom to shoot at the three standing up. At the word, all four of our rifles cracked like one gun.

Just as I drew the trigger on him, the big Indian was lifting a "chunk" of my maverick from the fire. At the crack of the rifle, the "chunk" flew up in the air, and the big Indian pitched headforemost on his face right among the hot coals and ashes, and before we left there was a stronger smell of roast meat than ever; but it was n't my maverick.

Jeff also killed his Indian dead in his tracks, but only one of those that Bill and Tom fired at was wounded, and not very badly at that. They retreated into the thick chaparral, and we never saw them again. However, we got all their bows and arrows, and one first-rate new flint-and-steel rifle, to say nothing of the maverick, which was done to a turn, for, to give the scamps their due, they do understand roasting meat to a fraction.

The big Indian that I got must have been a sort of

chief, for he had about twenty pounds of brass rings on his arms, and a "cue" that reached down to his heels, that "nipped and tucked" in the hot ashes like a burnt boot. The other Indians took the little hint I gave them, and have never camped on my premises since.

CHAPTER XXIX.

The "Mier Expedition."

DURING the fall of 1842, the "Mier Expedition," as it was called, was set on foot by the authorities of Texas, in retaliation, I suppose, for the then recent invasion of the Republic by General Wool, and the capture of the city of San Antonio. Of course, I was "on hand," as usual, and volunteered my services. Young men are always ready to volunteer on "wild goose" expeditions, and I was no exception to the rule; but as we grow older, we learn a thing or two, look some time before we leap, and don't "fly off the handle" quite so easily.

The place of rendezvous was the city of San Antonio, and the volunteers that assembled there for the expedition were placed under the command of Brigadier-General Somerville, an officer of good standing and considerable reputation. A motley, mixed-up crowd we were, you may be certain — broken-down politicians from the "old States," that somehow had got on the wrong side of the fence, and been left out in the cold; renegades and refugees from justice, that had "left their country for their country's good," and adventurers of all sorts, ready for anything or any enterprise that afforded a reasonable prospect of excitement and plunder. Dare-devils they were all, and afraid of nothing under the sun, (except a due-bill or a bailiff,) and if they had been managed with skill and judgment, they would undoubtedly have accomplished all that was expected from the expedition; but dissension, that bane of raw troops, which has so often brought to grief expeditions of this kind, prevailed among our leaders, and in a short time after we had marched on and taken possession of Laredo, a little village on the eastern shore of the Rio Grande, the greater portion of our men became dissatisfied with the way in which matters were managed, and returned home.

We found no troops in Laredo, and no attempt was made by the inhabitants to defend it. By the time we reached the place we had run short of provisions, and a requisition was made upon the citizens for a supply, and after obtaining a small quantity in this way, we marched out of town, and encamped for the night about three miles below it.

On our way to camp, a man named De Boyce was accidentally killed by the discharge of a gun in the hands of a messmate.

We remained at this camp all the next day, and the day after we took up the line of march down the left bank of the Rio Grande, keeping well to the eastward of the settlements on the river, so as to conceal our advance as much as possible from the enemy's scouts. We continued on southwardly for several days, through thickets of mesquite and other thorny shrubs, with which this country is covered, and then turning due west, soon struck the Rio Grande, about ten miles above Guerrero. Here we found two or three small boats, and at once proceeded to cross our whole force, now less than five hundred men, as Colonel Bennett, with all the "drafted men," had left us previously, and taken the "back track" toward home. The boats were quite small, and but few men could go in them at a time, and the day was pretty well gone before one-half of our force had landed on the opposite side.

About this time, General Green, who had been sent forward with a small force to reconnoitre in the direction of Guerrero, came back, closely pursued by a considerable body of Mexican cavalry. The men that had landed were at once formed in line of battle by Colonel Cook, and awaited the anticipated attack of the Mexicans; but, after circling round us and watching our movements from a respectful distance, they galloped off, and we saw them no more that day.

The next morning, the balance of our men were crossed over to the western side of the river, and we marched at once upon Guerrero. When within half a mile or so of the town, the alcalde came out to meet us, and begged us not to enter the place, as the citizens had been informed we intended to burn it and put them all to the sword. His request was complied with, and we encamped on the Salado, a small stream about a mile from the village.

The next morning, when we were all anticipating every moment the order to advance upon the town, we were astonished by receiving an order from our commander to "prepare to retreat, and to recross the river as soon as possible." We supposed, however, that of course our commander had received some information of the movements of the enemy that rendered this sudden retreat necessary, and we were soon in motion, and never halted until we were all safely landed again on the eastern bank of the Rio Grande, where we encamped for the night.

Rumors were rife among the men as to the causes of this retrograde movement, but nothing definite in regard to it seemed to be known to any one. Some said that our commander, General Somerville, had received orders from the President of Texas to abandon the expedition, but whether this was so or not I never knew; at any rate, he left us the next morning, and took back home with him a considerable number of the men. I had good reason afterward to regret that I had not continued my retreat with this crowd, for verily "discretion is the better part of valor."

Those of us that remained behind (I think, about two hundred and twenty-four, all told,) determined, as far as possible, to accomplish the objects of the expedition, and Colonel Fisher, an accomplished and tried officer, was selected for our "commander-in-chief."

The morning after our new organization we recrossed the Rio Grande again, eight miles from Mier, and marched at once upon the town, which we took possession of without any opposition. We found no troops there. The inhabitants were quite friendly apparently, and readily furnished us with such supplies as we needed; but had I known the Mexican character as well then as I do now, I should have suspected their sincerity precisely in proportion to the friendly manner in which they welcomed us. When I was at school, I learnt a Latin phrase, "*Timeo Danaos et dona ferentes,*"

(I fear the Greeks when they bring gifts.) And beware of the Mexicans, when they press you to hot coffee and "tortillas." Put fresh caps on your revolver, and see that your "shooting-irons" are all in order, for you will probably need them before long. They are a great deal more treacherous than Indians. If you can manage to get into an Indian's camp before he kills you, and can surprise him into offering you any little hospitality, even a drink of water, you are safe from him and his clan as long as you are with them. No temptation would induce him to "lift your hair."

But it is not so with the Mexican. He will feed you on his best, "señor" you, and "muchas gracias" you, and bow to you like a French dancing-master, and wind it all up by slipping a knife under your left shoulder-blade! And that's one reason I hate them so. I have respect for a bold and open enemy, but I despise your sneaking sort, who are forever hoisting "white flags" for the purpose of throwing you off your guard.

CHAPTER XXX.

Over the Rio Grande again — A Costly Exchange — Reception by the Mexicans — Firing an "Escopeta" — Fighting in Earnest — Captain Cameron and the Mexican Soldier.

WHEN we had got all the supplies we needed from the citizens of Mier, we recrossed the river once more and pitched our camp about four miles east of the town. No plundering was permitted while we were in Mier, and everything we took from the inhabitants was duly paid for according to our own estimate of its value, and of course the prices were quite reasonable.

The next day after our return to the east side of the river, some of the scouts we had left on the west side to watch the motions of the enemy, came into camp and reported that a large body of Mexican troops were marching into Mier. This we regarded as a banter for a fight; so we struck tents, crossed the river once more and for the last time, and marched on the city, which, as our spies had truly reported, we now found strongly garrisoned by a considerable Mexican force.

Before we crossed the river, a certain number of our men were detailed to remain at camp as a guard for our horses and baggage, and it was my luck to be chosen one of them. But I did not fancy that sort of business, and resolved, by some means or other, to make one of the detachment that was to advance on Mier. As it happened, one of my messmates, who had as little inclination for the front as I had for guarding horses in the rear, proffered to exchange places with me, to which I of course, readily consented, and at the time we were both, no doubt, well satisfied with the arrangement; but it was n't a great while before I rued the trade I had made with him, and would gladly have swapped back again and given considerable "boot."

Between three and four o'clock in the evening, our whole detachment had crossed the river, and we at once took up the line of march for Mier. We saw no signs of the enemy, except a few mounted scouts, who retreated expeditiously as soon as we came in sight, until we came to the Alcantro, a little stream a few hundred yards from the town.

Here we made all necessary preparations and advanced to the attack; but in place of hot coffee and tortillas, as in the former instance, we were received by the Mexicans with shouts of defiance, and heavy discharges from their "escopetas."

These "escopetas" are a short bell-mouth, bull-doggish looking musket, carrying a very heavy ball, which is "death by the law" when it hits, but that is seldom, for they shoot with little accuracy. They are good for nothing, except to make a noise, and a volley from them always put me in mind of the old saying about shearing hogs — "Great cry and little wool." I never fired one of them but once, and that was at the battle of the Salado, near San Antonio.

During the fight, I came across a dead Mexican with one in his hands, and as my rifle was empty at the time, I hastily caught it up, placed the breech against my shoulder, as I was in the habit of doing with my own gun, and fired at a party of the enemy who were retreating from the field. My first impression was that I had been struck with a nine-pound cannon-ball. It kicked me heels over head, and I suppose kept on kicking me after I was down, for when I "came to" I found that my nose was unjointed and two of my ribs stove in. I have since found that the Mexicans never place them to the shoulder, but hold them with both hands above their heads and fire at random, which accounts in a great measure for the little execution done by them.

But to come back to my story. The Mexicans received us, as I said, with heavy discharges from these escopetas, and after some sharp skirmishing we got possession of a portion of the town, and the fighting began in earnest.

Among us there were some of the best marksmen in the world, backwoodsmen from Kentucky, Tennessee, and Arkansas, and every "greaser" that ventured to peep at us above the parapets of the houses, and round the corners of the streets, was sure to get a bullet through his head.

In the mean time, with crowbars and picks, some of us were busily engaged in breaking through the stone walls of the buildings, and in this way we were rapidly advancing toward the "square," in the centre of the town. Night, however, came on and put an end, for the time, to the contest.

So far, we had lost but one man killed, (Major Jones, former Postmaster-General of the Republic.) The Mexican loss must have been considerable, but we had no means of ascertaining the extent of it.

Just as the fight ended, two or three of us had picked our way into a room, where we found a table well covered with various sorts of eatables — "chilicou carne," "tortillas," etc., several bottles of "pulque," and a box full of fine "puros," or Spanish cigars. At first, we were a little suspicious of these things, thinking the

Mexicans might have left them on purpose, for the *benefit* of the "gringos," and we touched them sparingly. But hunger at length got the better of our suspicions, for we had not eaten a bite all day, and we pitched into them, regardless of consequences, and made a jolly night of it.

At daylight the next morning the Mexicans began to blow their bugles and beat their drums, and to make a great to do generally; but Tom Hancock, a messmate of mine, who had been among the Mexicans a long time, and knew their character well, told us not to be alarmed, as they were merely playing a "game of bluff," and that he had always noticed that the more noise they made the less stomach they had for fighting. But it seems that the garrison had been greatly reinforced during the night, and, confident in their numbers, they charged us in the position we occupied with more spirit than we had given them credit for. The fire from our rifles, however, was so rapid and deadly that they at length fell back in confusion, leaving the streets and plaza strewed with their dead and wounded.

For some time after this repulse they contented themselves with firing upon us at "long taw," from their port-holes and the flat roofs of their houses, but gradually growing bolder, as reinforcements came in, they charged us again and again with great impetuosity and courage, but each time with the same result. The last time, they pressed us so closely that our men, in many instances, after discharging their guns, fought them with *rocks*, which they tore up from the streets, and from the walls of the surrounding buildings.

Captain Cameron, a man of extraordinary strength, having just discharged his rifle, was observed by several of us to seize a rock and dash out the brains of a Mexican soldier who was in the act of charging upon him with his bayonet.

Some of the Mexican soldiers told us subsequently that they were all drunk, having been furnished by their officers with as much "pulque" as they could drink, in order to stimulate their courage, which will account for their unusual intrepidity and daring.

I had a very narrow escape myself in this fight. After one of their charges upon us, in the excitement of the moment, I followed too far a party of retreating soldiers, when they suddenly turned upon me, and before I was aware of my danger, I was surrounded, and escape was apparently impossible. I was determined, however, to retreat at all hazards, and turned and dashed through their line. One fellow, as I passed, made a lunge at me with his bayonet, slightly wounding me in the left arm; but I made good my escape, and rejoined my comrades, who had given me up for lost.

The adventure had the effect of cooling my courage considerably, and during the rest of the fight I kept within supporting distance of my comrades.

The battle continued with great obstinacy on both sides, until perhaps one or two o'clock in the evening, when a temporary cessation took place of an hour or so, apparently by the tacit consent of both parties. And then affairs took a turn I have never been able to account for satisfactorily to this day. Everything seemed to promise us a complete victory, for we had evidently been getting the best of the fight all day long, when the Mexicans hoisted a "white flag," and sent it into our lines by a Dr. Sennickson, one of our men that had been previously captured by them. Sennickson was accompanied by two Mexican officers, Algereto and

Carasco. They bore a message from General Ampudia, requesting an entire cessation of hostilities for an hour longer.

This request was readily acceded to by our commander, for no doubt he was fully under the impression that the Mexicans intended surrendering the town to us. You can form some idea of our astonishment, then, when in a little while another officer came into our lines, with a message from General Ampudia to the effect "that it was a useless waste of life for us to contend longer against his greatly superior force; that he had received large reinforcements, and had us completely in his power; and if we would surrender at discretion, he pledged us his word we should be treated with liberality and clemency, but that if any further resistance was made, every one of us should be put to the sword without mercy."

I had but little knowledge at that time of the Mexican character, but I have since learned whenever they hoisted the white flag and succeeded in persuading the Americans into a "parley," they invariably got the better of them in some way or other. It was so at the storming of Monterey, during the Mexican war. There, after three days' hard fighting, and just when we got the whole Mexican army completely in our power, they hoisted that same white flag, and "bamboozled" General Taylor into a "parley," and then into an "armistice" of thirty days, and finally into a "capitulation," which enabled them to march out with the "honors of war," and with all their arms and equipments; and he had to fight them over again at Buena Vista under the most disadvantageous circumstances.

CHAPTER XXXI.

Surrender to the Mexicans — General Green's Proposition — Marched off to Prison — The Mexican Maiden — Off for Camargo — A Short Stay and off again — Reinosa.

A LONG "talk" followed between our officers and the messengers of General Ampudia, going and coming. Some of our officers were in favor of fighting to the last, but the "white flag" had produced its usual effect upon the majority, who were in favor of surrendering, providing General Ampudia would grant us such terms as they thought honorable and reasonable. These terms were at length decided upon, written out on paper, and forwarded to General Ampudia. After some further parleying, General Ampudia finally consented to ratify the capitulation upon the terms demanded.

It was at this stage of the proceedings that General Green stepped out of the ranks, and called for a hundred volunteers to go with him and cut their way through the Mexicans. But, the attempt seemed such a hopeless one, that no one responded to his call, and, mortified, the gallant soldier dashed his rifle to pieces against the ground, and resigned himself to his fate.

We delivered up all our arms to the Mexicans, who marched us off in double file to our quarters in some deserted stone buildings. Never shall I forget the humiliation of my feelings, when we were stripped of all our arms and equipments, and led off ignominiously by a numerous guard of swarthy, bandy-legged, contemptible "greasers." There we were, two hundred good men and true as ever shouldered a musket, (for we had lost only about thirty men killed and wounded in the fight,) for no earthly reason that I could see, bound hand and foot, and delivered over to the tender mercies of these pumpkin-colored Philistines, and all through the workings of that miserable little "white flag." I could have cried with a right good will if I had n't been so mad.

The force opposed to us in Mier, at the time of our surrender, as stated by the Mexicans themselves, amounted to something over three thousand men. Of these, upwards of five hundred, according to their own estimate, were killed in the fight. How many were wounded we never knew. In no other battle with the Americans, before or since, have the Mexicans ever displayed as much intrepidity and daring, and I have no doubt myself, that, as some of them told us, the greater portion of their soldiers were drunk on "pulque," with which they were liberally supplied by their officers during the fight.

The guard we had left on the east side of the river, in charge of our horses and camp equipage, it seems got information of our surrender, by some means, in time to effect their escape. They made their way safely back into Texas.

As I have before stated, as soon as we had surrendered, they fastened us up in some deserted stone buildings, like so many pigs, where we were kept for five or six days with nothing to eat except a little dried beef, which was so tough I gave one-half of my rations to a messmate, who had a remarkably strong set of teeth, to chew the other half for me; and, to wash this down, we were furnished with a limited supply of muddy water from the Rio Grande. However, there was no use to complain ; we knew we were "in for it," and principally through our own stupidity and folly, and we resolved to make the best of the worst situation in which we might be placed. As for myself, I was somewhat better prepared for this course of dieting than most of the men, having had, as I have already mentioned, a good meal the night before we surrendered.

Besides, on the morning of the second day after we were imprisoned, while I was sitting in front of a small grated window, looking out ruefully and hungrily upon the passers-by, a little Mexican maiden — bless her little tawny hide — came tripping along, and suspecting, from my woe-begone visage, the empty condition of my stomach, made signs to me to know if I did n't want something to eat. I could not speak a word of Spanish at that time, but I easily made her understand that she had guessed how matters were with me precisely, and she forthwith tripped off, and soon returned with a batch of the inevitable tortillas, some red peppers, and a considerable chunk of roast kid-meat, which she handed to me through the little window.

I made her a low bow, pulled my forelock, and smiled as sweetly and as amiably as I could with my powder-burnt and dirt-begrimed countenance. She went off laughing at my grimaces, and turning a corner, I lost sight of my little pumpkin-colored angel forever.

The tortillas were cold and tougher than army "flap-jacks," and the red pepper was as hot as mesquite coals; but I was as sharp-set as a new saw, and of course not inclined to "look a gift horse in the mouth." I felt just as grateful to the little saffron-colored maiden as if she had feasted me on roast turkey and plum pudding, and I hope her lot has been a happy one — tortillas, Chili pepper, and black-eyed papooses in abundance.

For five or six days we were kept closely guarded and watched in these miserable quarters, until the morning of the 28th of December, (I think it was,) when a pompous little Mexican official came into our prison and told us to get ready immediately for a march, as we were to start at ten o'clock that day for Camargo.

But this intimation was hardly necessary, for we were prepared to start at a moment's warning, as everything we had in the world was upon our backs. The extra wardrobe of our whole force could easily have been packed in a lady's bonnet-box.

At the hour designated by the little official, our Mexican guard made its appearance. It was commanded by General Ampudia in person, and consisted of about six hundred infantry and a considerable body of cavalry, and a small company of artillery, with two six-pound field-pieces. Certainly a most ample guard for two hundred half-starved, unarmed prisoners. After a fatiguing march of twenty-five or thirty miles, we reached the town of Camargo, and encamped in the vicinity, in commodious and well-ventilated quarters, at a corral or cattle-pen.

Camargo differs in nothing from every other Mexican town I have seen — the inevitable square in the centre, enclosed by lines of low, flat-roofed houses, with wretched "jacals," built of sticks and mud, scattered promiscuously about the suburbs.

Nothing that I remember now worthy of note occurred on our route to this place. Sometimes we were very roughly treated by the guard. Whenever a poor fellow lagged behind the column for an instant, they seemed to take an especial pleasure in accelerating his speed by the vigorous application of a bayonet. A bayonet is undoubtedly a powerful persuader. I have seen men when broken down and "beat out" by a hard day's march, wake up to new life and energy on the receipt of some welcome news, and, under like circumstances, I have seen renewed vigor instilled into them by the spirited strains of a fine band of music; but nothing is so effective in this way as one or two inches of cold steel in the body. I know this is so, for I speak from sad and personal experience of the fact.

In the morning, after our guard had paraded us several times around the public square, to give the good people of Camargo a chance to look at the "wild Texans," we bid them farewell, and again took the road down the river. Occasionally we were halted to rest for an hour or so at the "haciendas" and "ranches" on the way.

In some places the inhabitants, and especially the women, seemed to compassionate the miserable condition of the "Gringos," as they called us, and gave us water to drink, and sometimes more substantial refreshments. In others, we were hooted at by the mob, that was sure to collect around us whenever we stopped for a few moments, who would call us by all sorts of hard names, and pelt us with stones and clods of earth, and stale eggs.

Foot-sore and weary, we at length reached Reinosa, a town about fifty miles below Camargo. Here we were received with discharges of musketry, and a general ringing of cracked bells, and as we were marched "triumphantly" into the public square, where banners of all kinds were flaunting in the air, the flat roofs of the houses and the porches and the balconies were thronged with women and children, anxious to get a peep at the "terrible Gringos." It made us feel quite proud, to think that we were the cause of all this noise and bustle.

When they had paraded us around the square often enough to satisfy the curiosity of the good people of Reinosa, we were marched off to our quarters, in some old buildings just outside of the town.

CHAPTER XXXII.

Off for Matamoras — Distinguished Reception at Matamoras — An Oratorical Display — Again on the Road — A Serious Loss — Goat or Dog?

WE remained at Reinosa a day or two, and then took the road again for Matamoras. We never halted except at night, when we were "corralled," like so many cattle, on the bleak prairies, without any shelter, and scarcely food enough to keep body and soul together, until we reached the "Heroic City."

Is it any wonder, with the recollection of such treatment still fresh in their memory, that in the war which subsequently took place between Mexico and the United States, the Texans should have sent many a "greaser" "up the spout," without the formality of a court-martial to decide upon his guilt or innocence. However, I can say for myself that I never killed one in cold blood. I always turned them loose first and gave them a chance for their life; nevertheless, very few of them ever were heard of again, as in those days I was hard to beat in a "foot-race."

As we approached the city of Matamóras, a great crowd of men, women, and children came out to meet us, who were so anxious to get a look at the "wild Texans," that they could n't await our arrival. Some were in vehicles of various kinds, some mounted on mustang ponies, and not a few upon the backs of the little "burros," or jacks, that were hardly as tall as a good-sized Newfoundland dog. Escorted in this way, we entered the city of Matamoras, as at Reinosa, amid the firing of muskets, the waving of flags, and the clanging of bells, and after parading us, as usual, several times around the public square, we were marched off to our quarters in the outskirts of the city.

Our men were so worn down by fatigue and "short commons" that it was found absolutely necessary to remain in the city for a few days, to give them a chance to recruit. But our stay there could hardly have been considered an entire respite from the hardships and discomforts of the road, for at that time the lower classes of the citizens of the "heroic city" were exceedingly bigoted and intolerant toward all "heretics," and especially the Texans, and, consequently, whenever an opportunity offered, they never failed to render our situation as disagreeable as possible. Some among the better class of inhabitants, however, were very kind to us, as were many of the foreign residents, and furnished us with occasional supplies of food and clothing; indeed, if it had not been for these charitable individuals, we might have suffered considerably during our stay in the city, as the rations furnished us by the "commissariat" were remarkable neither for quantity nor quality.

One morning, a little bow-legged chap, dressed in uniform, and covered with stars and spangles, came into our quarters, and made us a regular set speech, which was interpreted to us by an attendant. What was his purpose I could never understand, unless, like some of our politicians, he was resolved to neglect no opportunity of bringing himself prominently before the public. He told us, among other things, what a great and magnanimous people the Mexicans were; that but for this fact, we would all have been taken out and executed as soon as captured, etc.; and he finally wound up by saying that if the United States did not cease giving "aid and comfort" to the rebels of Texas, this great and magnanimous nation would collect an irresistible army, that would march from one victory to another, until the Mexican flag would float proudly from the dome of the Capitol at Washington City!

Here some fellow in the crowd sang out, "Oh, spare the women and children!" and another, "You had better whip Texas first, before you tackle Uncle Sam!" But the little hero paid no attention to them. He continued in the same strain for some time, and then with a "grand flourish" turned on his heel, and stalked away majestically, his spurs clanking and his little sword trailing on the pavement behind him.

I wonder what he thought of the "magnanimous nation" when, a few years afterward, General Scott planted the stars and stripes on the "Halls of the Montezumas," with only ten thousand raw troops to back him!

Before we left Matamoras, a rumor reached the city in some way that General Rusk, with a considerable force of Texans, was on his way to attack it. In consequence of this report, General Ampudia and the detachment of troops that had guarded us from Mier were ordered away, and another guard of raw recruits, under General Canales, was substituted for it. This substitution of new levies for the regular soldiers, of which our previous escort was composed, emboldened us afterward to concert a plan to surprise them, and to make our escape into Texas.

The officer in command of our guard (General Canales) was well known to many of us by reputation as a cruel, cowardly tyrant, and we knew very well we had no favors to expect from him, or from the ignorant, undisciplined recruits of which his force was composed. We were detained at Matamoras for six days, and on the morning of the seventh took up the line of march again for Monterey. With all its hardships and discomforts, I much preferred being on the road to confinement in the filthy prisons and quarters of the towns and villages through which we passed. While marching, I could, at any rate, breathe the pure, fresh air of heaven without being hooted at and reviled by the mob or rabble that always collected around us whenever we were halted on the way.

On the first day's march I met with a serious misfortune in the loss of my "fine-tooth comb," which I had safely kept until then, in spite of our thievish Mexican guard, and which was my only "ark of safety" against the swarms of vermin with which they were infested. I have since lost articles of a thousand times more intrinsic value than that little horn comb, but never anything the want of which I felt so sensibly. The want of many things may be supplied by tolerable substitutes, but nothing will answer in place of a "ridding comb," under such circumstances.

Neither is there any substitute for tobacco. I have

tried all sorts of leaves, herbs, and roots, and have never yet found anything that would take its place. Ever since we were captured we had suffered as much for the want of tobacco as for lack of sufficient and healthy food. The miserable little "cigaritos," with which we were occasionally supplied by the Mexicans, (each containing about a good "pinch" for a snuff-taker,) only served to tantalize us. No one except an habitual consumer of the weed can appreciate or understand the soothing effects, after a hard day's march, of a pipe full of the genuine Virginia "cut and dried." It will even mitigate, to a considerable extent, one's grief for the recent loss of dear friends. But these wretched little cigaritos always reminded me of the old saying of "feeding a hungry man on soup with a fork." I never got a chance at a good old solid plug again until after we were liberated and landed at New Orleans, on our way home.

We encamped, the first night out from Matamoras, near a forlorn-looking little Mexican "ranch," where nothing was to be had to eat except a few scraggy goats, and naked, sore-eyed dogs. Even the inevitable tortillas could not be had for love or money. Some of the boys pressed one of the little naked dogs into service for supper, but according to their report, (for I did not taste it myself,) it must have been a poor substitute for roast pig. They said it was exceedingly tough, and when cooked, that "it smelt worse than a wet dog." The mess, however, to which I belonged was fortunate enough to *kid*nap one of the goats, which furnished us with a tolerable meal. If that goat has ever been paid for yet, I am not aware of the fact. The inhabitants of this "ranch" were certainly the most wretched-looking specimens of humanity (except perhaps the Digger Indians of California) that I have ever seen. Men, women, and children were squalid and filthy beyond description, and one would have supposed that the very height of their ambition, in a worldly point of view, was to make shuck cigaritos and smoke them, and loll all day upon a beef-hide, eating dried meat and red pepper. But this will apply equally as well to all the lower classes of the Mexican people as to the inmates of this ranch. If you wish to bring a Mexican to the lowest depths of despair, cut him off from cigaritos, red pepper, and tortillas. He might sustain existence for a little while under such distressing circumstances by the stimulus of gambling, but even that would afford him but a temporary respite.

If I were fishing for men, and wanted to catch an Englishman, I would bait my hook with the morning paper and a bottle of "London Stout;" if for an Irishman, I should use a small bit of the "blarney stone," and a "drop of the crathur;" if for a Frenchman, the customary frog and a little "eau sucre;" and for a Yankee I should put on a new copper cent and a "Congress penknife" for whittling; but if I wanted a "greaser," a cigarito, a pod of red pepper, and a tortilla would insure a bite at any stage of the tide.

CHAPTER XXXIII.

STILL ON THE ROAD — INHUMAN TREATMENT — WALLACE USES HIS "BIG FOOT" TO ADVANTAGE — PLANNING AN ESCAPE — DISAPPOINTMENT — MONTEREY — THE TARANTULA — CHANGE OF COMMANDERS, AND OFF AGAIN — RINCONADA — ANOTHER PLAN OF ESCAPE, AND ANOTHER DISAPPOINTMENT — ARRIVAL AT SALTILLO, AND OUR DETERMINATION.

THE last chapter left us on the road to Monterey. One day's march was pretty much the counterpart of another, ending at night by our being driven into some corral or other enclosure, like so many cattle, where we were left to recruit our exhausted energies as best we might, without any protection from the weather, and with barely enough food to keep us from an absolute state of starvation. On one occasion, while passing through a little village on the way (the name of which I have forgotten,) the customary crowd of men, old women, and boys flocked around us, shouting "death to the ladrones" (robbers), and "down with the hereticos" (heretics). One little scamp, in the excitement of the moment, ventured within reach of my foot, which you see is a No. 12, and I gave him a kick which would have done credit to a vicious mule, and of which, no doubt, he has a distinct recollection to this day. He went off howling like a full-grown cayote, but, fortunately for me, none of the guard noticed this little by-play, as otherwise I should certainly have been punished for it with a thrust from a bayonet, or a cut from a broadsword.

When shivering around our miserable camp-fire at night, exposed to the cold winds or pitiless rains, we frequently debated among ourselves the possibility of surprising and capturing our guard, and, with the arms and ammunition we expected to secure in this way, of effecting our retreat into Texas before a sufficient force to retake us could be collected together. We at length agreed that the attempt should be made at a little place called Sacata, one day's march ahead of us, and where we expected to be quartered for the night. Captain Cameron was chosen for our leader in the perilous undertaking, and it was understood, when the propitious moment for the attack should come, that he was to notify us of the fact by the command "draw," the usual order given when we were formed in line to receive our rations.

On our arrival at Sacata, we were turned into the corral as usual, and the guard took up their usual positions on the outside around us. Our plan for the attack was all arranged, and late in the evening, when our rations were brought in, every one fixed his eyes upon Captain Cameron, momentarily expecting him to give the wished for signal, but when he stepped out and said, "Draw your rations *first*," the men concluded that something had gone wrong, and every one quietly kept in his place. The rations were then distributed to us, and the attack postponed for a time.

I never understood what reason Captain Cameron had for giving up the attempt of surprising the guard at Sacata, but I have no doubt it was a good one, for he was as reckless of danger as any man that ever lived.

The next day we continued our march, and at length, wearied and worn down with the fatigues and hardships of our tramp, we reached the city of Monterey. A great crowd of persons, as usual, came out to meet us as we approached, by whom we were escorted into the city, but though they evidently regarded us as a species of wild cannibals, they treated us with more courtesy and respect than we had met with elsewhere, and on our arrival in the city we were at once conducted to our quarters. They were much more cleanly and comfortable than those that had been allotted to us in other places. Still they were not such quarters as one gets, for instance, at the St. Charles Hotel, in New Orleans. No sofas, no lounges, no chairs, no tables, nor even a common stool to dignify with the name of furniture — nothing, in fact, but bare stone walls, marked and scribbled over with pieces of charcoal by former occupants of these luxurious abodes.

Here one of our guard was bitten the first night of our arrival by a tarantula, a sort of large venomous spider, and although the Mexicans tried many kinds of "remedios" to relieve him, they all failed, and he died in a few hours. I can't say I lost much sleep from grief on account of his death, for he was a noted tyrant, and treated our men most cruelly whenever he could do so with impunity. Only a day or two before, I saw him cut one of our men severely with his sword, merely because he had loitered a moment behind the rest to tie his shoestring. On another occasion, when some of us were complaining of the scantiness of our fare, he went out and collected from the back-yard a quantity of old bones and other filthy offal, and returning, threw them on the ground before us, bidding us eat, as that was good enough for such abominable heretics as we were. Before he died, the priest was sent for to "confess" him, and if he only owned up to a tithe of the rascalities and crimes he had committed, I am sure the long list must have astonished even a Mexican padre.

Monterey was the handsomest Mexican town we had yet seen. It is situated in a rich and fertile valley, watered by clear cold streams that take their rise in the adjacent mountains.

In the suburbs I noticed a number of handsome private residences, with beautiful grounds and gardens attached, in which the orange, and the lemon, and the fig, and many other tropical fruits and plants were growing luxuriantly. The city seemed to be well fortified, and some years subsequently, when General Taylor attacked the place with his forces, I had the satisfaction of seeing them pretty well battered by our artillery. They would, no doubt, have been demolished if it had not been for that "same white flag" which the Mexicans always hoist when in a tight place, and with which they "bamboozled" General Taylor on that occasion in the same way they had so often done the Texans before him.

We were much more kindly treated while in Monterey than we had been in Camargo, Matamoras, and other places on our route. We were indebted particularly to many of the foreign residents in the city, who took pity on our forlorn condition, and supplied us with provisions and such articles of clothing as we stood most in need of. Among our men there were a few Roman Catholics, and we noticed, as a general thing, that they fared better and were allowed more privileges by the guard than the rest of us. Several sudden conversions to the Catholic creed were the result of this, but I remained constant to my "heretical opinions;" for I did not think it right to assume the garb of religion for such purposes.

Before leaving Monterey, to our great joy, Colonel Barragan, a kind and humane man, was placed in command of our guard, and the cowardly tyrant Canales assigned to some other duty. We remained in Monterey three or four days, and then took up the line of march once more — this time for Rinconada, a large hacienda about thirty miles distant, situated near the river San Juan.

On the route, the question of attacking our guard was discussed, and we determined to make the attempt the first good opportunity that might present itself. We knew that the farther we penetrated into the country the poorer would be our chances of making our way back safely to Texas after we had effected our liberation.

On our arrival at Rinconada we were quartered in an old building, and our guard in two adjoining ones, one on each side. After supper, our project of attacking the guard was talked over again, and it was resolved to carry it into execution at that place. The attack was to be made at daylight in the morning.

At the appointed time we were all up and ready for the fray, but just then we heard the rolling of the Mexican drums, and, looking through the chinks in our quarters, discovered the whole Mexican force filing out from the rooms they had occupied, and in a few moments we were ordered to fall into line and prepare to march.

There was no doubt in our minds that our plans had been divulged to the Mexicans by some one, but who it was we never knew to a certainty. What could have been his motive for betraying us it is hard to say, unless he thought by so doing he would secure better treatment from the Mexicans for himself. Had not our secret been divulged, it is more than probable we would have effected our intended surprise of the guard at Rinconada, from whence the chances are we could have made good our retreat into Texas, before a sufficient force of regular soldiers could have been collected to stop our advance. What a number of lives might have been saved, and what an amount of suffering avoided, if we had not been thus basely betrayed.

We at length reached Saltillo, without anything of particular interest transpiring on the way. Saltillo is a city of considerable importance, containing, I suppose, some ten or twelve thousand inhabitants. Here our guard was considerably reinforced, which satisfied us all the more that our intention of attacking them had been divulged by some one.

We remained at Saltillo but a day or two, and then continued our route through a desolate and barren country, toward the city of San Luis Potosi. Our guards were so wary and vigilant that we had no chance of surprising them, until we came to Salado, a little place about one hundred and twenty-five or thirty miles from Saltillo, near which we were quartered for the night. We were confined in some old adobe * buildings, and our guards, as usual, were posted in front of us. Here we were resolved to carry our plan of attack into operation, no matter what might be the result.

* Sun-dried brick.

CHAPTER XXXIV.

Successful Attack on the Mexican Guard — Bravery of Colonel Barragan — Retreat from Salado — Rapid Travelling — Bad Counsels — Suffering for Water — In Difficulties — Water at last — The Horses Killed and Eaten.

THE next morning about sunrise, observing that the guard had stacked their guns while engaged in cooking their breakfast, we held a hurried consultation as to what was best to be done, and proceeded at once to put it into execution.

Our plan was for Captain Cameron to "raise the yell" when he thought the proper moment for the attack had arrived, and at this signal our men were to rush out suddenly, knock down the sentinels stationed at the doors, and hasten to seize the guns that were stacked in front of the Mexican camps — all of which we hoped to accomplish before the Mexicans could recover from the disorder into which we thought the suddenness of our attack would throw them.

Captain Cameron took his seat near the open door, for the purpose of watching the movements of the Mexicans, who were scattered about here and there, busily engaged in cooking their breakfast, and totally unsuspicious of our designs. We anxiously waited for the concerted signal from him, and when it was given a "yell was raised" that might have been heard for miles, and out we poured from our dens like a pack of ravenous wolves. In an instant, the sentinels who were stationed at the doors were knocked down and trampled under foot and we dashed forward as rapidly as possible to where the guns were stacked. The Mexican soldiers made a rush for them at the same moment, and a fierce struggle took place for their possession. But the Americans generally had the advantage over their foes in strength and weight, and the contest was of short duration.

As soon as we had secured the guns, the Mexicans fled in the wildest confusion, leaving ten of their number dead upon the ground. Our loss was five killed — Dr. Brennan, Fitzgerald, Rice, Lyons, and Haggerty; wounded — Hancock, Captain Baker, Sansbury, Harvey, and another, whose name I have now forgotten.

Colonel Barragan made every effort to rally his men after they were thrown into confusion by the suddenness of our attack. He exerted himself manfully to retrieve the fortunes of the day, but without success, for the Mexican soldiers were thoroughly "stampeded," and nothing could stop their precipitate flight. At length he succeeded in rallying a small party of the fugitives, and with these he returned. Advancing fearlessly up to our lines, he addressed himself to Captain Cameron, telling him that if we would surrender ourselves to him, he pledged his word that we should be treated kindly, and not be punished for anything we had done. He said a good deal more to the same purpose, but we were deaf to all his arguments, and he finally rode off and left us.

Before Colonel Barragan left, in consideration of his bravery and of his kind and humane treatment when in command of our guard, Captain Cameron ordered his horse, sword, and other equipments, which we had captured, to be returned to him. Captain Cameron then recommended our wounded men to his care, and he promised us he would take charge of them and protect them to the extent of his power, and this promise we afterward learned he faithfully kept. And I here take great pleasure in giving my testimony of the fact that this Colonel Barragan was a clever fellow and a gentleman, although he had the misfortune to be born a Mexican. He was another example of the truth of the old saying, that bravery is always an ingredient of a magnanimous disposition. The domineering, tyrannical man is generally, though not always, a coward at heart. I have seen but few exceptions to the rule.

We captured all the guns the Mexicans had, and ninety-seven horses and mules, and all their baggage and equipments. Having selected the best guns for our own use, we broke up the balance. I think I destroyed nearly a cart-load myself. I took an especial pleasure in demolishing the "scopets," remembering the kicking I got from one of them on a former occasion.

After destroying the arms, and burning up all the tents and camp-equipage belonging to the guard, we put out from Salado with as little delay as possible, taking the road to Agua Nueva, and riding and walking by turns, as we had only one animal for every two men.

About midnight we stopped for a few moments at a "ranch" on the road, to get something to eat, and then continued our route and travelled until about sunrise the next morning, when we halted for several hours to rest ourselves and our jaded animals, having made upward of seventy miles from Salado, our starting-point.

On the road we went at a full trot the whole time, those on foot keeping up with the horsemen at that gait until exhausted, when they would take their turn in riding. The Mexicans, who are hard travellers themselves, particularly when an enemy is behind them, could scarcely believe we made so great a distance in such a short time, and under such circumstances. Our object, of course, in making this forced march, was to get so far ahead on the road as to render it next to impossible for a Mexican force to pursue us with any chance of overtaking and recapturing us; and had we followed the road from this on, as we ought to have done, there is every probability we would have succeeded in making our way back to Texas; but, as will be seen hereafter, rash counsels prevailed among our leaders, and we were persuaded to leave the high road and take our course through an unknown and barren country, in which neither food nor water could be found.

We remained but a short time at our halting-place, and then took up the line of march again. After travelling some eighteen or twenty miles, we quit the road, and turning to the left, entered a deep ravine that ran up toward the mountains. Passing for some distance along this, we at length came out upon an open plain, in which we discovered a ranche in the direction we were travelling. We hurried forward toward it, hoping to get a supply of water, but as we approached it more nearly, we saw that the housetops and windows were crowded with soldiers. We concluded it would be paying too dearly for a little water to storm such a strong position to obtain it, so we passed on. After crossing a spur of the mountain we came to a little pool of muddy water, from which we procured enough to quench our thirst.

Some miles farther on we came to a ranch, and finding out from the people living there that we were considerably to the east of the course we wished to pursue, we turned more to the west and travelled on till night overtook us, when we encamped at the foot of a mountain.

The next morning we were on the way again by sunrise, and after going some distance we came to the road running to Monclova. This we followed for a few miles, when we met an Englishman, (an old acquaintance of Captain Cameron,) who advised us to go with him to a ranch he owned near by, where he told us he could furnish us with provisions, of which by this time we were nearly destitute. He urgently advised us not to leave the road and go off into the mountains, as the majority of our men and officers were in favor of doing, and told us there were no troops along the road to intercept us, and that if we abandoned it and turned off through the desolate and mountainous country that lay in the direction we proposed travelling, we would inevitably perish for want of food and water. Well would it have been for us if we had done as this Englishman advised, for I am satisfied now that he was truly anxious to aid us in effecting our escape into Texas; but somehow the majority of us came to the conclusion that he was not to be trusted, and that he was merely seeking to delay us on the way until a sufficient force should have time to pursue and overtake us. So we declined accepting the friendly offers and advice of this Englishman, and continued our route until late at night, when we came to a little place called San Felipe, where we left the road and encamped at the foot of the mountains.

The next morning, we continued our course over the dreary-looking mountains that rose up before us, and their barren and desolate appearance disheartened even those who had been the warmest advocates for seeking the protection of their solitudes. All day long we toiled through this sterile region, until night overtook us again, when we encamped at the bottom of a "barranca" or deep cañon.

Several times during the day our progress was impeded by deep gulches and almost perpendicular walls of rock, through and up which we found it nearly impossible to force our jaded and broken-down hacks. Not a single drop of water had been seen upon the whole route, and, thirsty and dispirited, we wrapped our scanty covering around us and lay down upon the cold ground, and endeavored to forget our troubles in sleep.

Some time during the night, a small party, that had been sent in advance of the main body to reconnoitre, came into camp and reported an abundance of water within two or three miles of us. This was joyful news to us, and all hands were at once roused up, and without attempting to preserve any order in our line of march, we stumbled along in the darkness among the gulches and ravines, each one for himself, until we all safely reached the desired locality, and, after slaking our thirst with hearty draughts of the grateful fluid, we lay down once more and slept soundly until morning. We then went back to our first halting-place, gathered up our half-starved, broken-down horses, and such of our equipments as had been left behind, and returned with them to our "water-hole."

Here we concluded to remain and recruit ourselves for the balance of the day, and as it was deemed impossible to take our poor jaded hacks any farther through the rugged and mountainous country ahead of us, and as there was not a blade of grass in all that barren region, we determined, as a matter of humanity, to kill them all, and thus save them from the miseries of a prolonged death from starvation. This we proceeded at once to do, cutting the throats of the poor animals with our butcher-knives, in order to save our ammunition, of which we had but a limited quantity. This was a job I did n't fancy at all, and when I came to cut the throat of the wretched "Rosinante" that had borne my comrade and myself so faithfully and well ever since our escape from the guard, he looked at me so knowingly and pleadingly out of his sunken, hollow eyes, that my heart failed me entirely, and my comrade, who was not so "squeamish," had to play the part of executioner.

When the horses had all been killed, we selected a few of them that were in the best condition, (and a decent Mexican buzzard would have disdained to whet his bill upon any one of them,) skinned and cut them into small strips, which we "jerked" over fires made of a sort of weed, the only fuel to be found in many places in these barren mountains. When we had prepared as much of the meat in this way as the men could conveniently carry in their knapsacks, it was divided out among them, and at daylight the next morning we were again on the march.

Little did we think, when we left this camp, that we had tasted the last drop of water that was to moisten our parched lips for six weary days and nights; but so it was. Oh, those wretched, wretched days and nights! I shall never forget them as long as I live. After toiling all day over broken, barren, rugged mountains, suffering the agonies of torturing, excruciating thirst, we laid down at night upon our hard rocky beds, to dream in broken and disturbed slumbers of bubbling springs and rippling brooks, which somehow always mysteriously disappeared when we were just in the act of quaffing their sparkling waters.

CHAPTER XXXV.

A Dreary Prospect — No Water — Dying by the Wayside — Hunger and Thirst — Dreaming of Water — Hopes and Disappointments — Captured by the Mexicans — Water at last — Wretched Condition of the Survivors.

WITH much difficulty, even on foot, we at length forced our way up the almost perpendicular walls of the mountain that rose up in the direction we proposed travelling. When, at length, we had reached the top, we were appalled by the dreary prospect that presented itself to our view. Behind us lay the dismal valley from which we had just emerged, over the surface of which, scattered here and there as they had fallen, lay the dead carcasses of our animals, looking like little specks in the distance; and the thin columns of smoke, rising up from some smouldering fires we had left burning, and the naked rocky hills that encircled it, gave it a remarkable resemblance to the crater of some slumbering volcano. Before us, as far as the eye could reach, mountain after mountain rose up, rough, rugged and broken, and the total absence of everything like vegetation too surely indicated that no water was to be found in the parched-up valleys that lay between them; and over all this dismal prospect a burning sun poured down its scorching rays from a cloudless sky, with an intensity that greatly aggravated the thirst from which we had already begun to suffer excessively, before the toils of this weary day had ended.

We were much depressed in spirits by the barren and desolate appearance of the country ahead of us;

still there was no alternative but to go forward, for we knew if we retraced our steps we would inevitably be recaptured by our vigilant foes, and anything, we thought, was preferable to that. And so we went on all through that weary day, up one rugged, rocky mountain, and down, and up another, still hoping and trusting that in some of the ravines or cañons that lay between them, (for they could not be called valleys,) we would, at length, come across a stream or pool of water sufficient to slake our thirst. But everywhere we were continually disappointed. No murmuring streams rippled over the sandy beds of the gulches and cañons we passed—all were parched up, and as dry as if a drop of rain had not fallen in that dreary region since the days of the Flood. And thus we struggled on till darkness closed over the scene, when, abandoning all hope of finding water that day, we encamped for the night among the broken rocks and debris at the bottom of a deep cañon.

In the morning, dispirited and unrefreshed by our comfortless bivouac in the cañon, we again took our toilsome way over gulches and ravines, and up and down the steep and scraggy sides of the mountains, that everywhere impeded our progress. And thus we staggered on for several days in succession, through this desolate wilderness, still hoping for, but never finding, the cooling stream or pool of water, in which we longed to slake the intolerable agonies of thirst that was consuming our very vitals.

On the morning of the fifth day we made an early start, in order to get over as much ground as possible before the sun should acquire its full power. But, by the time it had risen above the tops of the mountains to the eastward of us, the sufferings of the men became so intolerable that many of them, to relieve themselves of all superfluous weight, threw away their guns and equipments, and what remained of their rations of jerked meat — for hunger was not felt or feared — our whole craving was for water! water! Many of the men gave out entirely, and laid down on the wayside to die, but no one paid any attention to them, for great suffering, such as we were enduring, is apt to render men callous and unfeeling toward each other. Still the rest of us struggled on, hoping that our strength might hold out until we came to water; but we toiled up one rugged, barren mountain, only to see another as rugged and barren rise up before us.

The way appeared interminable, and no change of scenery varied the tiresome monotony, or gave us any indication of our approach to the long-wished-for stream or pool of water. Not a tree nor a sprig of grass was to be seen anywhere. Nothing like vegetation, except in a few localities, where a species of leafless, withered weed managed, in some way, to draw a precarious sustenance from the parched and gravelly soil. All was barren, desolate, and scorched up by the long-continued drought that had prevailed in that country. Not a living animal was to be seen, nor was the song of a bird, or even the chirping of a cricket ever heard during all our wandering in this wilderness, which might appropriately have been termed anything but "howling;" for even a "cayote" could not, by any possibility, have existed there for many days. Night at length overtook us again, and, worn out, despairing, and suffering indescribable tortures from thirst, we threw ourselves upon the ground to pass away, as best we might, the wretched hours till morning.

All night long I could hear the men moaning in their uneasy slumbers, and crying out for water! water! I had heard that by chewing a leaden bullet thirst could be partially alleviated, and I tried it upon this occasion, but without success. It may afford some relief when the thirst is not excessive, but in the extremity to which we were reduced for the want of water, it did not seem to have the least effect.

The suffering caused by hunger is not comparable to that resulting from long-continued thirst. I had rather starve a week than go two days without water in warm weather, especially when compelled to travel on foot. Hunger comes by "fits and starts." There are intervals, even after starving for days, when one is comparatively free from pain or suffering, and in sleep one can occasionally find temporary relief from its pangs. But with thirst it is very different. There is not a moment's cessation of the suffering, but, on the contrary, it increases regularly in intensity, until the tongue becomes black and swollen and protrudes from the mouth, and the eyes, bloodshot and bleared, seem as if they are about to start from their sockets. Even sleep affords no respite whatever from this terrible anguish. Horrible shapes gibber and moan around the wretched slumberer, and frighten him away from the gushing spring or rippling brook, that forever haunts his mind, waking or sleeping.

One spring in particular haunted me in my dreams—one that I had often frequented in my boyhood's days, in one of the gorges of the Blue Ridge in Virginia. It poured out from the mouth of a small cave, at the foot of a high bluff, in a bold rivulet larger than my arm, which ran off through an old mossy trough six or eight feet long to the edge of a ravine, down which it pattered and splashed with a musical sound very agreeable to the ear of the passer-by on a hot summer's day. During my disturbed slumbers that night, if I attempted to take a drink at that spring *once*, I tried it a thousand times, but something always prevented me, just as I was on the eve of placing my parched lips to the mossy spout.

In 18—, many years after this, when I went back to "Old Virginia" to see my relatives, I visited this spring again, and there it was, still pattering and splashing down into the ravine below, just as I had seen it so often in imagination during my wanderings in the mountains of Mexico; and I took a last drink from the mossy spout, though I was not in the least thirsty, just for old acquaintance' sake.

On the morning of the seventh day after our entrance into these dismal solitudes, we resumed our cheerless march again, or rather, I should say, those of us that still remained together under the leadership of Captain Cameron; for by this time many had fallen by the way from exhaustion, and others singly or in small squads had wandered off in various directions in their search for water. Mechanically as it were, and scarcely knowing or caring whither we went, we crawled up the side of the sterile mountain ahead of us, frequently pausing on the way to recover our breath and strength. At last, when with much labor we had gained the top of the mountain, a joyful prospect presented itself to our view, and instilled new life and vigor into our worn-down frames. Below us lay an extensive valley, covered in places with thick chaparral, and in others with clumps and groves of trees, indicating certainly, as we thought, the proximity of water.

Resting for a few moments, we hastened down the mountain as rapidly as we could, toward this "land of promise," but the distance to it, and the difficulties of the way were much greater than we had at first supposed, and the day was pretty well advanced before we reached the level plain. But even then, in vain did we search every gully and ravine for the long-wished-for element. Not one drop of water could we find. Some of the stoutest and strongest men now "gave in" entirely, and dropped down by the way, either exhausted by the fatigue they had undergone, or else utterly overcome by the sufferings they endured from the intense thirst that preyed upon them. Others wandered off into the dense "chaparral" in their frantic search for water, and were lost.

When the sun went down, on this wretched day, only fifty or sixty men still dragged their weary limbs after our gallant leader, Captain Cameron, of which remnant I was one. But so terrible were our agonies from the internal fires that consumed our vitals, that we never thought of halting as usual when night overtook us, but staggered on, like drunken men, scarcely conscious of what we were doing. Some wandered in their minds, and prayed, or cursed, or sang, as their different dispositions prompted.

I noticed one poor fellow, as he stumbled along in the dark over the stones and bushes that beset our path, cheerily singing, in a very faint voice, "And who'll be king but Charlie." He was as crazy as a bed-bug, of course.

About ten o'clock at night, we discovered some fires burning ahead of us, and supposed that they were the signal fires of some one of our straggling parties, to let us know that water had been found. We pushed on toward them as fast as we could, and scarcely had the foremost men reached them, when a large Mexican force rose up on all sides of us, and enclosed us in their lines.

No attempt at resistance was made; indeed, we would have been utterly incapable of anything of the sort, even if we had been armed, but as well as I remember now not more than ten or a dozen of our men still carried their muskets with them — the rest having thrown them away while in the mountains. The Mexicans seized us at once, tied us in pairs together, and laid us on the ground. We begged and implored them, in the most piteous terms, to give us some water, and they measured out from the gourds they had brought along with them a very small drink for each one of us, not venturing to trust them in our hands for fear we should take too much at one time. Though not the twentieth part of what would have been sufficient to quench our thirst, I shall never forget as long as I live the delicious taste and coolness of that drink of water! If you want to know what that "nectar" is which is said to be imbibed by the gods alone, travel for six days under a burning sun, without a drop of water to cool your "coppers," and then take a long "swig" at a Mexican gourd, filled to the brim with the pure element. Then, and not till then, can you fully appreciate its great superiority over all other drinks.

At early dawn the next morning, the Mexicans untied us, and we all started for the nearest water. From the place where the Mexicans recaptured us, as well as I remember, it was fifteen or twenty miles distant, and without their guidance and assistance we could never have made half the distance, even if we had known in what direction to travel. But such of us as were the weakest and least able to walk were mounted on horseback, and in this way we reached the "water-hole" by twelve or one o'clock in the day. On the route, the Mexicans gave us two or three times a small drink of water from the gourds they had brought along with them, but this only seemed to aggravate our thirst the more, though I have no doubt it was better for us than it would have been if we had been supplied with all we wanted at one time. I am inclined to think so from the fact that, soon after we were recaptured by the Mexicans, one of them carelessly left his gourd, filled with water, within reach of one of our men, who instantly snatched it up and drained it dry before he took it from his lips. He was seized with terrible pains a little while afterward, and for several hours we thought he would die; but he eventually recovered.

CHAPTER XXXVI.

Encampment at the Water-Hole — Wretched Appearance of the Men — March Back to Saltillo — Mexican Vermin — How Wallace was Dressed — Mexican Vegetation — The Tiger Thorn — Conflicting Rumors.

WHEN at length we came to the water, (which was contained in a sort of artificial tank or reservoir,) we were led down to it under guard, and only permitted to drink for a few moments; but before they succeeded in "horning me off," I am confident I secured at least a gallon "under my belt." But I experienced no bad results from having drank so freely; on the contrary, my strength was rapidly restored to me from that moment.

Here we found encamped the main body of the Mexican cavalry that had been sent in pursuit of us. The wretched appearance we presented seemed to touch, to some extent, even the callous hearts of our enemies, and with the exception of again tying us together in pairs, they offered us no indignity. In truth, we were as woe-begone a looking set of "scarecrows" as were ever congregated together, I suppose, at one time. Some were without hats, some without shoes, and one could scarcely tell from the shreds of clothing that still hung about us to what garments they originally belonged.

I noticed one fellow who was hatless, and with but one shoe on, with one leg of his pantaloons torn entirely off, and nothing left of his coat except the collar and sleeves, and a few little strips of the lining still dangling behind his back. Our beards were rough and unshaven, and our matted and uncombed locks hung down in "swads" around our faces, pinched and sharpened by long abstinence from food and water, from out of which our sunken hollow eyes glared with a wild and demoniac expression not at all pleasant or assuring to the beholder.

We remained at this tank, or water-hole, for three days, during which time most of the men that had wandered off from us in the mountains, singly or in squads, were hunted up by the Mexicans and brought into camp. Only thirteen, I think, were missing, and as nothing was ever afterward heard from them, it is reasonable to suppose they ultimately perished from thirst, and no doubt their bones are bleaching to this day in some of the dreary gulches and ravines of those inhospitable mountains, from which we had made such a narrow escape ourselves.

Early on the morning of the fourth day, we were told by our guard to prepare for the march, and in a few moments they started off with us on the road toward Saltillo.

To prevent all chance of another "uprising" on our part, (of which they seemed to be continually in dread,) they tied our hands securely behind us with raw-hide thongs, and thus "hampered" we had to march all the way back to Saltillo.

I never knew before how necessary a free use of the arms was, to enable one to walk with ease and celerity. A twenty miles' march, with our arms pinioned down in this way, fatigued us as much as twice the distance would have done if they had been unfettered.

We were several days on the road, during which time nothing of interest that I remember now occurred. On our arrival at Saltillo, we were taken again to our old quarters, in which we were once more securely fastened up and closely guarded. I had been but a day or so in these dirty barracks when I fully appreciated the extent of the misfortune I had met with in the loss of my fine-tooth comb.

And here I may as well say to over-sensitive readers, that perhaps it would be as well for them to skip to the bottom of this chapter, as it is not my wish or intention to say anything offensive to "ears polite;" but I have started out with the determination of telling my story my own way, and I must do it, or abandon the attempt altogether. With this fair warning, I shall resume the story of what I endured from the loss of my fine-tooth comb.

Vermin swarmed in countless numbers in the miserable quarters in which we were confined. Even the bare floors at times were thickly covered with them. Our Mexican guard did not seem to mind them much; in fact, I rather think they liked them, and that, in some way or other, they were absolutely necessary to their health and comfort. I verily believe, if one of them had been suddenly freed from all sorts of the vermin with which they were infested, that he would not have slept soundly for a week afterward. They never use a comb, and of course it is only the larger and overgrown fellows they succeed in capturing by the primitive method of "looking each others' heads." These they "crack" between their teeth, apparently with much gusto and relish, by way, I suppose, of retaliation — "bite for bite."

For want of a comb myself, I was compelled to have my hair cut off short and permit my finger nails to grow untrimmed. With these I became so expert, after long practice, that I could rake out a fellow above a certain size with unerring certainty, whenever by biting or crawling he designated sufficiently his exact locality. By this primitive method, I kept myself pretty well rid of all the full-grown chaps, but the "small fry" dodged the question entirely, and unfortunately it is the nature of the "brute" to commence the propagation of his species the moment he is hatched. Often when a fellow, by hard raking and combing, (if lucky enough to be the possessor of a fine-tooth comb,) has come to the conclusion that at last he has entirely freed his head from these disgusting occupants, he wakes up the next morning to find it as densely populated as ever. I speak advisedly on this subject, for I had many opportunities, while imprisoned in Mexico, of studying the "habits and customs" of all kinds of "vermin."

The evil was aggravated by our want of a change of clothing and the scanty supply of water furnished us for our ablutions. As for myself, I had worn from necessity the same suit of clothes I had on when we made our escape from the guard, and after travelling in them all this time over dusty roads, and sleeping in them at night upon the ground, it can easily be imagined that my costume was not exactly a suitable one for a ball-room or a fashionable assembly. But little was left of my shirt. My hat had long since gone by the board, and in place of it my head was partially protected from the sun by a red cotton handkerchief, wrapped around it somewhat in the fashion of a Turkish turban. I had but one shoe left, which was in a very dilapidated condition, and in lieu of the other a raw-hide sandal was strapped on my foot with leathern thongs. My coat

18

was tattered and torn by thorns, and like Joseph's, from frequent mending with all sorts of materials, was of many colors, but the dirt or drab color predominated over all. It is impossible to describe the remnant of my pantaloons. They hung upon me in shreds that were inextricably bound together by thongs and strings, and upheld by a system of "tackling" as complicated as that of a seventy-four gun ship, to compare small things with great; and from out of these habiliments a countenance presented itself that had been guiltless of a thorough cleansing for — I am ashamed to say how long. "Such a beauty I did grow!" If my old sweetheart, Jenny Foster, could have seen me then, I am sure her heart would have relented, and that she would have reversed that cruel decision that sent me "packing off" to Texas some years before.

Everything that grows in Mexico, or at least in that portion of it in which I had travelled, has thorns upon it, which will account satisfactorily for the dilapidation of my clothing in such a short space of time. Even the very grass has thorns or spurs upon it, as we frequently found to our cost, whenever, forgetful of the fact, we seated ourselves upon it for a moment's rest or repose. I remember once seeing a shrub in Mexico which at a little distance appeared to be covered with dense green foliage, but upon a nearer approach I discovered that it was leafless, and simply a mass of thorns, thorns growing out of thorns.

The prickly pear, or cactus, the varieties of which comprise three-fifths of the vegetable kingdom in that part of Mexico, are all armed with spears, pikes, and thorns, of all lengths and sizes, from the minute prickle, so small that it is impossible to ascertain its locality when fixed in the flesh, except by the irritation it causes, to pikes and spears long enough for a buffalo to impale himself upon.

Everything in this wretched country seems to be constituted for a state of continual warfare, as if nature herself sympathized in some way with the normal political condition of its inhabitants. The cattle have the longest horns; the snakes all have fangs; every insect you touch stings or bites you, or both at the same time; and, as I have said before, the trees, shrubs, and grasses are all thorny: even the frogs and toads, so soft, moist and flabby in other countries, are here protected by hard, dry, scaly hides, and horns upon the head.

There was one species of shrub, with long, crooked, cat-like talons, which was dubbed by our men the "tiger thorn," from the fact that its slender elastic branches were frequently held in a constrained position by the twigs and foliage of other shrubs, and when loosened by the passer-by, they would spring up voluntarily, as it seemed, and seize him with their crooked claws, very much as the tiger springs from the jungle and seizes upon its prey. I have left many a rag fluttering in the breeze upon the branches of this terrible "tiger thorn," proud trophies of the numerous contests we had had, and showing that I had always retreated from the field with the loss of part of my baggage and equipments.

We remained at Saltillo several weeks, awaiting, it was said, orders from Santa Ana, the President of Mexico, as to our further disposition. During this time many and conflicting rumors reached our ears as to what was to be our ultimate fate. For some days it was generally believed that we were to be sent on to the city of Mexico, where we were to be immediately released or paroled and shipped back home by the way of New Orleans. Then again it was reported among us, that a despatch had been received from Santa Ana ordering the immediate execution of every one of us, but that General Mexier had refused to carry out the barbarous mandate.

I am inclined to think there must have been some truth in this report, as General Mexier, before we left Saltillo, resigned his joint commission of Commandante and Governor of the State. Besides, I learned afterward, when a prisoner in the city of Mexico, that all the foreign ministers resident there, as soon as they heard of this order, remonstrated against it as barbarous and inhuman, and Santa Ana revoked the order, substituting in its place the one requiring the "decimation" or execution of every tenth man. We had no intimation, however, that any of these orders had been actually passed until both of the latter were read to us subsequently at Rancho Salado, where the "decimation" took place.

CHAPTER XXXVII.

Sudden Change of Quarters — Rancho Salado once more — Brutal Order — The Drawing of the Beans — "Dip Deep, Boys" — The Baboon-faced Mexican Officer — Indifference of the Men — The One Exception — Wallace Draws a White Bean — "Ould Ireland Forever" — Speedy Execution — A Miraculous Escape and Subsequent Death.

AFTER our long sojourn at Saltillo, we were one morning roused up by our guard, and told to get ready to march, as we were to start that day to the city of Mexico. A few moments afterward the guard paraded in front of our quarters. We were taken out and formed into line, and marched off on the road back toward Rancho Salado, where, some weeks previously, we had risen upon and surprised the guard under the command of Colonel Barragan. Handcuffed and bound together in pairs, to cut off all chance of our escaping or making another attack upon the guard, we were driven along the road at a gait that would have been "killing" even to men that were not fettered as we were.

On the evening of the fourth day, I think it was, after leaving Saltillo, we came in sight, once more, of the lonely, desolate Rancho Salado. The officer now in command of the guard, Colonel Ortez, had spoken kindly to us frequently during the day, telling us to "be cheerful and walk up fast, for that the sooner we arrived at the city of Mexico, the sooner we would be liberated and sent back home." Notwithstanding these assurances, from the first moment the men caught sight of the dismal old ranch, whether it was the dreariness of the locality, or the recollection of what had happened there when we rose on the guard, and of the sufferings and disasters that followed in the wake of that event, or whether it was some dim foreboding of the "bloody scene" that was to be enacted there again so soon, that weighed upon the minds of the men, I know not; but not a word was uttered by any one, as we trudged along silent and depressed, until we reached the hated spot, and were once more securely fastened up in the same corral we had occupied before.

But a few moments elapsed before an officer, accompanied by an interpreter, entered the corral, and calling our attention, proceeded to read to us from a paper he held in his hand, a mandate from the "Supreme Government of Mexico," ordering the instant execution of every tenth man. Some of the more sanguine among us fully thought that the paper contained an order for our release, and eagerly crowded around the interpreter to hear the joyful news; but when the purport of the writing was explained to us by the interpreter, this barbarous decimation of our number came upon us so unexpectedly that we stood for a moment stunned and confused by the suddenness of the shock. Then a reaction took place, and if our hands had only been unshackled, unarmed as we were, the old Rancho Salado would have witnessed another up-rising, ten times as bloody as the first; but when we looked upon our manacled limbs, and the serried ranks and glittering bayonets of the large guard drawn up around us, we saw at once that any attempt at resistance would be utter folly, and we quietly submitted to our fate.

It was determined that the seventeen men to be executed should be selected by lottery, and in a little while

DRAWING OF THE BEANS. — Page 211.

a squad of Mexican officers came into the corral, preceded by a soldier bearing an earthen vessel, which he placed upon a low stone wall bounding the farther side of the corral, and which was intended to hold a number of white and black beans, corresponding to the number of men and officers in our command. The Mexican officers stationed themselves near the earthen pot, to overlook and superintend the lottery, and see that every one had a fair chance for his life. One of them then proceeded to count out so many white beans, which he poured into the vessel, and then dropped in the fatal seventeen black ones on top of them, covering the whole with a thick napkin or cloth. We were then formed into line and drawn up in front of the low wall on which the earthen pot had been placed.

Before the drawing began, they informed us that if any man drew out more than one bean, and either of them should prove a black one, he would be regarded as having drawn a black one solely, and be shot accordingly.

Our commissioned officers were ordered to draw first. Captain Cameron stepped forward, and without the slightest visible trepidation put his hand under the cloth and drew out a white bean. He had observed, when the Mexican officer put the beans in the pot, that he poured the white in first and the black ones on top of them, and then set it down without shaking, possibly with the intention of forcing as large a number as possible of the black beans upon our commissioned officers, who were to have the first drawing. When he returned to his place in the line, he whispered to those nearest him, "Dip deep, boys," and by following his advice all the officers drew white beans except Captain Eastland.

After the officers had all drawn, the "muster-rolls" of the men were produced, and we were called forward as our names appeared upon them. Some of the Mexican officers present were evidently much affected by the courage and nonchalance manifested by the men in this fiery trial; others, on the contrary, seemed to enjoy the whole proceedings hugely, particularly one little swarthy baboon-visaged chap, that looked as if he had subsisted all his life on a short allowance of red pepper and cigaritos. He appeared to take an especial delight in the hesitation of some of the men when they put their hands into the vessel, for even the bravest felt some reluctance to draw when he knew that life or certain death depended upon the color of the bean he might select. Whenever there was the slightest hesitation, this officer would say, in apparently the most commiserating tone: "Take your time, mi nino, (my child;) don't hurry yourself, mi muchaco, (my boy;) be careful, mi pobrecito, (poor fellow;) you know if you get a black bean you will be taken out and shot in ten minutes," — a fact we had already been fully apprised of.

"Ah! that's unfortunate," he would say, when a poor fellow drew a black bean; "but better luck to you the next time."

Yet, all the while he was talking in this way, in the kindest accents, a devilish grin on his baboon-face indicated the great pleasure he took in the anxiety and distress of these "poor fellows."

I am not of a revengeful disposition, but if that Mexican had ever fallen into my power, his chances of living to a "good old age" would have been miserably slim, and I could have recognized him among ten thousand, for his weazen features and his diabolical grin were indelibly impressed upon my memory. I 'll tell you how I would have served him. I would have bought a bushel of black beans, cooked them about half done in a big pot, and made him sit down upon it and eat until he bursted. I 'd have given him a dose that would have stretched his little tawny hide as tight as a bass-drum. He should have had his fill of black beans for once, to a certainty.

Those who drew black beans seemed to care very little about it. Occasionally one would remark, as he drew out the fatal color, "Well, boys, the jig is up with me;" or, "They have taken my sign in at last;" or something of a similar character, and then give way to the next, apparently as unconcerned as if he had no interest whatever in what was going on around him.

There was but a single exception to this. One poor fellow, a messmate of mine, too, appeared to be completely overcome by his apprehensions of drawing a black bean. He stood until his own time to draw came round, wringing his hands and moaning audibly, and continually telling those near him that he knew he should draw a black bean; that he had a presentiment such would be his fate. When his turn came, he hung back, and absolutely refused to go up at all until a file of Mexican soldiers forced him forward at the points of their bayonets. He hesitated so long after he put his hand into the vessel containing the beans that a Mexican officer near him pricked him severely with his sword to make him withdraw it. All this, of course, was immensely gratifying to the little baboon-faced official, who "ninoed" and "pobrecitoed" him in his kindest tones, all the while, though, evidently snickering and laughing in his sleeve at the fears exhibited by the "pobrecito."

At last the poor fellow was forced to withdraw his hand, and his presentiment proved too true, for in it he held the fatal black bean. He turned deadly pale as his eyes rested upon it, but apparently he soon resigned himself to his inevitable fate, for he never uttered a word of complaint afterward. I pitied him from the bottom of my heart.

My name beginning with W, was, of course, among the last on the roll, and when it came to my turn to draw, so many more white beans than black had been drawn out in proportion, that there could have been no great difference in the number of each. I observed twenty-four white beans drawn out in succession. The chances of life and death for me were, therefore, not so very unequal. I will frankly confess, when I put my hand into the pot and this fact recurred to my mind, a spasm of fear or dread sent a momentary chill to my heart, but I mastered it quickly, and before even the lynx-eye of the little baboon-faced official detected any sign of such weakness. At any rate, he bestowed none of his endearing epithets upon me.

All the time the drawing had been going on I stood pretty close to the scene of operations, and I thought I could perceive a slight difference in the size of the black and white beans — that the former were a shade larger than the latter. This difference, I know, may have been purely imaginary, but at any rate, I was eventually decided by it in my choice of a bean.

When I first put my hand in the pot I took up several beans at once in my fingers, and endeavored to distinguish their color by the *touch*, but they all felt precisely alike. I then dropped them and picked up two more, and after fingering them carefully for an instant, I thought that one of them seemed a little larger than the other. I dropped that one like a hot potato, and drew out the one left. It was a white one, of course, or I should not now be here to tell my story — but not a *very* white one, and when I cast my eyes upon it, it looked to me as "black as the ace of spades."

I felt certain for a moment that my fate was sealed, but when I handed it to the Mexican officer who received them as they were drawn out, I saw that he put it on the wall with the white beans, and not into his waistcoat pocket, as he had done the black ones. I knew then that I was safe, and the revulsion of feeling was so great and rapid that I can compare it to nothing except the sudden lifting of an immense weight from off one's shoulders. I felt as light as a feather, though I weighed at least one hundred and seventy pounds net, (after all my hardship and starvation,) exclusive of the remnant of clothing I had on me.

Among the last to draw was an Irishman, by the name of W——, a fellow noted for his wit and humor, as well as for his reckless, dare-devil character. He put his hand into the pot, and feeling around, discovered that there were but few beans left in it.

"Arrah now, my hinnies!" he said, "and is this the way you would thry to desave an innocent man to his destruction? Faith, and there 's not a dozen beans left in the pot, and I 'll not draw one at all."

He was peremptorily ordered to take one out immediately.

"Oh, it 's for murtherin' me ye are, ye bloody spalpeens," said Pat, "widout judge or jury. I see that as plain as the nose on my face. Yees let the ither men pick and choose as it suited 'em, out of scores of beans, and now there is n't a dozen left in the pot, and I 've no choice scarcely at all. Divil take such a lotthery, say I. But I suppose there 's no help for it, so here goes."

And Pat drew forth his bean, and everybody, even the Mexican officers themselves, I believe, were rejoiced when it proved to be a white one.

"There, you bloody nagurs," said Pat, handing the bean to the officer, "it *was* a black one, but I offered up a short prayer to Saint Pathrick, you see, and in the twinkling of an eye, he convarted it into a white one! Hooray for Saint Pathrick and Ould Ireland forever."

When the drawing was completed, the white and black beans were carefully counted over again, and the number found to tally with that of our men. Those that had drawn black beans were kept separate from the rest of us, and, in a few moments after the drawing was concluded, they were marched off in two squads, and shortly afterward repeated volleys of musketry were heard, and we knew that their cares and troubles were forever ended in this world.

One of them, however, a man by the name of Shepperd, as we learned subsequently, made a most miraculous escape for the time being. When they were fired upon by the guard, Shepperd fell and pretended to be dead, though, in fact, he was only slightly wounded. He was left on the ground with the dead bodies of his companions, and when night came he got up and went off without being observed. The next morning, when the Mexicans examined the bodies again, they were greatly astonished to find that one was missing, and could not be accounted for satisfactorily in any way. Shepperd wandered around for several weeks without being recaptured, but at length he was discovered, taken back to Saltillo, and shot to death in the public square, and his body carried out and left unburied on the commons.

CHAPTER XXXVIII.

San Luis Potosi — Queretaro — Tuli — The Black Hole of Calcutta — Murder of Captain Cameron — Arrival at the City of Mexico — Put to Work on the Public Road — How Wallace Got his Pay—How one of the Men "Played Horse"—Escape of Prisoners — Why Wallace was called "Big-Foot" — "Texas Cannibals."

THE next morning we took up the line of march for San Luis Potosi, but before leaving the dreary old rancho, we were taken out and drawn up in line in front of the bloody and stiffened forms of our murdered companions. For what purpose this was done I know not, unless it was to inspire us with a wholesome dread of a similar fate should we ever attempt to rise upon our guard again.

In four or five days we arrived at San Luis Potosi, the largest city we had yet seen in Mexico. It has a population of perhaps fifty or sixty thousand. Here we remained several days, during which time our handcuffs, or "bracelets," as we termed them, which we had worn constantly for more than a month, were taken off.

We then went on to Queretaro, also a considerable city; and thence to Tuli, a little village, containing a few hundred inhabitants.

At Tuli we were all crammed into a small room, without ventilation, and came near suffocating before we were liberated. It gave me a vivid conception of the horrors of the "black hole" at Calcutta.

At a little place beyond this, the name of which I have forgotton, the gallant Captain Cameron was taken out and shot by order of Santa Ana. I understood the plea for this second murder was, that in the lottery of the black and white beans, there was a fractional part of our number (not quite ten men) for which no additional black bean had been put in the pot, and Captain Cameron was shot to make amends for the omission. The truth is, however, the Mexicans were afraid of him, and no doubt had determined to put him out of the way "by fair means or foul." No braver or better man than Captain Cameron ever lived or died. His death was universally regretted by the men.

In two or three days we arrived at the City of Mexico, and were furnished with quarters in the prison of Santiago, just outside its limits. A description of the city of Mexico has been so often given, by those better qualified for such a task than I am, that I shall not attempt it.

We remained at Santiago but a few days, and were then transferred to the prison of San Angel. Nearly everything and every place in Mexico is named after some Saint; and among them, some of the most unmitigated rascals I have ever known have rejoiced in the patronymic of "Jesus," or "Hasoos," as they pronounce it.

From San Angel, at the expiration of nine or ten days, we were taken to Molino del Rey, where we were supplied with picks, spades, and shovels, and put to work on the public road between Tacubaya and the Bishop's

Palace. We remained in the city of Mexico from about the first of May until the last of October, during all of which time we were kept pretty constantly employed on the public works, for which we have never received one dime in the way of compensation to this day. On reflection, however, I am wrong in making such an assertion, as far as I am individually concerned, for when General Taylor captured Monterey in 1846, I was amply repaid for all the work I had done for the Mexican Government, in witnessing the defeat and discomfiture of their "grand army" at that place, to say nothing of a few "pesos" I picked up in the row.

If the truth must be told, though, we never injured ourselves much by work while in Mexico. We resorted to all sorts of expedients that would enable us to slight the tasks imposed on us. For instance, when carrying small rocks or pebbles in the sacks furnished us for that purpose, we would tear holes in them and let our loads *drip* out gradually on the way, so that by the time we arrived at our destination, there probably would n't be material enough left in the sack to make a "dirt-dauber's nest."

On a certain occasion, when we were all employed in transporting earth and other materials from one part of the road to another, the Mexicans hitched up some of our stoutest men to little carts, to enable us to carry on the work more rapidly. Among them was a stout active fellow by the name of J——, who soon became so disgusted with "playing horse" that he resolved to "fly the track." While the train of carts was travelling slowly along the edge of the embankment, he suddenly pretended to "take fright" at some object on the roadside, and giving a snort that a mustang would n't have been ashamed of, he started off with his cart at railway speed. In vain the Mexican guard that were stationed along the road at intervals, hallooed to him to stop, and even placed themselves in his way in their endeavors to arrest his flight. But nothing could stop his headlong career after he had once got his cart fairly under way, for the road was smooth and hard and down hill in the direction he was going.

At length he came to a favorable spot, and kicking himself out of the traces, he gave the cart a dexterous twist, that sent it whirling down to the bottom of the embankment, where it was dashed to pieces on the rocks. This was all the work of an instant; and continuing his flight down the road with increased velocity, when freed from the cart, he ran on a hundred yards or so farther, when he suddenly halted, whirled round, and gave another snort that might have been heard for a mile.

I verily believe the Mexicans thought at first that he had run off involuntarily, supposing, perhaps, it was one of the natural characteristics of the "wild Texans" to stampede occasionally like wild horses; but when the fun of the thing gradually dawned upon them they laughed heartily, and as soon as the runaway was captured and brought back, instead of punishing him severely, as we anticipated, they gave him his shovel and told him to go, and never afterward hitched him in the traces again.

While in the city of Mexico, nine or ten of our men succeeded in making their escape from prison, and eventually the most of them, in various disguises, from the country. They got out of their cells through a small tunnel they had dug with their knives under the foundations, barely large enough for one man to pass through at a time. They worked at this tunnel by turns during the night, packing off the dirt and other material excavated in their haversacks, when they went out to their daily tasks. There is no doubt that they labored much more faithfully at this little private job than they ever did upon the public works.

Among the men who escaped was one named Thompson, who had played "old soldier" upon the Mexicans the whole time. When we were recaptured in the mountains, he bound up one of his legs with old rags, and pretended to be too lame to walk, and the guard was compelled to furnish him with a horse. He never walked a foot of the way from there to the city of Mexico. The Mexicans were, therefore, much astonished, when these men made their escape from prison, to find that the "pobrecito coxo," as they called him, (the "poor lame fellow,") Thompson, was one of the number. I knew all the while there was nothing in the world the matter with him, but, of course, I felt no disposition to betray him.

It was while we were prisoners at the city of Mexico that I acquired the name of "Big-Foot," which has stuck to me like Texas mud ever since. It happened in this way: Some of the foreign residents of the city, observing that we were almost in a shoeless condition, made up by contribution among themselves a sufficient sum to purchase a pair of shoes for each of us. Every one was fitted with a suitable pair except myself; but I searched in vain every shop and "tienda" in the city for even a pair of No. 11's, though 12's fit me best, and finally I had no alternative left me but to buy the leather and have a pair put up on purpose for me by a "zapatero," or go barefooted. The Mexicans are generally a small people compared with the Americans, and their feet are still smaller in proportion; consequently they were much astonished at the size of mine, and from that time forward, and as long as I remained in the city, I was known among them as "Big-Foot."

I flatter myself, however, that my foot is not a very large one, taking into consideration the fact that I am just six feet two inches in height, and weigh upward of two hundred pounds net. But, even if it were otherwise, there is nothing dishonorable in the appellation, and I would rather be called "Big-Foot Wallace" than "Lying Wallace," or "Thieving Wallace." Such handles to my name would not be agreeable.

During our stay in Mexico, on one occasion, when five or six of us were being taken by a guard from one part of the city to another for some purpose, a mob of old men, women, and boys gathered around us, shouting "Death to the Gringos!" "Down with the heretics," etc. Our guard endeavored in vain to keep them back, and they were pressing closer and closer upon us in the most threatening manner. At last the sergeant in command of the guard told the mob if they did not give way he would turn the "Texas cannibals" loose among them. We heard and understood very well what he said, and to carry out the joke, and make a diversion in our favor, three or four of us grabbed as many old women and boys who had ventured in reach of us, and made out we were going to eat them up at once, without salt or pepper.

I clinched an old wrinkled squaw, who had been making herself very "prominent" in the "mêlée," and took a good bite at her neck, but it was tougher than a ten-year-old buffalo bull's, and though I bit with a *will*, and can crack a hickory-nut easily with my grinders, I could make no impression on it whatever. However, this unexpected demonstration on the part of the "Gringos" took the mob completely by surprise, and they scattered like a flock of partridges, and we were molested no more that day.

CHAPTER XXXIX.

PUEBLA—PEROTE—WALLACE HAS "JAIL FEVER"—THE SURGEON-GENERAL SAVES HIS LIFE—SEEING THE ANIMALS—MORE MEN ESCAPE—FINAL RELEASE, AND START HOME—STOPPED BY ROBBERS, WHO PROVE TO BE VERY CLEVER FELLOWS—YELLOW FEVER—HOME AGAIN.

AT various times during our stay in the city of Mexico, all of our men who claimed to be British subjects were released, at the request of the English minister, Doyle. The United States minister, General Waddy Thompson, I believe made every effort in his power for our liberation, but for a long time was altogether unsuccessful.

I could easily lengthen out my narrative of the "Mier Expedition" by entering into a detailed account of the cities and countries we passed through while in Mexico; and by commenting upon, and censuring or applauding the motives and conduct of the prominent men or leaders in this disastrous expedition. But I had no idea of attempting to write a professed history of the "Mier Expedition." My sole object has been to describe such scenes and incidents as came under my own observation, and to relate such anecdotes and occurrences connected therewith as I thought would be interesting or amusing to my readers. This I have done to the best of my ability, and I shall now hasten to the close of my story.

On the last day of October, we left the city of Mexico for Puebla, and thence on to Perote. Between Pueblo and Perote we were confined one night in a house in which the small-pox was raging, but, strange to say, none of us contracted the disease.

At Perote we found the prisoners that had been captured at San Antonio when General Woll took possession of that place. Some time after our arrival at Perote, I had a violent attack of the "jail-fever," as it was called — a sort of epidemic prevailing among us, produced, I suppose, by confinement in illy-ventilated quarters, and the want of wholesome and sufficient food. I soon became delirious, and in that state was removed to the hospital, with many others suffering from the same disease.

In the height of my delirium, I am told, I became entirely unmanageable, and several times "cleaned out" all the guard and other attendants of the hospital. They were compelled at last to "lasso" me, and tie me down to my bed, which was effected with great difficulty, for my strength (and I am no chicken at ordinary times) was increased fivefold under the excitement of fever.

One day, after my frenzy had somewhat abated, one of the attendants of the hospital came to dress some blisters that had been placed upon me when I was delirious. The rascal coolly proceeded to handle me as if I had been as devoid of feeling as a "knot on a log," tearing the blisters from my arms by main force, and causing me thereby the most horrible torture. A heavy copper stew-pan happened to be within reach of me, which I grabbed instantly, and, exerting all the strength I had, I gave him a "clew" on the side of the head with it that knocked him senseless to the floor. The guard stationed in the room immediately rushed upon me with their drawn sabres, and no doubt would have made mincemeat of me, if luckily the surgeon-general had not at that moment stepped in and interposed his authority in my behalf, and saved my life. He said that I had served the fellow I knocked down exactly right; that he richly merited the chastisement, for the harshness and cruelty with which he had always treated the sick and helpless.

This old surgeon-general was one of the best-hearted men I ever knew, and I shall never forget his kindness to me when I was sick and a prisoner at Perote. For some reason, he took a great fancy to me, and always favored me as much as he could, and when I left there he made me a handsome present of money and clothes. He was a Castilian, or Spaniard, by birth, and not a Mexican, which may account satisfactorily in a great measure for the fact that he was not a bigoted tyrant in disposition. At any rate I hope he may live a thousand years and never lose his front teeth, for a Spaniard or Mexican cannot manage the "cigarito" very well without them.

While at Perote, the "Dons" of the city frequently came into our quarters to get a look at the "Texas barbarians." They would poke us up from our lairs with their walking-sticks, just as I have seen the beasts stirred up with a long pole in a menagerie, now and then applying some such remarks to us as "Carrambo! look at that fellow's teeth, will you!" "Did you ever see such feet and hands?" "Carrajo! what red hair that fellow 's got! I wonder if he would n't give me a lock to light my cigaros with?" "Cuidado! don't go too near that chap with the big mouth and bushy beard; he has a ravenous look!" "I wonder when they are going to feed them? I should like to see that cannibal there devour five or six pounds of raw beef!" and other like expressions.

Some time in March the Bexar prisoners were released, by order of Santa Ana, and furnished with passports to go home. We sincerely rejoiced in their good fortune, but our own lot seemed more cheerless and hopeless than ever after their departure.

Not long after this, sixteen of our men escaped from one of the dungeons in which they were confined in the castle. When the guard entered it in the morning, they were astonished to find a huge black hole burrowed down in one corner, and leading down beneath the foundations of the castle and out into the moat or ditch that surrounded it. Most of these men eventually got out of the country without being recaptured.

For a long time after the escape of these prisoners, we were much more strictly guarded, and subjected to harsher treatment than had previously been the case.

I remained at Perote from some time in November until the 22d day of August, when I was liberated, together with five or six others, and furnished with passports to return home. The balance of our men were, I believe, all set free shortly afterward.

From Perote my companions and myself went on to Jalapa, where we rested for a day or two, and then took the road to Vera Cruz.

A few miles beyond Jalapa we were stopped by a

company of robbers on horseback, (eleven in number,) who demanded our money. We told them that we had been prisoners for a long time, and had just been liberated, and of course we were not particularly flush of funds. The one who seemed to have command of the party then asked me if we were Texans, and if we had passports. I told him we were Texans, and handed him my own passport, signed by Santa Ana. He looked at it and pronounced it all right, but said that Santa Ana was a scoundrel, and wished to know why the Texans did not kill him when they had him in their power. I told him if I had had the keeping of him, he never would have troubled Mexico any more.

This reply appeared to tickle them amazingly, and the robber chief then asked me to what place we were travelling. I told him to Vera Cruz, and he said they were going in the same direction, and would keep us company and protect us from any further molestation on the way. I thought to myself that such protection as they would be likely to give us was of a very questionable character. However, we travelled along sociably together for seven or eight miles, and night coming on, they turned off the main road and conducted us to a large ranch or hacienda, that appeared to be a sort of rendezvous for gentlemen of their profession.

The inmates of this ranch seemed to be well acquainted with the robbers, and when they entered, it was "How are you, colonel?" and "How are you, major?" from all sides. Titles were as plentiful among them as they are in Texas when a closely contested election is about to come off. Here an excellent supper was soon prepared, and we were cordially invited to partake of it. Supper ended, a variety of fruits and some excellent wines were placed upon the table. I asked the robber chief if that was their usual style of living, and when he replied that it was, I told him if there was any vacancy in the corps I should like to enlist.

This little politic speech of mine appeared to please the robbers exceedingly, and they drank the health of the "Gringo" in a full bumper.

After a night of general jollification, the next morning they filled our haversacks with provisions, gave us half a dollar apiece, and escorted us back to the road, where they bid us "adios," with many expressions of good will. I told the boys I wished the robbers would attack us every day in the same way these had done until we reached Vera Cruz.

We arrived at Vera Cruz without the happening of any further incident worth mentioning. A few days after our arrival I was taken with the "vomito," or yellow fever, and came very near "shuffling off this mortal coil" again. When I recovered sufficiently to travel, we took passage on a vessel bound to New Orleans, where we landed safely about the 24th of September. Just as our vessel (which was a crazy old hulk and totally unseaworthy) was towed over the bar at the mouth of the Mississippi, a tremendous hurricane came on, which would assuredly have sent us all to "Davy Jones's locker" had we been half an hour "behind time." In a few days I took passage on a steamer for Texas, and arrived at San Antonio in December following, after an absence of little more than two years.

CHAPTER XL.

WALLACE HEARS FROM VIRGINIA—CIVILIZED COMPARED WITH UNCIVILIZED LIFE—HE DETERMINES TO TAKE A TRIP TO "THE OLD STATES"—LAYS IN A "CIVILIZED" WARDROBE—AN OLD FRIEND FINDS HIM DISGUISED IN HIS NEW CLOTHES—STARTS ON HIS JOURNEY—WALLACE'S OPINION OF THE SEA—AT NEW ORLEANS, AND WHAT HE SAW THERE.

SOME years after the Mexican war, a stranger stopped at my "ranch" one night, and gave me a letter which he said the postmaster at San Antonio had requested him to deliver. I opened it, and found that it was from one of my relatives in Virginia, advising me to come on there at once, as my presence was necessary in the division of an estate, of which I was one of the heirs.

I had never been back to the "States" since I left Virginia in 1837, and made up my mind at once that I would go—not so much for the purpose of securing what property I might be entitled to, as to see how people managed to live in those old countries, without the excitement of an occasional Indian fight, or a "scrimmage" with the Mexicans, or even a "tussle" with a bear now and then to keep their blood in circulation. I thought to myself, it must be a mighty humdrum sort of a way of living, but I suppose custom enables one to get used to almost anything. The happiest people I ever saw on earth were the Keechies, who were at war with all the neighboring tribes, and ran a great risk of having their hair lifted, even when they went to the spring for a drink of water.

I don't say this to recommend a state of warfare, but only to prove that people can get used to almost everything but skinning. I once saw the Keechies skin some of their prisoners alive, and they did n't live twenty minutes afterward. Nothing can survive that operation long, except a snake.

But, to come back to my story: It was necessary, before I started on my trip, to replenish my wardrobe, as what I had on hand was n't exactly suitable for civilized countries. Leather hunting-shirts and leggins are just the things for the prairies and chaparral; but I had a sort of idea they would n't be considered the "height of the fashion" by the people of the "Old States."

I had a splendid suit of buckskin given me by my old friend "Bah-pish-na-ba-hoo-tee," (which means "Little blue whistling thunder" in the Tonkawa language,) made of the skins of the "big-horn," and rigged off with buffalo tags and little copper bells, that jingled musically as I walked along; and when I was dressed up in them, and had my coonskin cap on, with its tail hanging down behind, I do believe there was n't a young woman in the settlement that could look at me with impunity. But even that, I concluded, would n't be exactly the thing for my travels; so the next day I got on my horse, and rode into San Antonio, to supply myself with such articles as I required.

A city friend, who was posted in the fashions, went around with me to the shops, and bought for me such things as he said I would want — a stove-pipe hat, and coat and pantaloons, and a pair of patent-leather boots that were as slick and shiny as a darkey's face after a dinner of fat 'possum, and a pair of gloves that I never wore but once, for they "choked" my hands so that they made me short-winded. He bought me also a number of other little traps, combs, brushes, etc., and a two-story trunk to hold them all.

A day or two after I had made my purchases, I thought it advisable to rig myself out in my "toggery," so as to get a little used to their "hang" before I started on my journey. I squeezed myself into a pair of pants that fitted as tight as candle-moulds, and into a blue coat with metal buttons that was tighter still, and which split from stem to stern the first time I sneezed, and finally forced my feet into the shiny boots, without bursting either them or a bloodvessel, which was the greatest wonder of all.

When I had rigged myself out from head to foot, I felt as I suppose a man would feel who had a layer of "daubin" plastered over him, that had hardened in the sun. I could n't bend my knees, nor crook my elbows; could n't do anything except sit bolt upright in a chair, with my legs straight out before me. Even when I smiled at the ridiculous figure I cut, no matter how faintly or sweetly, I could hear a seam crack somewhere. If the shanty had caught fire just then, I would have been roasted to a certainty, before I could have made my retreat.

It so happened that while I was "trussed up" in that style, a fellow with whom I had a slight acquaintance came in to see me about buying a horse. I asked him to take a seat, which he did, all the time staring at me in a way that convinced me he did n't know me. At length he inquired if "Big-Foot" was at home. I laughed outright, at the expense of two buttons and a rent in my pants, and he then recognized me at once. "Why, 'Big-Foot,'" he said, "what do you mean by disguising yourself in that way? Are you crazy, or are you going a-courting?"

"Neither," I replied. "I am tired of tending stock, and fighting Indians, and intend to play the gentleman awhile, and as a commencement of my new career, I have bought this suit of 'store clothes' on tick, which I am trying on to see how I feel in them. Though my education has been considerably neglected in these backwoods, just as soon as I can learn to play poker and cut-throat loo, swear like a trooper, and can run off with some man's wife, I have some hopes the fraternity will admit me as a member. It is true I have n't killed a man as yet in a duel, but I have 'got' 'severial' in fights with the enemies of my country, and perhaps they will consider that a fair offset. What do you think?"

My friend said he had no doubt I would do with a little training, and asked me when I proposed to make a start in my new line of business.

"I am off in the morning," said I. "I have just five hundred dollars in my pocket, and when I have got through with that and my 'inheritance,' I shall come back to my ranch here, put on my old buckskins, and run after stock and fight Indians for a livelihood the balance of my life."

My friend bid me good-by, and the next morning, leaving my "ranch" in the care of my old compadre, Jeff Bond, I went into San Antonio, and took the stage for Indianola. There I got on board a steamer that was just ready to start, and in two or three hours we were rolling and tossing on the Gulf.

Anybody can have my share of the sea that wants it. I had rather have ten acres of the poorest ground in Texas than the whole Gulf of Mexico. I want something solid under me, and not miles of slippery, sloshy water, that is forever heaving and setting, and swelling, and sinking, and sliding and slipping from under a fellow, until his head grows dizzy, and his stomach is turned inside-out.

I am very fond of oysters, and ate about a peck of 'em raw, and four or five dozen fried, for dinner, just before I left Indianola; but I returned them all to their native element as soon as we got over the bar. How the sailors manage to live for six or seven months at sea, without ever seeing land, is a wonder to me. Two days were enough for me, and I was truly glad when at the end of that time I found myself on the "levee" in the city of New Orleans.

What a sudden change from the quietness and solitude of the little "ranch" on the borders of Texas, where I had lived so long, to the noise and bustle of a big city like New Orleans! I put on my "sombrero," for I had thrown away the "stove-pipe" as a useless concern, (I would as soon wear a Dutch-oven on the top of my head,) and walked out to see the sights and lions of the city. Everything was new and strange to me! The clatter of the hundreds of drays and omnibuses, tearing through the streets; the piles of merchandise and cotton-bales heaped up along the levee; the long line of steamers and vessels moored side by side, and loaded with the productions of every quarter of the globe; the eager crowds rushing here and there, as if life and death depended on their reaching some particular spot at a certain minute, (and maybe so in some cases they did, for the "police" was in full chase after some of them,) and the many foreign languages that I heard on all sides, Dutch, French, Spanish, Irish, etc., all brought forcibly to my mind the fact that I had got a long ways from the prairies and chaparrals of Texas.

At the corner of one of the streets I stopped to look at a foreigner of some sort, who was turning a crank fixed in a hollow box, by which he ground out occasionally a pretty fair tune, but with a sort of drone to it, like the Methodist hymns that are sung at camp-meetin's when the weather is damp and everybody has got bad colds. On top of the box a monkey sat, making faces at the crowd, and poking the nuts and cakes into his mouth, which were now and then thrown to him by the boys. By the side of the man stood a little girl dressed in a faded, seedy-looking muslin gown, and beating on a wide hoop covered with a piece of dried deerskin, and hung round with little metal plates about the size of those the Indians usually wear in the nose. They all had a melancholy and jaded look, (even the monkey, except when he cracked a nut,) especially the poor little girl, who beat on the hoop with the jangles in a mechanical sort of way, as if she was heartily sick and tired of the whole concern — and no wonder. I felt sorry for her, and slipped a new fifty-cent piece into her hand; but the man with the box saw me do it, and it enlivened him so that he gave the thing another screw, and ground out "Hail Columbia" about as easy as I could grind a peck of hominy on a steel mill.

Just then a tolerable genteel-looking chap, who had been watching me for some time, stepped up and requested a word with me in private. We went a little way off to ourselves, when he told me that he was a stranger in the city, (left there by some accident, I have forgotten now what,) and that he was entirely without money, and had not eaten a bite for more than two days; and if I would only give him fifty cents for a gold ring, which he fished out of his pocket, I would be doing him a great favor. I told him we didn't consider a two days' fast, on the prairies of Texas, a thing of much consequence, (and, really, he didn't seem to be much the worse for it himself,) but that if he was in want of something to eat, I would freely give him the fifty cents, as I did not want the ring, never having worn one in my life, except a large copper one in my nose, out of compliment to my friends the Lipans, when I was on a visit to the tribe. The fellow, however, generously insisted on my taking the ring, and actually forced it on one of my fingers, and as he did so, he remarked that it was well worth five dollars. It may have been worth five dollars in some markets, where brass was exceedingly scarce, but in New Orleans they sell a better quality at about three cents a dozen, for window-curtains. However, the fellow left me with many thanks, and in a few moments I saw him go into a "saloon," where drinkables on the "tangle-leg" and "bust-head" order were sold at five cents a glass to flat-boat-men and men of that stripe. Two or three hours afterward I found him lying dead-drunk in a gutter, and it occurred to me that perhaps he had mistaken his case — that he had been two days without drinking instead of without eating. However, I kept the ring as a memento of the poor fellow, and have got it yet, though it is now covered with verdigris, and smells louder than an old brass candlestick.

CHAPTER XLI.

Wallace goes to the Theatre — His Opinion of "Play-actors" — The Dancing Woman — Wallace gets Excited — The St. Charles "Tavern" — How he Registered his Name — Wallace is Afraid of a Fire—He Breakfasts at the St. Charles, and gets up an Excitement — The Bill of Fare — Fried Bullfrogs.

IN the evening I went to the theatre, and saw a play acted for the first time in my life. One or two of the actors I thought performed pretty well, but the most of them stormed and blustered out of all reason. When a man is in earnest he don't generally say much. Once two fellows that were after the same young woman came out on the stage and had a regular "set-to" with their swords. Twenty times a minute exactly they hit their swords together, first on one side, then on the other, and never drew a drop of blood. It was the poorest attempt at a fight I ever saw, and when at last one of them quit cutting the others' sword, and stuck his own through his body, I thought he might just as well have done it at the start — there was nothing to hinder him that I could see. I'll bet a gallon of "bear's ile" I could have given the Tonkawa war-whoop, jumped on the stage, and cleaned them both out in two minutes with "Old Butch," with "ease and elegance." If play-actors generally don't know anything more about fighting than these did, they ought to come out to Texas and attend the polls during an exciting election, and they would learn more about it in a week than they could on the stage in forty years. It would n't be click! click! as regular as the ticking of a wooden clock, and nothing done for half an hour, but it would be "pop" here, and over he goes — "bang" there, and down he drops; and in less time than it takes me to tell it, the whole green would be covered with "bits of skull and tufts of hair," and as red with blood as a slaughter-pen.

Between two parts of the play, a young woman came out on the stage and made a low bow to the people, who yelled and shouted as if she had done something extra. Her dress was very low above, and very high below, and a very scanty pattern in the middle, and so thin, if it had n't been for the spangles on it, you would n't have suspected she had on any dress at all. When the people kept on yelling and shouting ever so long, she brought a whirl on the tip of one toe, and made another bow so low that the hem of her dress almost touched the floor, and as she straightened up she stuck one foot straight out before her, and "pinted" it right at me, and kept on "pinting" it so long, that although I 'm not generally a very bashful man, I rather caved in and drew my sombrero over my face. All at once she made another whirl and brought the straight foot down against the other with a slap, and at it she went in earnest — cross over, right and left, heel and toe, backward and forward, "likety-clicket," up one side and down the other, till it almost made a fellow feel dizzy to watch her little feet shuffling in and out so fast, that you could only see them now and then when the bottoms were turned up toward you.

I thought I had seen pretty fair dancers among the Mexican señoritas, but none of them could hold a candle for that young woman. At last she brought another whirl on the tip of her toe, made another low bow, and as she rose stuck her foot out again, and "pinted" it right at me. The people yelled louder than ever at this, and threw bouquets and half-dollars on the stage till the floor was almost covered.

By this time, I had got considerably excited myself, and as I had no bouquets or money about me, I threw her every thing I had in my pockets, among which was a plug of tobacco about a foot long, three New York pippins, and my coarse comb; and not feeling entirely relieved by that, I jumped up on the seat and gave the Tonkawa war-whoop till the rafters of the house fairly shook again. There was a dead silence at once. The young woman looked frightened and skipped off the stage, and everybody stared at me. Then, such another hurrah began as you never heard, some hollering "Encore! encore!" and others, "Put him out—put him out!" but just then the little bell tinkled and the curtain was hoisted, and the play commenced again.

At last it all came to an end, and the young man married the young woman he had been courting so long; an old uncle of his fortunately "pegged out" about that time, and left him a power of money, and everything else wound up and "dovetailed in" in the luckiest way for the happy pair.

As soon as the play was over, I went to the St. Charles tavern, to hunt up quarters for the night, as I had been told it was the best in the city, and I was determined to have the best of everything going while I was on my travels. Some one had pointed the tavern out to me in the daytime, and as it was but a little way off, I soon came to it, and went up the broad steps in front, and then into a room where several men were putting their names down in a book.

I asked a fellow standing behind the railing at a desk,

if the landlord was in, as I wanted to see him. He laughed a little, though I did n't see anything funny in the question, and told me the landlord was out just then, but that he would attend to any business I might have with him. I told him all I wanted was a room to sleep in, and as much "grub" as I could eat as long as I staid in New Orleans.

"Certainly," said he, "you can be accommodated. Will you please register your name?"

I took the pen and wrote down "Big-Foot Wallace" in the first column, "Buffalo-Bull Ranch, Texas," in the second, and "Old Virginny" in the third. Then the clerk, or whoever he was, struck something that sounded like a clock, and a fellow jumped up from the corner of the room, and came up to where we were.

"Show this gentleman to No. 395," and he handed the waiter a little piece of candle that did n't look to me nigh long enough to last us through three hundred and ninety-five rooms. But the whole tavern was lighted up with little brass knobs, that made every place as bright as day.

The waiter took me up one pair of stairs, and then up another and another, until I thought I was in a fair way to get to heaven at last, providing my breath did n't fail me. We then wound about through half a dozen lanes and alleys, until at last we came to No. 395. The waiter unlocked the door, lit my candle, and told me good night.

"Stop a minute, my friend," said I; "if this tavern should catch fire to-night, how am I to find my way back again to where we started from?"

"Oh," said he, "there's no danger of fire, for it is all built of rock; and besides, it's insured."

"Devil trust it," said I, "with that gas stuff burning all over it. If it can set fire to a brass knob, why can't it burn a rock, too? I'd rather trust myself in a dry prairie, with a stiff 'norther' blowing, and the grass waist high, and hostile Indians all around: my chances of being roasted alive wouldn't be half as good as they are up here in No. 395; and besides," said I, "I'm not insured!"

"Well," said he, "if the house catches fire, all you've got to do is to pull that string hanging down there with the tassel on the end of it, which rings a bell, and I'll come up and show you the road down."

"Look here, my friend," said I, "you can't satisfy me in that way. This is room 395, and I suppose there's at least 395 more of 'em, and when 790 bells are all ringing at the same time, how are you going to tell which one is mine? You might as well try to tell the bellowing of a particular buffalo-bull in a gang of ten thousand. No, sir; you stay up here with me, and when the row commences, if you are lucky enough to find your way down, I won't be far behind you."

"Well," said he, "when my watch is up, which will be in about half an hour, I'll come back."

"'Nough said," I replied, "and I'll stand treat in the morning."

So I turned into bed, and in five minutes was fast asleep. I never knew whether the fellow came back or not, but I suppose he did, for he claimed the "treat" off me the first thing in the morning. I gave him a bran-new fifty-cent piece, and he said he'd like to take the job by the week at half the price: so I engaged him regularly at twenty-five cents a night, and considered it dirt-cheap at that.

I made an early start in the morning, for I knew I had a crooked way to travel and a dim trail to follow; and about nine o'clock I found myself in the room where I had registered my name the night before, and feeling considerably snappish after my long tramp.

I inquired of one of the porters sitting there, how long it was till breakfast. He said any time I wanted it, and showed me the way into the breakfast-room. It was almost as large as a small prairie, and, instead of one long table, as we have in our taverns at home, there were at least forty or fifty little round ones scattered about all over it.

Being of rather a social disposition, although I have lived so much in the woods by myself, and seeing a tolerably jovial little party of ladies and gentlemen sitting around one of these tables, I walked up and took a seat with them. I saw in a minute I was n't welcome, for the gentlemen looked as ill-natured as a sulky bull, and the ladies all tittered; but I pretended not to notice it, and called to one of the waiters who was running round, to bring me a pound or so of beefsteak and the "condiments."

At this, one of the men spoke up, and said "he presumed I was under a mistake, as that was a private table."

"Yes, sir," said I, "I am. I presumed you were gentlemen; and as to this being a private table, all I have to say is, it 's the first one I ever saw in a 'public house.' However," I continued, "I 've no wish to force my company where it is n't wanted," and I got up and took a seat at another table.

If a man had spoken to me at a tavern in Texas the way that chap did, I would have introduced him to "Old

Butch" at once; but thinks I, maybe things are different here, and I bothered myself no more about it.

There was nothing to eat on the table where I had taken a seat but a plate of butter and a bowl of sugar; but in a minute or so a waiter stepped up and handed me a paper. I took it, folded it up, and laid it on the table.

"My friend," says I, "I'm 'remarkable' hungry just now, and I'll read that after I get something to eat, if you say there's anything special in it."

After a little while he says, "What'll you have for breakfast, sir?"

"Well," I answered, "anything that's fat and juicy. What have you got cooked?"

"If you'll read the 'bill of fare,'" says he, "you can see for yourself."

"Well! let's have it," said I.

"That's it you have just folded up and laid on the table there," he replied.

"Oh, yes," said I. "I understand now;" and I picked it up, and the first thing I saw on it was '*Café au lait*,' and it's late enough too, for it, heaven knows," said I; "for I am used to taking a quart cup every morning just at daybreak!"

"What else?" said the waiter, and I read on:

"*Pâté de fois gras*"—some sort of yerbs, thought I, and I never went high on greens, especially for breakfast. I found most of the names of the things on the 'bill of fare' were French, or some other foreign lingo, and they were all Greek to me; but, to make the waiter believe I knew very well what they were, only I wasn't partial to their sort of "grub," I told him to bring me some "crapeau fricassee" and "gumbo filet," and I wish

I may never take another "chaw" of tobacco if he did not bring me a plateful of fried bullfrogs' legs, and another full of their spawn, just the same sort of slimy, ropy stuff you see around the edges of shallow ponds. I might have known that everything French had frog in it in some shape or other, just as certain as "Chili pepper" is found in everything the Mexicans cook. However, I made out a tolerable breakfast on other things, but would have been much better satisfied if I could have had four or five pounds of roasted buffalo-meat and a "*marrow gut.*"

CHAPTER XLII.

WALLACE MEETS WITH AN ADVENTURE—GOES TO A QUADROON BALL, AND TEACHES THEM "THE STAMPEDE"—WALLACE TAKES A "WHITE LION," AND PAYS FOR IT—HAS HIS FORTUNE TOLD—WHAT FOLLOWED.

AFTER breakfast, I loaded my pipe and took a seat on the front porch, with my legs hoisted up on the iron railings, and while I was sitting there puffing away, as comfortable as an old sow in a mud-hole on a hot day, a young woman came along on the opposite side of the street, and stopped awhile to look at some pictures in a window. Presently she looked up, and beckoned me to come to her! I couldn't believe my eyes at first, but she kept on motioning her hand to me, until I knew there was no mistake about it.

I thought maybe she takes me for some acquaintance of hers, and I'll go down and let her know she is on the wrong trail, just to see how foolish she will look when she finds she has been making so familiar with a stranger. So I went down the steps and crossed over to where she was standing. When I got up close to her I noticed that her dress didn't look overly neat, and that her eyes were as red as if she had been on a burst for the last week. I made her a polite bow, however, and remarked that I supposed she was mistaken; but before I could finish my speech, which I had "cut and dried," like the politicians, she ran up to me and grabbed me by the hand.

"Oh, bosh!" said she, "not a bit of it: you are the hardest fellow to take a hint I ever saw. I've been beckoning to you for the last half-hour. Come along, Johnny Green, I want to introduce you to some particular friends of mine."

"My name ain't Johnny Green," said I, trying to get my hand loose from her; but she held on to it like a vice.

"Oh! never mind that," said she; "come along with me, and we'll have a jolly time of it."

Thinks I, if you ain't a brazen piece I never saw one; for all the time she was talking she kept dragging me on, though there were half a dozen fellows on the stoop of the tavern, killing themselves laughing at us. This made me desperate, and I jerked my hand away by main force, though I hated to serve anything like a woman in such a rough way.

"Won't you go?" said she.

"No," said I, "not just now; I haven't time."

"Well," she answered, "if you won't go, I reckon you won't refuse to 'treat.'"

"Certainly not," said I. "What'll you take—a lemonade, or an ice-cream?"

"To the old boy," said she, "with your lemonades and ice-cream! I'll take a glass of brandy with a little schnapps in it."

"There," said I, and I threw her a slick quarter; "that'll buy you one;" and I turned on my heel and made tracks for the tavern as fast as I could.

Geminy! what a "cussin'" she gave me as I went! I thought I had heard the rangers on the frontiers of Texas make use of pretty hard language, but they couldn't hold a candle to that young woman. The farther I went the louder she "cussed," and I never got out of hearing of her until I found my way at last up to 395, where I bolted myself in, and never came out till dinner-time.

After supper, I fixed up a little, slicked down my hair with about a pint of bear's grease, (some of my own killing,) and went off to a "Quadroon Ball" in the French part of the city, for I was determined to see a little of everything going. Just as I entered the door of the house where the ball was given, a man stopped me and told me I would have to be searched before I could enter!

"What for," said I; "anything been stolen about here?"

"No," said he; "but if you've got any weapons about you, you must give 'em up to me before you can go in, and I will be responsible for them."

"Well," said I, "the truth is, I am partially 'heeled,'" and I handed him out a pair of Derringers and 'Old Butch.'

"I don't care so much about the Derringers," said I, "but take good care of 'Old Butch,' for I have a sort of affection for him, on account of the many scrapes he has helped me out of, and the amount of hair I have lifted from the heads of Indians with it."

The doorkeeper looked at me and then at 'Old Butch,' as if he didn't know what to make of either of us exactly; but he took the weapons, and told me I could have 'em when I left; and said he, "If you have any money about you of account, you had better leave it with me; else you may n't be able to put your hand on it when you want it."

"I 've only a few Mexican dollars in my pocket," I answered, "and if anybody can get them, they are welcome to them."

"Very well," said he, "you can go in."

So I went up a pair of stairs, and into a long room filled with people, and lighted up as bright as a prairie on fire with gas-knobs. 'Most everybody had masks on, so you could n't tell who they were, but that made no difference to me, for, of course, all there were strangers to me.

There were two or three sets on the floor dancing, besides a great many little squads scattered all about, laughing and talking, and making fun of themselves and everybody else. I sauntered about among 'em for some time, amusing myself with looking on as well as I could. I had begun to get rather tired of the concern, as I had no one to dance with, when a genteel-looking chap with a parrot-bill mask on, came up to me, and said "he presumed I was a stranger in the city."

I told him he had hit the nail on the head exactly.

"And how do you like our little fandango?" he asked.

"Oh! very well," said I; "but I see you have n't yet introduced the Texas national dance — the Stampede."

"No," said he; "have never heard of it before

Would n't you be kind enough to describe it to me, and I'll introduce it immediately; we are very much in want of something new just now."

"Of course," said I, "if you wish me. The 'Stampede' is danced in this way: The ladies range themselves on one side of the room, and the gentlemen on the other. Then one of the gentlemen neighs, and if a lady 'whinnies' in answer, they both step forward, and become partners for the dance. If the gentleman is very homely, and, after neighing three times, no lady should answer, he steps out of the 'ring,' and hopes for better luck next time.

"When the couples are all paired off in this way, the manager calls out, 'Gallopade all,' and all 'lope' around the room briskly three or four times. Then the gentlemen 'curvet' to their partners, and the ladies coquettishly back their ears and kick up at the gentlemen. Then the ladies canter up to the gentlemen, who rear and plunge for a while, then seize the ladies' hands, and pace gracefully off in couples around the room. First couple then wheel and go off at a two-forty lick, second couple ditto, and so on till the race becomes general, when the manager calls out, 'Whoa!' and everybody comes to a sudden halt. The manager then calls out, 'Walk your partners;' 'pace your partners;' 'trot your partners;' and 'gallopade all' again, faster and faster, until the 'sprained' and 'wind-galled' and 'short stock' begin to 'cave in,' when he calls out 'Boo!' and throws his hat in the 'ring.' A general 'stampede' follows; the gentlemen neigh, curvet, and pitch; the ladies whinny, prance, and kick, chairs and tables are knocked over, lights blown out, and everybody tumbles over everybody else, till the whole set is piled up in the middle of the room; and so the dance ends."

"By jingo," said my new friend, grabbing my hand, "it's glorious! It's the very thing for this latitude, and will create a sensation, you may depend. I'll introduce the 'Stampede' this very night."

"Very well," said I; "but you had better wait till it's time to go home, for, generally, things are smashed up so after the 'Stampede,' that it's hard to get the ball going again."

My new friend and myself soon got pretty thick with each other, and before I suspected what he was up to, he had pumped me dry of all the information I could give him about myself, where I was from, what was my name, where I was going to, etc.

After a while, he asked me if I ever indulged. I told him I was indulgent to a fault, providing the liquor was n't certain death, like the most of it in Texas. (I once drank some in Castroville, that was so awful bad that it burnt a hole in my sleeve when I wiped my mouth afterward.) My friend, however, said they had pretty fair liquor there; and he took me to a little room off to one side, where refreshments of all sorts were ladled out to the crowd.

"What'll you take?" asked my new friend.

"Well, I don't care," said I; "I'm not particular, so it ain't stronger than fourth-proof brandy."

"'Spose," said he, "we try a 'white lion?'"

"Agreed," says I, off-hand like, just as if I knew perfectly well what he meant by a 'white lion,' though, of course, I had n't the least idea what it was.

The bar-keeper took a tumbler, poured a little water in it, then put some sugar, and a good deal of brandy, then a little old Jamacia rum, and some pounded ice, and then clapping another tumbler to it, mouth downward, he shook 'em backward and forward till everything in them was well mixed up. He then slipped a slice of fresh pine-apple into the tumbler, and handed it to me. I put it to my lips, intending just to take a sip, to see how it would go; but it never left them till I had drained the last drop.

It was hard to beat, I tell you. I never tasted anything equal to it but once, and that was a drink of muddy water out of a Mexican gourd, after having been without any for five days and nights. I had already seen most of the 'lions' of the city, but the 'white lion' took the lead of them all. If I had joined the Temperance Society only the day before, I should have backslidden at once. There's no use at all of joining it, when you have to encounter one of these 'lions' in the path every day. Father Mathew himself could n't scare one of them out of the way!

Well, I was so much taken up with my "lion," I forgot my new friend for an instant, and when I turned to look for him he was gone. I started off to hunt him up, but the bar-keeper called to me and told me I had forgot something.

"What is it?" I asked.

"To pay for those 'lions,'" said he.

I handed out the change without a word. In Texas, when a man asks you to drink, it is expected that he will pay, of course; in the Old States, it seems the rule is reversed. But customs differ everywhere. I looked all around the room, but could n't find my new friend anywhere, nor a buckskin "puss," filled with "six-shooter" bullets and percussion caps, that somebody had cut out of my coat-pocket. I did n't mind losing the bullets much, for I would freely have given them to the fellow that took 'em, if he had told me he needed 'em, but he had split my new coat about six inches on the side, and ruined it entirely. I suppose he thought he had got a purse full of California nuggets, from the weight of it; and I rather think he must have felt a little disappointed when he emptied it and found what it was filled with. I would have given a "slick quarter" just to have seen how he looked when the bullets and percussion caps rolled out.

But, he was n't the first fellow, I thought to myself, by a long ways, that got only bullets from me when he expected something more agreeable. A good many others have carried off my lead with 'em, and some not very far, at that. I ain't in the habit, you know, of bragging in this way, but you see it was all owing to the "white lions" that somehow had got into my head, for by this time I had "repeated."

Well, I was beginning to get somewhat tired of the "fandango," and was just about to despatch another "white lion," with the full intention of exterminating the breed at once, when a young woman, dressed in a fanciful sort of costume, came up to me, and said "she presumed I was a stranger in the city."

"How in the world," thought I, "does everybody know I 'm a stranger in the city? Perhaps it 's my 'sombrero,' with its broad brim, and silver tassels hanging down behind;" and I remembered then I had n't seen anybody else in the city with one on.

"Yes," said I, "Miss; I have n't been in the place long."

"I thought not," said she; "you look like you had

lately been transported from your native soil; you have n't wilted a bit yet."

"I am afraid I will, though, now," said I, "since I have met with you;" for there was something about that young woman that was 'monstrous' taking! She was built up from the ground, and she walked as springy as a 'spike buck.' Her foot was n't longer than my thumb, and the prettiest sort of pigtail curls hung down all around her neck.

"Cross my hand," said she, holding out a little paw about the size of a possum's, with a flesh-colored glove on it, "and I'll tell you your fortune."

"My dear," said I — for by this time I was n't afraid to say anything, the "lions" had made me so bold — "I don't care about having my fortune told; but I'll give you a two-and-a-half-dollar gold piece if you will take off that mask and let me have a peep at that pretty face of yours."

"Agreed," she answered. "But I must tell you your fortune first, anyhow, just to convince you that I understand my trade. Hold out your hand;" and I poked out a paw that will span the head of a flour-barrel 'with ease and elegance.' She took it in both of hers, and examined it closely for some time.

"You are from Texas," she said; and she followed a wrinkle on my hand with one of her little soft fingers till my blood tingled all the way up to my elbow. "That line runs straight back to that State."

"You are a witch, sure enough," said I.

"You are not married," said she, "but you will be before long, for that line," (following another with her finger that ran up to the bottom of my thumb,) "reaches all the way to Cupid's dominions."

"Right again," said I; "I see you understand your 'trade,' sure enough."

"And this line," she went on, tracing another from the middle of my hand till it sprangled out toward the roots of my fingers, "shows you've roamed about a great deal in the prairies and backwoods of Texas. You have been a great hunter, and no doubt have taken the scalps from the heads of many an aborigine."

"No," said I; "we have n't any of those varmints in Texas; but I've lifted the hair from the head of many an Indian; and if I only had 'Old Butch' here, I 'd show you the little instrument I did it with; but the fellow down stairs has got it. But how in the world did you find out all this? You are a witch to a certainty."

"Of course I am," she answered, "and therefore I can easily tell that you are now on your way to 'Old Virginny.'"

"That'll do," I said; "I see you know it all; and I won't let you read any more of the lines on my hand, for some of 'em, you see, run into places where I would n't like to be trailed up. Come, I'm as dry as a 'buffalo chip,' and wish you would ask me to take something."

"Why don't you ask me?" said she.

"Because," I answered, "it seems to be the custom here for the one that's invited to pay; and I don't want you to settle the bar bill."

"Oh, very well," she said, "suppose we do have something."

So we went up to the bar, and she asked me what I'd take.

"I'm after big game now," said I, "and we'll take a 'white lion.'"

She called for "a lemonade with the privilege," and

the "privilege," I noticed, (which was Cognac brandy,) filled up the tumbler pretty well of itself. Well, we stood there laughing and talking, and sipping our liquor, until we got on the best of terms, and at length I ventured to take her hand in mine and give it a gentle squeeze; but I had drunk so many "white lions" I could n't regulate the pressure exactly, and I squeezed harder than I intended.

The young woman gave a keen scream, and jerked her hand away, and said I had crippled her for life. I begged a thousand pardons, laid the blame on the "lions" and "love at first sight," etc.; and finally got her in a good humor again. A woman will forgive a fellow anything, if he can only make her believe that it 's all owing to her good looks or winning ways.

"And now," said I, "that we are friends again, I must have a peep at that pretty face of yours, as you promised," and I handed her the two-and-a-half-dollar gold piece.

"Well," says she, "it 's about time to be going home, anyhow, and I suppose it will make no difference."

So she took off her mask, and—what do you think? If she was n't a full-blooded "mulatto" I wish I may never lift the hair from another Indian! I was so astonished I could n't say a word; and what I would have done I don't know, but just then I heard a terrible row going on, and looking round, I saw my first friend sitting on a table, and calling out the figures of the "Stampede." Nearly everybody in the room had joined in, and such neighing, curvetting, and prancing, and pitching, and kicking up, I never saw or heard on the prairies of Texas. At last the manager threw his hat among 'em and called out, "Stampede all," and the "rippit" commenced. The women screamed and made tracks down stairs, while the men kicked over the chairs and tables and pitched into each other right and left.

One fellow came along by where I was standing, and planted his boot-heel with all his might on the top of my toes! I gave him three or four pounds of my fist right in the middle of his forehead, and he tumbled over on the floor, and did n't take any more stock in that "scrimmage." By this time the police came in and took a hand in the row, and things got livelier than ever. Two fellows grabbed me at once: I took an "under crop" out of the ear of one of 'em, and about half the hair off the head of the other. (It was well for him I did n't have "Old Butch" about me, or I should have got it all.) Pretty soon I saw a mahogany chair flying straight toward me, and I rather suppose, from the bump that was on my head the next morning, that it had finally stopped the chair. At any rate, that 's the last thing I recollect about the "Quadroon Ball."

CHAPTER XLIII.

WALLACE IN TROUBLE — LEAVES NEW ORLEANS — ON THE MISSISSIPPI — A BOAT RACE — WALLACE ROARS LIKE A MEXICAN LION — HE "SELLS" A DANDY — "RUNNING AGAINST A SNAG" — ANCHORED ON A SAND-BANK — DAMAGE REPAIRED, AND ARRIVAL AT CINCINNATI.

IN the morning when I woke up, I found myself lying on the floor of a room with little grated windows to it, and two or three policemen walking backward and forward before the door. There were at least a couple of dozen besides myself in the room, all looking very much the worse for wear: an hour or so afterward, the police came in, and took us all before the justice of the peace. He fined some of us considerably, especially those that seemed to be old acquaintances, and sent off all that couldn't pay to the "calaboose." When he came to me, and found that I was a stranger in the city, he only fined me five dollars, and gave me lots of good advice gratis, which I forgot ten minutes afterward.

This scrape rather sickened me with New Orleans, and after dinner I paid my bill at the St. Charles tavern, and hired a porter to take my trunk to a steamboat that was to start up the river that evening for Cincinnati, and in an hour or two after I went aboard she raised steam and put out.

She was a splendid boat, and everything belonging to her was of the finest sort, just as if the owners had no idea she would ever "bust up," or run into a snag or a sawyer, which I believe is the end, sooner or later, (generally sooner,) of all Mississippi steamboats. There was a crowd of passengers aboard, and the ladies' cabin was filled with women and children. Such eating and drinking as there was on that boat I never saw before! They were n't satisfied with three meals a day, but had to have another, between breakfast and dinner, they called "lunch." I thought of the times when I was a ranger, and used to ride hard all day, and then breakfast, lunch, dine, and sup, at night, on a little dried beef and a cake of "hard-tack," and I wondered how these city-folks would make out on such fare!

The river was very high, and had overflowed all the bottom lands, and it looked strange to see people going from one house to another in pirogues and yawl-boats. I thought I would rather live on one of the high-and-dry prairies of Texas, where I had to haul my drinking-water five miles, than in such a place, where I could neither ride nor walk, nor do anything but paddle about in a "dug-out." Water is a good thing in moderation, but it can be "overdid" like everything else, just as it is in the Gulf of Mexico, and in most of the liquors we get in Texas!

The next morning after leaving New Orleans, we noticed a large steamboat come puffing on behind us. She appeared to be rapidly gaining on us, and it was soon reduced to a certainty that if we did n't "hurry up the cakes," she would pass us before long. I saw the captain of our boat and the mate with their heads together, and shortly afterward three or four old tar-barrels and half a dozen sides of bacon were thrown into the furnace by the firemen. Pretty soon the black smoke began to rise out of the chimneys, and the old steamer quivered and shook like a green hunter with the "buck-ague." By this time the other steamer had got nearly opposite to us, and everybody on it and on our boat hurraed and waved their hats and handkerchiefs.

The captain of our boat walked up and down the guards, and tried to look as unconcerned as if he did n't know there was another boat in ten miles of him, but I saw plainly enough that he was n't easy in his mind. The mate ran up and down the stairs every five minutes, till his face was as red as a turkey-gobbler's snout, and the firemen poked everything into the furnace they could lay their hands on. I do believe if we had taken the bran-new piano out of the ladies' cabin and handed it over to them, they would have shoved it in along with the tar-barrels, and never thought anything strange of it! Some of the passengers were afraid the boat would blow up, but they soon got over their scare, and "hurraed" as loud as the rest. And such a fizzing and whizzing and sputtering of steam you never heard. I tell you it was almost as exciting as a running fight on the prairies with the Comanche Indians!

At last we began slowly to gain on the other boat, and as soon as the passengers noticed it, they "hurraed" louder than ever, and I was just as crazy as the balance. I do believe, if I had known positively that our boat would have blown up the next minute, I would have yelled out, "A little more grape, Captain Bragg," to the fellows that were poking the fuel into the furnaces. I danced the "war dance," gave the Comanche death-yell, and then roared like a Mexican lion; and as soon as I saw that we were fairly leaving the other boat behind us, I ran up to the captain and grabbed him by the hand. The captain tried to look as if he thought the whole affair a small matter, but I could see well enough that he was tickled to the backbone. However, he was "sensible to the last," for the first words he said to me were, "Let's go and take something," and we went.

After we had taken a horn, the captain said to me, "See here, my friend, what sort of a yell do you call that you gave just now as we passed the other boat?"

"That," said I, "was the *bona fide* screech of the genuine Mexican lion."

"Well," said he, "I would n't begrudge five hundred dollars if I had a steam whistle on my boat that would blow in that style." From that time the captain seemed to take a great fancy to me, and always asked me to "liquor" whenever he went up to the bar, which was about every half-hour on a "low average," for he was n't a hard drinker by any means.

One day, we stopped a little while at a place called Vicksburg, in Mississippi, where the gamblers were all hung some years ago. Pity we have n't got half a dozen Vicksburgs in Texas! At this place a fellow came on board and took passage for somewhere up the river. He was a dandified-looking little fellow, dressed up in the height of the fashion. How he kept his shirt-bosom and his clothes so smooth, was a mystery to me. He looked as slick and as shiny all over as a newly varnished cupboard. He had a great many rings on his fingers, (and on his toes too, for all I know,) and wore a big gold chain looped up in his vest pocket, and the half of a pair of spectacles hung round his neck by a black ribbon. Every now and then he would put this up to his eye, and take a sight through it at the ladies in the cabin. He was evidently laboring under a disease which we call in Texas the "swell-head," and I saw plain enough if something was n't done for him pretty soon, there would be no chance for him ever to get over it; for it's a hard complaint to get rid of, anyhow!

The first time he dined on the boat, he happened to take his seat at the table right opposite to where I sat; and what do you think he did? He took out a silver knife and fork from a little morocco case he had brought along with him, and ate his dinner with them, instead of the knife and fork by his plate, which were good enough for anybody. Thinks I, old fellow, here's a fine chance to do something for your case, and I'll see if I can't take advantage of it.

The next day we stopped at a wood-yard to take in fuel, and I went on shore, and, while the deck-hands were getting in the wood, I whittled out a wooden case-knife about three feet long, and a fork in proportion. When I had finished them, I hid them under my coat, and carried them to my state-room without anybody seeing them. There was a gentleman occupying the state-room with me, and I had to let him into the secret, but he was mightily tickled at the idea of "doing the dandy," and lent me the case of his double-barrel gun, which was just about long enough to hold my knife and fork.

When the dinner-bell rang, I took my seat at the table right opposite the chap with the "swell head," with my "gun-case" hid away under my frock coat, and waited for him to begin operations. He carefully laid the knife and fork by his plate to one side, and took out his own silver ones from the little morocco case, and began to eat in a "finniken" sort of way! I followed suit precisely, laid my knife and fork to one side, placed my "gun-case" on the table, and drew out my three-foot butcher-knife and "pitchfork," and began eating with them as sober as a judge. As soon as the folks at table saw what I was up to, the ladies all "tittered," and the gentlemen "haw, hawed," right out—the captain especially laughed till the tears ran down his cheeks; but I never cracked a smile, and kept on eating as "solemn" as a parson at a funeral.

After dinner, the captain came up to me, and says he, "Texas," (for that was what he always called me,) "you are a trump, sure," and he made me a present of a fine bowie-knife, which I have got yet, but it don't lift hair like "Old Butch;" and besides, when I went to settle for my passage, he knocked off five dollars, just for the effectual way in which he said I had "done for" the dandy. What went with "Swell Head" nobody knows, for he disappeared from the boat that day, and we never saw him afterward.

The next day, as we were going along "full clatter" against the swift current of the Mississippi, we ran head on against a snag, and stove a hole in the bottom of the boat as big as a flour barrel. I had often heard of running against a snag, and I understood the meaning of it pretty well after I tackled an old she-bear once, and got three hugs and a bite from her before "Old Butch" had the least show; but this was the first time I ever actually came in contact with the *bona fide* article! I tell you it made everything hop, and the old boat quivered from stem to stern like a dying buffalo! The ladies all came pouring out of the cabin, screaming like wild-cats, and some crying out, "Oh! we are lost! we are lost!" "The boat is sinking;" and some of the men, I noticed, were worse scared than the women. Such a "hubbub" and "to do" you never saw!

I was n t the least bit frightened myself, for I learned to swim (like a puppy or an Indian papoose) before my eyes were open; and I stood on the guards, quietly waiting for the boat to sink, when I intended to strike out for the nearest shore. Most of the women screamed, and prayed, and wrung their hands, as if they thought it was the best way to keep the boat from going down; but I noticed one young woman that never "took on" at all the whole time; and a mighty good-looking one she was too! She was as pale as a lily, but as calm and quiet as a morning in May, and did n't seem the least bit frightened for herself, but only on account of a lame old gentleman, who, I suppose, was her father. She held on to his hand all the while, and looked up at him so lovingly and affectionately, I would n't have minded being her "pa" myself for a short time.

I determined, when the time came to "strike out," to take that young woman and the old gentleman into my especial keeping, and see 'em safe to shore; but just then a fat old lady, who weighed perhaps about two hundred and fifty pounds gross, came waddling by in a great fright, and grabbed me by the arm; and then another woman came along and hitched on to my other arm, while another clinched my coat tail, and they hung on to me like leeches till the alarm was over! If the boat had gone down I would n't have had a chance even to kick when I was drowning — they "hampered" me so!

The minute the boat struck the snag, the pilot backed her off, and steered for the nearest shore; but she filled so fast, we never could have made half the distance. Luckily for us, though, and particularly for me, with three women hanging on to me, we had n't gone more than two or three hundred yards before we ran on to a sandbar in the middle of the river, and settled down on it hard and fast! and that was all that saved us. We laid there two days and nights, pumping out the boat and stopping up the hole the snag had made in the bottom. When everything was put to rights, we raised steam up to the high-pressure point and backed off, and once more went on our way rejoicing. Two or three days afterward we landed at Cincinnati, without any further accident.

CHAPTER XLIV.

CINCINNATI — WAITER GIRLS AT THE HOTEL — WALLACE DISCOURSES ON POLITENESS — SOUTHERNERS AND YANKEES — A LITTLE DISH OF POLITICS — GOES TO DAN RICE'S CIRCUS — RIDES A REFRACTORY HORSE, AND MAKES TWENTY DOLLARS — WHAT WALLACE THOUGHT OF CINCINNATI.

ARRIVED at Cincinnati, I hired a hack and went up to the —— tavern, where I took a room, as I intended to stay long enough in the city to see all the sights.

Pretty soon the gong rang for dinner, and I went in and took a seat at the table. A handsome young woman stepped up to me and asked me "what I'd take!" I did n't understand exactly at first what she said, and I got up from my chair and offered it to her. She looked a little astonished, and everybody around laughed right out. Would you believe it, she was only a waiter, and I then noticed that every one of the waiters at the table was a young woman, and all dressed exactly alike. There must have been twenty of them at least, and a pretty sight they were, too, and one well calculated to give a fellow an appetite. No wonder that tavern was the most popular one in Cincinnati!

I took my seat again, and of course felt a little foolish, but it did n't take away my appetite; and when the young woman asked me again what I 'd have for dinner, I told her about five pounds of roast beef, rare, (my usual allowance,) and the "condiments." In a twinkling the roast beef was smoking before me, with the "condiments" piled up all around it in little dishes, about the size and mostly in the shape of a big oyster-shell. I have seen all sorts of waiters in my travels, negroes, Mexicans, French, and Dutch, but these young women were the spryest and handiest I ever met with. All I had to do was to wink or make a motion with my head, and what I wanted was there!

When I had finished the beef and "condiments," the young woman asked me what I 'd take for dessert. I looked at her pretty little red pouting lips, and wanted to say that I 'd taper off on them; but I did n't, for if there 's anything in the world I despise more than anything else, it is a man who will make rude and insulting speeches to a woman, just because he can do so with impunity. Such a man is the most contemptible of all animals, and is n't fit to be cut up into bait to catch mud-cats with.

Well, I suppose every country has its particular fashions, but this was the first time I ever was at the table where the men were waited on by the women! It did n't seem right to me to hear great, coarse, rough fellows ordering these nice young women about as if they had been "niggers." A low-bred dog, that sat opposite to me, told one of them to bring him some fried chicken, and because she did n't bring him the hind leg or some other particular piece he wanted, he told her she was a "good-for-nothing minx," and sent her back to get it. If I could have had that *gentleman* to myself in the "chaparral" for about five minutes, I would freely have given a couple of Spanish ponies — just for the privilege of teaching him some of the rudiments of common politeness! You bet I would have given him a distaste to fried chicken the balance of his natural life.

I'll tell you what is a fact: The Yankees may brag as much as they please about their refinement and education; but with all of it, they are not near so polite to the women as the Southerners are. They are a "go-ahead," energetic, enterprising people, full of vim and vigor, and shrewd, smart, and calculating, the very sort of people to get along in this world, the way it is "put up" at present; but it seems to me they lack a something that the Southerners have, that is necessary in the making up of a number-one gentleman. I can't tell, to save me, what that is, (and maybe, after all, it 's only a notion of mine,) but at any rate it 's one that can't be changed very easily. I don't say this out of prejudice to the Northern people, for we have our faults as well as they; and I think it probable, taking into consideration the different way in which they have been taught and brought up, that, if a correct balance was struck between them and us, the remainder of sterling, substantial qualities would be in their favor. But I give this opinion more to let the Southern people know I've studied arithmetic, than for any great weight I expect them to place on it. That the Yankees are an ingenious people, I know all will admit at once. Give one of them a Barlow knife and a piece of white pine for his stock in trade, and he 'll make money out of it; if he can't do anything else, he 'll whittle it up in wooden nutmegs, that will be better than the imported ones, only they won't flavor a toddy or a mince-pie quite so well!

A great many Southerners are mightily "down on" the Yankees for the way they have treated us since the war ended — and the Yankees ought not to be surprised at it. When a fellow comes to your house, and beats and bangs you about, because he is able to do it, and takes the most of your property, and leaves you as poor as a "church mouse," you ain't going to love him, that 's certain, no matter how much you may have done to excuse such treatment — it is 'nt human nature; and besides, many of the Southerners really think they were in the right from the start. For my part, I can forgive them everything they have done since the war began, except turning the negroes loose among us, and giving them the right to vote and make laws for us. I do not mind their being set free, for that was the natural consequence of the war; but to take four millions of ignorant darkeys out of the sugar-fields and cotton plantations, and give 'em the right of voting and making laws to govern this great country, was a crying shame; for hardly one of them could tell J from a bandy stick, or knew anything more about the principles of our government than they did about mathematics or algebra.

Besides, any one who will notice the way in which the "nigger" is "gotten up," will be satisfied that he is not the equal of the white man in mind or body. When we see a white man with a low forehead, pop eyes, and no chin to speak of, and what head he's got bulging all out toward the back part, we generally find he is n't overburdened with sense; but this is the case with nearly all the "niggers;" and, besides, they have wool on their heads instead of hair, blubber lips, bandy legs, jaybird heels, thick skulls, and an odor that the rankest abolitionist I ever saw did n't fancy on a hot day. "Cuffee" has some good points, I won't deny, (and I hope, since he has been set free, that the white people will give give him all the "showing" he deserves;) but statesmanship, and the abilities necessary for legislating for this great country ain't among the number!

But as the French say, (which I learnt from 'em when I was in New Orleans,) "*Revaw noo ah noo crapo,*"—"let us return to our frogs." After dinner, I asked one of the landlords of the tavern (for I believe there were at least six of them) if there was anything amusing going on in town.

"Nothing just now," said he, "except Dan Rice's circus."

I had been to a circus once at San Antonio, but as it seemed there was nothing else on hand, I concluded to go to this one too. So I went, and found that it was the same old thing over again. The clown had the same old jokes, cut and dried, I had heard ten years before, and the "ring-master" walked around in a circle, cracking his whip, and letting the clown fool him continually in the same old way, for which he paid him off every time by a cut upon the shins. A handsome young woman, dressed in tights and a little, short dress, that looked about as substantial as a puff of tobacco-smoke, came out, and did some pretty fair riding on one foot, and jumped over the ribbons and through a hoop that was held up for her, without ever making a slip. I thought, how nice it would be if a man only had a wife like that young woman, to ride around the yard of a summer's evening, and amuse him when he felt low-spirited and gloomy. She was mighty good-looking, too, in the bargain; but when I came to inquire more particularly about her, of a gentleman who was well acquainted with all these circus-people, he told me she had already had three husbands, and was about through with the fourth, who was then on his last legs; so I concluded she was n't as interesting and amusing a creature as I had taken her to be.

I had begun to get pretty well tired of the concern, when the ring-master led out a horse, and offered ten dollars to any one who would ride him around the circle. A negro boy got on him, but had hardly fixed himself in the saddle when the horse made a lunge or two, and pitched him right against a Shetland pony that was hitched near by. Fortunately his head struck first, and of course he was n't hurt; but the Shetland pony was killed dead on the spot, and had to be "drug out." Two or three others tried to ride the horse, but he threw them all before they got him half round the ring. I did n't like to make a show of myself, but then I hated to see the horse come off winner, when I knew I could ride him, so I stepped into the circle, and told the ring-master that I would try him a small "hitch" myself. I sprang into the saddle, and in a moment the fellow discovered, from the way I manœuvred, that I was going to "stick" him; so he made some excuse to take hold of the bridle, and said to me, in a low voice, "Where are you from?"

"From Texas," said I.

"The d—l!" said he. "I'll give you twenty dollars if you will let the horse throw you."

"Done!" said I, for I knew what he was up to; so after a pitch or so, I pretended to lose my balance, and rolled off upon the sawdust. The ring-master picked me up, and slipped a twenty-dollar gold-piece into my hand, which paid me pretty well for all the damage that had been done; but I could have ridden the lights out of that horse if I had been a mind to, and he might just as well have tried to pitch his own hide off, as to "oust" me, after I had once got fixed in the saddle. The ring-master made me an offer to join the circus; and if that young woman had n't had so many husbands already, I might have "enlisted" with 'em for a spell; but as it was, I declined.

Cincinnati is as handsome a city as I ever saw, and the streets are as clean as if they were scoured every Saturday night. The people do a lively business in the "pig line," and the first question they ask one another when they meet on the streets, is, "How 's pork to-day?" and they are gay and jolly, or dull and low-spirited, just as "pork" is "lively" and "looking up," or "heavy" and "flat." I think a good coat-of-arms for Cincinnati would be a fat shoat "rooting" upon an "azure field," and a keg of lard "couchant" on its side, with bunches of sausages and "adamantine dips" hanging around, and the motto underneath,

"Root, pig, or die."

I heard that there was one establishment in the city for packing pork, where they had a sort of mill, into the hopper of which you can throw a hog alive and squealing, and by the time you can run round to the other side a couple of canvas hams will roll out, then a couple of sides and shoulders, then fifteen or twenty pounds of souse, and two or three strings of sausages, and lastly a few dribblings in the way of stearine candles, bar-soap, and bristles done up in bundles ready for the brush and shoemaker! Everything that went in at one side comes out at the other in some shape—except the "squeal." I did n't see this machine in operation myself, but I was told about it by a member of the church, and of course it 's all so!

CHAPTER XLV.

Off for Wheeling — Everybody Smoking — Wallace's First Trip in the Cars — What he Thought of Railroad Travelling — Richmond — The Dime Restaurant — Wallace goes to a Fire, and gets "Put out" — What he Thought of Prince Albert — Wallace Leaves Richmond, and goes to Lexington — What his Relatives Thought of him — The "Wild Texan" at a "Fandango," where he Tells some "Big Stories" — Miss Matilda, and What she Heard — Wallace gets Tired of Civilization, and goes back to Texas.

AFTER I had seen pretty much all the sights in Cincinnati, I went on board of a steamer and took passage for Wheeling, where we landed safely without anything worthy of note happening to us on the way. I went ashore at once, and took up my quarters at —— House. Wheeling is a dull, smoky-looking town. The air was smoky, the houses were smoky, the trees were smoky — even the people were smoky; and when I went into supper I found that that was smoky, too, particu-

23*

larly the coffee, which tasted as if it had been boiled on a sobby fire in a pot without any lid to it. I did n't fancy the "lay-out" of the place at all, and, finding that the cars left that night for Richmond, I had my trunk taken to the depot, and about twelve o'clock I bid good-by to the city of Wheeling, and if I never see it again I shan't grieve myself to death, certain!

I never had travelled on a railroad before, and the whole "lay-out" was new and strange to me—the puffing of the engines, the clatter of iron wheels, and the rapidity with which we scudded by every object on the wayside. I could n't get over the idea for some time, whenever I looked out, that the horses were running away with the stage! Whenever the cars gave a harder jolt than usual, I shut my eyes and clenched my teeth, expecting the next instant I would be shot to "the other side of Jordan," at the rate of forty miles a minute. But I noticed that the people on the cars who were used to railroads, laughed and talked, and seemed as unconcerned as I would on the back of a wild mustang; although we had been told that, only a few days before, a train had run off a high embankment, and smashed up everything at such a rate, that one poor fellow who got jammed between two of the cars, was flattened out so they had to roll him up like a sheet of paper before they could get him into his coffin; and another that was caught somehow endways, was driven up into so small a lump that they buried him just as he stood, in a box no bigger than a five-gallon demijohn! I don't know which would be the most "unpalatable," the "flattening out" or the "driving up" process; but for my part, even if I was killed, I should prefer to retain my usual dimensions, six feet four in length by two in breadth across the shoulders.

There is another thing about this railroad travelling I don't like at all! They don't give a fellow half time enough to stow away his "grub" decently at his meals, but compel him to bolt everything he eats like a starved cayote wolf. We stopped at a fine tavern for breakfast, and I paid a man at the door fifty cents to let me in; but just as I had sweetened my coffee to my notion, and buttered four biscuits, and peppered and salted half a dozen boiled eggs I had broke into a tumbler, the whistle was blown, and everybody bolted for the cars, and I along with them, and I had just time to jump on the platform when off they started. I hope some clever fellow got my breakfast, for it was fixed up "all right," sure — particularly the eggs. But I concluded that sort of game would n't pay in the long run; so when we stopped for dinner I bolted my provisions whole, (a trick I had learned when I was a prisoner in Mexico,) and trusted to the strength of my gizzard, which was "equal to the emergency," as the politicians say.

When I had n't time to bolt my rations before the whistle was blown, I grabbed up a plate of fried chicken, or something else, and a "pone" or two of bread, and walked off with it, plate and all, and finished my meal at my leisure in the cars. By the time I reached Richmond I had a pile of dishes and plates in my corner of the car, enough to have set out a small table decently, if they had only been washed!

Just before we got to Richmond, a fellow I had got acquainted with on the cars advised me to stop at the "Dime Restaurant," where, he said, I would be much better accommodated, and on more reasonable terms, than at the "first-class hotels." So, when I got to the depot, I hired one of the hacks and told the driver to take me to the "Dime Restaurant." When I got there I asked the clerk for a room, and he gave me a very comfortable one, with a good bed in it, and everything else a fellow needed; and for this I paid fifty cents a day. He gave me the key of this room, which he said was mine as long as I wanted it, and that I could go or come whenever it suited me.

After I had washed and slicked up a little, I went down into the dining-room and took a seat at one of the tables, and in a minute a waiter brought me a "bill of fare," which is a sort of "muster-roll" of all the kinds of grub on hand. There was hardly a thing in the "eating line" that was n't put down on this "muster-roll." The only "absentees" I noticed were "buffalo-hump," "marrow-gut," and bear-meat; but I suppose they can't always be had in a city like Richmond. On one occasion, out of curiosity, I attempted to call for all on the roll regularly through, but though I only tasted a mouthful of each, by the time I had got half through the list, before I got to "fried oysters," of which I am "remarkably" fond, I "caved in" completely.

Each separate dish (except bread and coffee, which were n't counted in,) cost a "dime," and from this I suppose the restaurant took its name. A man could breakfast, dine, or sup there just according to the length of his purse. Forty cents would pay for a dinner good enough for any one, and if a fellow was getting down pretty near his "bottom dollar," he might make out to satisfy himself on a single dime. It was n't like those big taverns where a fellow has to pay three or four dollars a day, besides perquisites to waiters and chambermaids, and shoe-blacks, even if he should never eat a bite in the house the whole time; for, at the "Dime" you paid for just what you got, and no more! It was one of the best taverns I met with in all my travels, and I only wonder there ain't more of 'em kept on that plan. All the drinkables in the house were a "dime" a glass also, and it was a curious thing to me that a man with a common appetite was just able to eat or drink a dime's worth of anything. But I thought, perhaps there might be some sort of proportion between a man's stomach and the tenth part of a dollar!

One night, a house just opposite to the "Dime" caught fire, and there was such a ringing of bells and rattling of fire-engines, that it was enough to have woke up one of the Seven Sleepers. It put me in mind of a "feast-day" at San Antonio, when the bells on the old church always set up such a jangle that it invariably put my teeth on edge.

I got up and went out to have a look at the "row." People were running backward and forward on the street, hallooing "Fire!" as loud as they could bawl, and a number of steam-squirts were throwing streams of water up to the very roof of the building as big as my arm. I walked up to where one of 'em was in operation, and after watching it for some time, I thought what a great thing one of 'em would be to water a "truck-patch" with in a dry season; so I asked the man who was working it, as polite as I knew how, "how much one of those 'steam-squirts' would cost?" Instead of answering me, he turned the nozzle of the thing right toward my bosom, and in a second I was lying on my back in a puddle of muddy water!

I "riz" with a brick in my hand, and took him just on the "burr" of the ear with it, and down he went! As soon as the other firemen saw this they all levelled their steam-squirts at me and knocked me over again, and kept on squirting at me, until they washed me clean over the curbstone and on to the side-walk, when I scrambled up and dodged into an alley, and made my way back to the "Dime," as wet as a drowned rat. That "soured" me on fires completely, and I went to no more of 'em.

It was while I was in Richmond that Prince Albert paid a visit to the city. I only got a sight of him once, when he was riding in his carriage through the Cemetery grounds, and I must say that I think I have seen many a Dutch boy about New Braunfels and Fredericksburg that was better looking. He did n't show the "blood-royal" half as much as "Little Blue-Whistling-Thunder," the young Tonkawa chief. Some of our good democratic people took on mightily about this sprig of royalty, and gave him big dinners and soirées and tea-parties; but for my part, though he bowed politely to me when I met him in the Cemetery grounds, I did n't feel in the least "cowed" or confused by the compliment. I bowed politely back to him, and wished him well, and hoped he would remember me to his "ma" when he returned home. I have since heard that the poor young man died soon after he got back;* but his "ma," Queen Victoria, was a prudent woman, and had made ample provision for all such accidents, so that even if five or six of the "heirs apparent" were to die, she would still have "a few more of the same sort left."

From Richmond I went on to Lexington, where my

* Mr. Wallace is mistaken; the Prince is still living.

relatives lived. They were all glad to see me, and did all they could to make my time pass pleasantly while I was with them; though I could see very plainly that they all looked upon me as a sort of half-civilized savage that never could be entirely tamed; and perhaps they were right. I had lived too long the free and independent life of a ranger, to be contented a great while with the steady habits and humdrum existence of the people of the "Old States." I longed for the excitement of the chase, an Indian foray, a buffalo-hunt, or a bear-fight. However, everything for a time was new and strange to me, and I enjoyed myself as much as I could have expected.

A few weeks after my arrival I went to a "fandango" that was given for my especial benefit. There was a great crowd there, and everybody was anxious to see the "Wild Texan," as they called me. I was the "lion" of the evening, particularly with the young ladies, who never tired of asking me questions about Mexico, Texas, the Indians, prairies, etc. I at first answered truly all the questions they asked me; but when I found they evidently doubted some of the stories I told them which were facts, I branched out and gave them some "whoppers," which they swallowed down without "gagging." For instance, one young woman wanted to know how many wild horses I had ever seen in a drove. I told her perhaps thirty or forty thousand.

"Oh! now! Mr. Wallace," said she, "don't try to make game of me in that way. Forty thousand horses in one drove! well, I declare you are a second 'Munchausen!'"

"Well, then," said I, "maybe you won't believe me when I tell you there is a sort of spider in Texas as big as a peck measure, the bite of which can only be cured by music."

"Oh, yes," she answered, "I believe that's all so, for I have read about them in a book."

Among other "whoppers," I told her there was a "varmint" in Texas, called the "Santa Fé," that was still worse than the tarantula, for the best brass band in the country could n't cure their sting; that the creature had a hundred legs and a sting on every one of them, besides two large stings in its forked tail, and fangs as big as a rattlesnake's. When they sting you with their legs alone, you might possibly live an hour; when with all their stings, perhaps fifteen or twenty minutes; but when they sting and bite you at the same time, you first turn blue, then yellow, and then a beautiful bottle-green, when your hair all fell out and your finger nails dropped off, and you were as dead as a door-nail in five minutes, in spite of all the doctors in America.

"Oh! my! Mr. Wallace," said she, "how have you managed to live so long in that horrible country?"

"Why, you see," said I, "with my tarantula boots made of alligator-skin, and my centipede hunting-shirt made of tanned rattlesnakes' hides, I have escaped pretty well; but these don't protect you against the stinging scorpions, 'cow-killers,' and scaly-back chinches, that crawl about at night when you are asleep! The only way to keep them at a distance is to 'chaw' tobacco and drink whisky, and that is the reason the Temperance Society never flourished much in Texas."

"Oh!" said she, "what a horrible country that must be, where the people have to be stung to death, or 'chaw' tobacco and drink whisky! I don't know which is the worst."

"Well," said I, "the people out there don't seem to mind it much; they get used to it after a while; in fact, they seem rather to like it, for they chaw tobacco and drink whisky even in the winter-time, when the 'cow-killers' and stinging-lizards are all frozen up!"

I had been introduced to one young woman by the name of Matilda, who was as pretty as a pink! Her teeth were as white as an alligator's, and her eyes were as bright as two mesquite coals, and her mouth looked like a little gash cut in a juicy peach. She was a "deadener," I tell you, and a regular "knee-weakener," in the bargain; and I wanted to have a little talk with her the worst in the world; but somehow I felt a little afraid to venture. After a little while, however, she came up to me of her own accord, and began to ask me a great many questions about Texas and the Indians, wild horses, and the prairies, etc. Among other things, she asked me if young women were in great demand in Texas.

"I should think they were," said I. "The day the first young woman came into our settlement there were fourteen Spanish horses badly foundered on sedge-grass, by the young men who flocked in to see her, from forty miles around; and the next morning she had seventeen offers of marriage before breakfast! The young woman was a little confused by so many applications at once, and before she could make up her mind which one to take, one of the 'rancheros' watched his chance, and the first time she walked out he caught her up behind him on his horse, rode off full speed to San Patricio, drew his six-shooter on the padre, and forced him to marry them on the spot. This saved the young woman all further trouble on the subject, and they are now living happily together on one of the finest cattle ranches in the County of Karnes."

"Oh! I declare," said Miss Matilda, "that is delightful! How romantic to be run off with in that way by a handsome young 'ranchero.' I think, Mr. Wallace, I shall have to go to Texas."

"You might do worse," said I; "and besides, you would stand a chance of being run away with by some great Comanche or Tonkawa chief, with a bow and quiver on his back and eagle's feather on his head, and nothing else to speak of in the way of clothes."

Miss Matilda did n't seem to hear the last part of my speech, for she jumped up and clapped her little hands: "Oh," said she, "would n't that be fine? To gallop over the flowery prairies, free as the wind, from morning till night, and listen to the feathered songsters pouring forth their untaught melodies from every grove and shady dell! Oh, it would be splendid, Mr. Wallace!"

"Yes," said I, "it would. One of the handsomest young women in our settlement was carried off, three or four years ago, by 'He-che-puck-sa-sa,' the 'Bellowing Bull;' and when I went on a visit to his tribe, not long ago, she was the favorite wife and head squaw of the wigwam, and had brass rings enough on her arms and legs to have made a pair of 'dog irons,' if they had been melted up, besides one in her nose as big as the palm of my hand."

"Why! how many wives did the Mormon have?" asked Miss Matilda, looking a little down in the mouth.

"Oh! I can't say exactly," I answered; "I only saw six; but he had another wigwam at the village below. But," said I, "Miss Matilda, after riding over the flowery prairies all day, and listening to the cayotes howling in every grove and dell, where will you *put up* at night; and how will you manage to get along without hot rolls for breakfast, and baked custard for dinner?"

"Oh," said she, "I don't care for them; I can do very well without them; all I want is a nice cup of coffee in the morning, and a biscuit or a slice of toast, and a little fresh butter, or a few fresh-laid eggs; and for dinner a few vegetables and wild fruits, and now and then a nice beefsteak or a saddle of venison roasted before the fire!"

"Yes," says I, "that's all reasonable enough, and you could get them, I suppose, at any time; but you see, the Indians don't cook their meat."

"The cannibals!" exclaimed Miss Matilda; "they certainly don't eat it raw, do they?"

"Yes," said I, "as a general thing; only sometimes, when a fellow feels a little squeamish, he fastens a beef or mule steak under his saddle, and after riding and jolting on it all day, he finds it nicely 'done' when he stops at night; and it's a very convenient way of cooking, too, especially when a fellow is in a hurry, (which the Indians always are, for they are always after somebody, or else somebody is after them;) and besides, they say it is the best thing in the world for a sore-back horse!"

"Oh! dear," said Miss Matilda, "I don't believe I'll go to Texas, after all; for if I do, I must put up with a 'ranchero'—they don't eat their meat raw, do they?"

"No," said I, "except when they are out on the plains, and can't find buffalo-chips enough to cook it with."

"Oh! tell me, Mr. Wallace," said she, "did you ever see a 'mirage' on the plains?"

"A mirage?" said I, rather taken aback, for I had n't the least idea what she meant, unless it was a drove of mustangs or a herd of buffalo; "why, certainly, I have seen a thousand of 'em."

"I did n't think they were so common," said she.

"Oh, yes," I answered; "the last one I saw was just back of Santa Fé, and it stampeded when we got in about a quarter of a mile of it; and such a dust as was kicked up you never saw, for there had n't been a drop of rain there in six months."

"Well, I declare!" said Miss Matilda; "I always heard that the mirage would disappear as you approached it, but I never heard of one kicking up a dust before."

"No," said I; "they don't in other countries, where the ground is kept wet by constant rains; but in Texas, you see, it is different."

Just then a dapper-looking young fellow came up and asked Miss Matilda if he might have the pleasure of dancing with her that set, and she walked off with him. I took a dislike to that young fellow at once, and felt for "Old Butch," without knowing what I was about! The fact is, I rather fancied this young woman, and I determined, the next time I met up with her, to give her a better account of Texas, and leave out all about the centipedes and "raw meat."

Well, sir! I staid with my kinsfolk in Old Virginny till I began to pine for the prairies and woods once more. They were as kind to me as they could be, but feather beds, tight rooms, and three meals a day were too much for me, and, like old General Taylor, when he was taken from "camps" to the "White House," I fell away daily, and "went off my feed" entirely; and, like him, I suppose I should have gone up the spout, if I had staid much longer. I helped matters a little by taking a camp-hunt of a couple of weeks in the Blue Ridge Mountains, where I killed the last bear, I suppose, that was ever seen in that part of Old Virginny, for when his carcase was hauled in, people came from twenty miles around to have a look at it. But I never got entirely to rights again till I returned to Texas and got into an Indian "scrimmage," and lifted the hair off of one or two of them, with the aid of "Old Butch." That night, for the first time, my appetite came back to me, and I ate six pounds of buffalo-hump, a side of ribs, and a roasted marrow-gut, and ever since I have been "as well as could be expected."

CHAPTER XLVI.

Wallace gives Jack Dobell his Opinion of Farming — Uncle Josh — The Jews a Sensible People — Wallace makes his Arrangements for a Crop — He and "Keecheye" try Ploughing — Both Disgusted — Queer Muskmelon — Ruined by the Drought — How Wallace was Cheated out of his "Roasting Ears" — Living on Watermelons and "Poor Doe" — Wallace's Future Prospects — Conclusion.

SOME years ago, while on my way to the city of San Antonio, I lost my road, and after wandering about the prairies till nearly sunset, I concluded to strike camp, and make a fresh start in the morning. But, just as I had made up my mind to pass the night at "Sprawls," and put up as well as I could with such accommodations as are usually furnished by that extensive establishment, I thought I saw some faint symptoms of a "settlement" ahead of me. Spurring on my jaded horse, I at length came to a sort of hybrid between a log cabin and a half-faced camp, in front of which a man was seated on a fallen tree, busily engaged in rubbing up his rifle.

"Can you give me such directions, my friend," said I, "as will enable me to find my way back to the main road to San Antonio?"

The man looked up as he replied to my question, and to my astonishment I recognized my old friend and messmate, Big-Foot Wallace.

"Why, hello, Foot," said I, "have you forgotten your old 'compadre,' Jack Dobell?"

Big-Foot looked at me dubiously for a minute, then, springing up from the log, he seized me by the hand and gave it such a grip that my fingers stuck together for five minutes afterward.

"Get down, Dobell," said he, "and rest your face and hands. You must stay with me all night, and in the morning I'll pilot you out to the road myself. It's a fact, though," continued Big-Foot, looking ruefully around upon the apparently scant accommodations afforded by his 'ranch,' "it's a fact though, I haven't got much to offer you. Crops have failed entirely, but there's pretty smart of good grass in that hollow yonder for your nag; and my partner, Jackson, was lucky enough to kill a fat buck to-day. So get down at once, for I have a heap to tell you about what has happened to me since we last met, and particularly about a scurvy trick my partner, Jim Jackson there," (pointing to a remarkably homely individual who was busily engaged near by in "peeling" the hide from the aforesaid buck,) "played off upon me about a month ago."

Without further "palaver," I dismounted from my

horse, and, under Big-Foot's guidance, proceeded to stake him out in a snug little valley, where the mesquite grass grew rank and luxuriantly.

"You need n't be afraid to stake him so far from camp — there 's no Indians about here now," said Big-Foot, with a melancholy expression of countenance, as if he was heartily sick of "these piping times of peace," and longed to see once more the stirring scenes of bygone days. "I do believe there has n't been an Indian in ten miles of this place for the last twelve months."

"Why, you don't tell me, Big-Foot," said I, "that you have been all that time without a single 'scrimmage' with the Mexicans or Indians?"

"Yes," said he, "with the exception of a little 'tussle' I had with the 'Tonks,' about six months ago, on the Llaño, I have n't had a row of any sort since I 'drove my megs down' in this settlement. And no wonder, neither, for the people are 'piling in' here as thick as pig-tracks around a corn-crib door; and they have fenced up the prairies in such a way that the Indians won't venture in, for fear of being 'hemmed up.' If I only knew where all these people come from, I 'd go there right off, for there can't be any one left behind, and a fellow would n't be 'scrouged' to death, as he is here now. Of all things in the world, I hate being 'fenced up;' I want plenty of elbow-room and plenty of 'out-let,' but here you can't travel half a dozen miles in any direction, without being headed off by somebody's fence."

On our return to the "ranch," we took a seat on the log which answered Big-Foot in place of a sofa, and he said to me, "Well, in the first place, I suppose you would like to know how I came to settle here, and take up with the business of farming.

"You see, after the Mexican war had ended, and that chap with the gold epaulets on his shoulders and the 'chicken fixings' on his coat-sleeves had mustered us out of the service and paid us off, Jackson and I concluded, as we had saved up a smart pile of money between us, that we would try our hands at 'ranching.' Neither of us knew anything about it, but we thought it would be plain sailing enough, as things appeared to grow in this country pretty much of their own accord anyhow, without requiring a great deal of hard work, of which neither of us were 'overly' fond. So we bought two hundred acres of land here, from Uncle Josh, (and by the same token, he made us pay a 'swingeing' price for it — twenty-five cents an acre, half cash down.)

"You know Uncle Josh, don't you? There never was a better-hearted fellow in the world, and he has but one little failing: whenever he can get to where there's liquor, either the liquor gives out, or he gets 'Ingin drunk' certain — one or the other. I have often taken him out in the chaparral, and talked to him with tears in my eyes as big as glass marbles, about his carrying on so in that way; but all I can ever get out of him is, 'that it's all owing to the high price of putty,' which, he says, 'riz half a cent on the ton, just as he had sold out.'

"But, as I was telling you, after Jackson and I had bought this piece of land from 'Uncle Josh,' the first thing we did was to build this shanty, and fence in that 'truck-patch' you see yonder; and long before we got through with the job, I tell you I had taken a perfect disgust for farming. To sit here comfortably on this log, and look at that little shanty and the truck-patch alongside of it, you would think them a mere circumstance; and, in fact, they don't make a very imposing show in the way of improvements; but just you try your hand at riving a few hundred boards out of these knotty post-oaks, that split just as well crossways as lengthways, and if you don't lather 'a few,' and cuss a few more, then I'm mistaken. And, if that don't satisfy you, just pitch into that chaparral out yonder, where the thorns are as sharp and as crooked as cats' claws, and perhaps, by the time you are tattooed all over like a New-Zealander, and there's nothing left of your pants but the waistbands, and only the collar of your shirt, you will come to the same conclusion that I did, that farming ain't quite so pleasant a business as following an Indian trail on an easy-going horse, with a fair prospect of overtaking the women and children.

"In my opinion, the Jews are the most sensible people about 'farming,' after all. You'll find 'em everywhere making money at all sorts of trades and occupations; but whoever heard of a Jew that followed 'grubbing the ground' for a living? Even in the time of Moses, you know, they went 'scootin'' around the country for forty years, living on manna and grasshoppers, just for an excuse to keep from building shanties and hoeing corn. They are a shrewd, smart people, and I'd join 'em at once, only I'm opposed to their 'earmarks,' and don't like being circumscribed and hemmed up, as I told you. Besides, I don't want to give up 'old Ned,' * of which I am remarkably fond.

* A Southern term for bacon.

Take my advice, Dobell, and never do you try 'farming,' unless you have got half a dozen darkeys and a small 'trash gang' to clear away the 'roughness.'

"Well, as I was saying, after we had worked and 'fussed' around here more than a month, and got the shanty built and the ground fenced in, I went into town and bought a plough, shovels, spades, hoes, and all sorts of farming ammunition, so as to have everything ready when the planting season came round. I went to a drug-store and bought all kinds of seeds, done up in little brown paper parcels; for, thinks I, maybe farming is like shooting at ducks with mixed shot: if a No. 4 don't hit 'em in the body, perhaps a No. 7 will take 'em in the head. If parsnips don't do well, maybe beets will. I did n't forget muskmelons and watermelons, (for I am powerfully fond of 'em, I am;) and well it was I did n't, as I 'll tell you before I 'm done.

"The first thing I did, when I got back from town, was to hitch my saddle-horse, old 'Keecheye,' into the plough; and if ever I saw a shame-faced brute, he was one. He looked as if he thought he had got down to 'the lowest notch' at last. He was so cowed he went off as quiet as a lamb, and never cut up the first 'shine.' I had never tried ploughing before in my life, but I had seen other people at it, and I thought it was the easiest thing in the world; but I 'm blamed if I have got the 'hang' of it rightly to this day. Sometimes the crazy thing would scoot along the top of the ground for a yard or so, and then, kerwhoop! it would come up against a grub, and jar the very nails off my fingers. Then again it would dive right down into the earth, as if it thought I was engaged in digging cellars by the job; and whenever I tried to bring it up, I was sure to overdo the thing, and away it would go again scooting along the top of the ground, until another grub would bring it up all standing. I pledge you my word, Dobell, after I had run the first furrow, and looked back at it, it made me dizzy, it was so monstrous crooked. However, we at last got through with the job; though, if you had seen the field after we had it done, you would have thought a gang of wild hogs had been rooting in it for the last month.

"Well, we planted the most of it in corn, and the rest we planted with the seeds I had bought at the drug-store. Among them was a paper labelled 'muskmelon seed,' (and I am remarkably fond of muskmelons, I am;) so I planted them in the richest part of the patch, and tended them well till they began to grow finely. But, one day, as I was passing through the patch, I saw a young melon sprouting on one of the vines, and as it appeared to have a rather queer look, I stooped down to examine it closely, and may I never scalp another Indian if it was n't a regular bottle-gourd! I turned in right away and dug all the vines up, for fear strangers might think I had a touch of nigger blood in me, for you know the old saying, 'A poor man for posterity, and a nigger for gourds.'

"Well, everything grew off splendidly for a spell, and the corn seemed to do just as well in the crooked furrows as if they had been straight; but after a while the drought set in, and the drier it got the more the corn turned 'yaller,' until at last it wilted right up. I tried my best to make it rain, but it was all no use. Sometimes, the frogs croaked powerfully in the 'slash' over yonder, but it never rained for all that; and at last the slash went dry, and the frogs would have died if they had n't turned to highland toads. Sometimes the wind was due east, and my corns hurt me terribly, but still it did n't rain. Sometimes there was a great 'hello' around the moon, as big as a wagon-wheel, and I made sure we would have rain then; but we did n't, and never did until everything was as dry as this long yarn I am spinning now.

"But to cut it short, the crop turned out a perfect failure. And now I will tell you about the scurvy trick that Jackson there played off on me, not long ago. I wish my rifle may snap the next fair chance I get at an Indian, if I thought there was as much meanness in 'human natur.' You see, though it is true the crop had failed teetotally, there were about roasting-ears enough in the patch to make one pretty fair mess; and I told Jackson one morning that I would go out and kill a fat buck, and when I got back we would gather the crop, and have one good 'bait' out of it, anyhow. So I swabs out old Haco, as I call my rifle, and off I put up one side of Doe Run and down the other, then over to York's Creek, and from there to Little Sandy, but not a single deer could I find. At last, however, when I had given up all hopes of killing a deer that day, and was making tracks for home, just after crossing Burnt Boot, I 'upped' as fine a buck as you ever saw. I peeled his hide off in short order, cut out the 'saddle,' and started for home at a double-quick, for by this time I was getting as hungry as a cayote wolf. When I got in about two hundred yards of the camp, I thought I smelt 'fried corn,' and mistrusted something was wrong immediately; and, sure enough, when I walked into the ranch, there sat that rascal Jackson 'shovelling' the last grain from the skillet down his throat.

"He had taken advantage of my absence to gather and eat up the whole crop we had been working four or five months to make! He had n't left a nubbin as big as my thumb in the field, and consequently all my share of that crop was just one smell of fried corn; and I suppose I should n't have got that much if I had n't happened to have the wind of Jackson as I came up.

"Well, from this time on, things got worse and worse. The potatoes took the dry rot—and who could blame 'em, as a drop of rain had n't fallen in three months? — and everything else we had planted wilted right up, except the watermelons. They did finely, I suppose because they carry their own water along with 'em, and of course are independent of the weather. By this time, what with buying ploughs and hoes and other implements, etc., our money gave out entirely, and we were compelled to live on watermelons, with now and then a dish of 'poor doe,' which, as you know, is n't much stronger diet than the watermelons. I admit that watermelons are first rate in their way, but when a fellow has nothing but watermelons for breakfast, watermelons for dinner, and watermelons for supper, he fairly hates the sight of one after a while. I pledge you my word, Dobell, that after I had lived for a week or so on 'em, I could hear the water 'jug' in me whenever I stumped my toe as I walked along! And then they are such unsatisfying and 'ill-convenient' diet! In fifteen minutes after eating a fellow that would weigh twenty pounds, I was just as hungry as ever.

"Once there came along some travellers here, who wanted dinner, and I tell you, Dobell, I have never felt so mean in my life since the time Polly Jenkins said, 'No, sir-ee, horse-fly, Bob,' to a little question I asked her, as I did when I took the travellers out to the 'patch,' and, giving them a butcher-knife apiece, told them to 'pitch in,' as their dinner was before them. However, I see Jackson has got the steaks ready for supper; so draw up a 'chunk,' Dobell, and take a 'bite.'

"No, Dobell," he continued, as he helped my tin platter to about a pound of juicy steak, "I 'd rather be that old chunk you are sitting on, sailing forever round and round in a 'dead eddy,' than live here as I have done for the last six months."

"But, Big-Foot," said I, "if you are going to give up 'farming,' what will you go at? There won't be any more rangers wanted, you know, because the Government has settled all the Indians upon their 'reserves,' where they are learning them to farm and to eat fat beef in place of horse-meat."

"Yes," said Big-Foot, with a melancholy shake of the head, "all that is very true, I know, and I hear the Indians take to it kindly—least ways, to the beef. However, Jackson tells me there 's a couple of 'gals' moved into the settlement down below here, that are as rich as 'cow-yards,' and we have concluded to 'slick up' a little and hunt stock awhile in that neighborhood. I think I shall stand a pretty good chance to get one of them, seeing as how there are worse-looking chaps than I am; but as for Jackson there, he is so uncommonly ugly, that if a 'gal' was dying of some sort of sickness that could only be cured by marrying, I 'm doubtful, if he was to offer himself, if she would n't rather 'kick the bucket,' and him, too. Look at them teeth of his, will you, how they stick out in front, just as if he had been made on purpose to 'eat pumpkins through a fence.'"

"But, Big-Foot," said I, "if you *should* accidentally fail in the 'gal speculation,' what will you do then?"

"That is what I call a 'poser,'" said he; "but there's one thing you may depend on: just as soon as I hear of a Comanche starving to death for want of a horse to eat, I'll try 'farming,' again, and not before. Jackson, bring out the bottle-gourd — there's a little 'wake robin' left in it yet, and I have talked till I am as dry as a 'buffalo-chip.'"

FINIS.